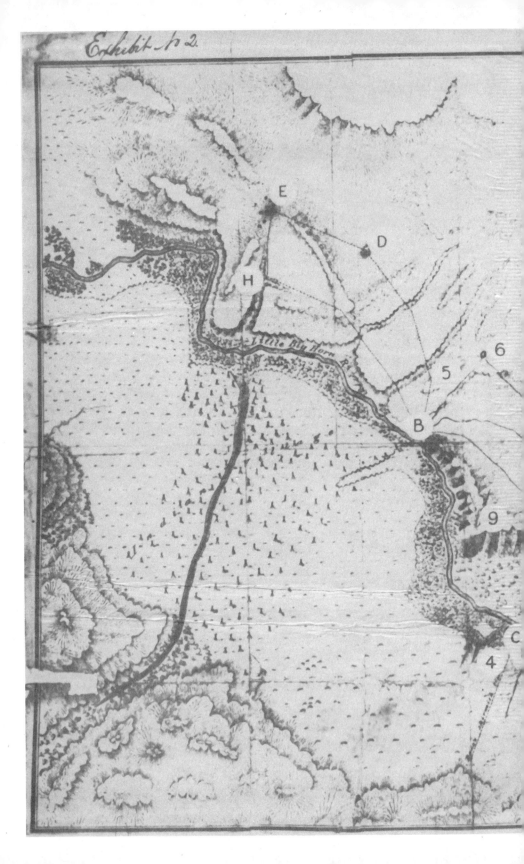

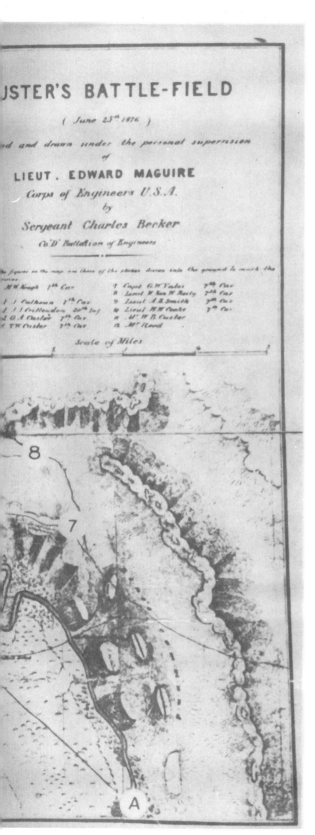

THE MAGUIRE MAP

(a) *Lettering, by* Lt. Maguire.

   A. Reno's first crossing and advance.

   B. The middle ford.

   C. Right of Reno's skirmish line.

   D. Calhoun Hill.

   E. Custer Hill, scene of "the last stand."
(N.B. See p. 8 for enlargement of D & E terrain)

   H. Ravine where many "E" Company bodies were found.

(b) *Figures, pencilled in by witnesses to clarify their testimony.*

   1. Girard encouraged Reynolds here, and gave him whiskey.

   2. Girard's guess on Custer's position at time of Reno's retreat.

   3. Girard saw Reynolds killed here.

   4. Herendeen dismounted here.

   5. Hare's guess on Reno's farthest advance toward Custer.

   6. Hare's guess on Weir's farthest advance.

   7. DeRudio, from valley position, saw Custer here.

   8. Martin turned back with "Come On" message to Benteen.

   9. Edgerly's guess on Reno's advance toward Custer.

(c) Short lines to front and rear of "Reno's Skirmish Line" pencilled in by witnesses who thought Maguire's placement of the line incorrect.

Note: Letters and numerals have been retouched because some were illegible on the original map, which otherwise has been reproduced exactly.

MAJOR MARCUS A. RENO, *Seventh Cavalry*

The Reno Court of Inquiry

Abstract of the Official Record of Proceedings

W. A. Graham

New introduction by
Brian C. Pohanka

STACKPOLE
BOOKS

Published by
STACKPOLE BOOKS
5067 Ritter Road
Mechanicsburg, PA 17055

Printed in the United States of America

10 9 8 7 6 5 4 3 2 1

Library of Congress Cataloging-in-Publication Data

Graham, W. A. (William Alexander), 1875–1954.
    [Abstract of the official record of proceedings of the Reno Court
of Inquiry]
    The Reno court of inquiry : abstract of the official record of
proceedings / W. A. Graham : new introduction by Brian C. Pohanka.
        p.   cm. — (The Custer library)
    Previously published: Harrisburg, Pa. : Stackpole, © 1954.
    Includes index.
    ISBN 0-8117-1416-0
    1. Reno, Marcus A. (Marcus Albert), 1835–1889 — Trials, litigation,
etc.   2. Courts-martial and courts of inquiry — United States.
3. Little Bighorn, Battle of the, Mont., 1876.   I. Pohanka, Brian
C., 1955-   .   II. Title.   III. Series.
KF7642.R46G73   1995
343.73′0143 — dc20
[347.303143]   94-24679
                                                             CIP

ACKNOWLEDGMENTS

I am indebted—

To E. A. Brininstool of Los Angeles for his permission to use as a Frontispiece for this volume, a portrait of Major Reno presented to him many years ago by the Major's sister, Mrs. Cornelia Knowles of Peoria, Illinois, then in her 96th year. Mr. Brininstool is widely known for his many contributions to the history of the Indian War period, and for his stout defense of Major Reno.

To Anita Benteen Mitchell of Atlanta, Georgia, granddaughter of Benteen of the Old Seventh, who during May 1954, discovered, and has permitted me to present herein, a battle map drawn and annotated in the field by her famous grand-father, only a few days after the fight.

To Hugh Shick of North Hollywood, for his generous help in preparing an analytical table of contents, lacking which the reader might easily find himself lost in a labyrinthine maze of conflicting statements.

To my wife, Helen Bury Graham, without whose able and untiring assistance, this trans-substantiation of an echo of 1921 would have remained an echo only.

W. A. GRAHAM.

vii

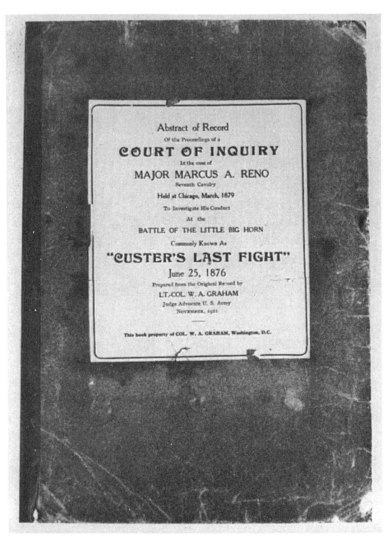

The Original Abstract—An Echo of the Year 1921.

PREFACE

THE battle of the Little Big Horn, in which the popular and spectacular General George A. Custer, together with every officer and man of five companies of the Seventh Cavalry were exterminated by hostile Indians, occurred on the 25th and 26th of June 1876. Few events in American history have more profoundly shocked the American people, or have caused more controversial discussion and debate. Almost immediately after news of the disaster reached the press and public, efforts to find a scapegoat upon whom to fix the burden of responsibility were initiated in many quarters.

Failing in attempts to pin the blame on General Terry, who was in general charge of the operation, and on the morning of the 27th relieved the survivors of the regiment, Custer's partisans turned upon Major Marcus A. Reno, the regiment's second in command, and upon Captain Frederick W. Benteen, the senior captain, to both of whom were assigned three-company battalions on the 25th of June. Despite their desperate struggle some four miles distant from Custer's battlefield, Reno and Benteen were accused of cowardly failure to go to his relief. The latter was in large degree cleared in the public mind; but not so Reno, upon whom at length was concentrated all the censure and crimination that partisanship and prejudice could muster.

Chief among Reno's critics—head and front of the accusing legion—was Frederick Whittaker, who late in 1876 had published a "Complete Life of Major General George A. Custer," a paraphrased version of Custer's own "Life on the Plains," with a few added chapters which purported to describe his last campaign, and in which Reno and Benteen were bitterly assailed as recreant to their duty.

On the 13th day of June 1878, Whittaker released through

the public press, an open letter dated 18 May 1878, addressed to the Delegate to Congress from Wyoming Territory, the Hon. W. W. Corlett, in which, after reiterating his charges against Reno and Benteen, he demanded an investigation by the Military Committee of the House of Representatives. Notwithstanding Major Reno joined in the demand, Congress adjourned without action, and on the 22nd day of June he addressed a letter to the President, asking that a Court of Inquiry be convened to the end that the truth or falsity of Whittaker's charges be established. His letter, together with that of Whittaker to Corlett, which he attached, was made the basis of the inquiry which, in response to Reno's request, was duly approved and ordered.

WHY THERE WAS NO INQUIRY UNTIL 1879
[W.A.G.]

Among the many undeserved criticisms leveled at Major Reno throughout the years is the charge that he did not demand a Court of Inquiry until after the Statute of Limitations had barred trial by court-martial for acts of cowardice and unofficerlike conduct during the battle of June 25-26, 1876.

As a matter of fact, Reno did demand a Court of Inquiry before the Statute of Limitations had run. *He could not demand trial by court-martial* in any event, and the fact is that no charge cognizable by court-martial was ever filed against him throughout the two years following the battle, two years after the event being the statutory limit for prosecutions.

His request for a Court of Inquiry, however, was addressed to the President June 22, 1878, and had The-Powers-That-Then-Were so desired, charges based upon the allegations contained in the Whittaker letter (see Exhibit 1, pp. 5-7) could easily have been formulated and arraignment accomplished before the statutory period of limitation had elapsed, just as in the past it has many times been done to my personal knowledge, and is still being done. But the military authorities had no charges or accusations to make against Major Reno, and none were made.

It must not be forgotten that during the 70's the Army was small, and action could be had within the hour if deemed desirable or necessary. Charges against Reno could easily have been formulated in the War Department in half a day, a court ordered to convene within twenty-four hours, and all by order of the President, to whom access then was easy. All that was necessary to stop the running of the Statute of Limitations was an arraignment: trial could then follow at the government's own convenience. There were then no interminable quantities of red tape to unravel —no maze-like channels of approach. It has been only since the first World War, when we had a look-in at European methods, that present day complexities were superimposed upon our erstwhile simple military system.

A Court of Inquiry, unlike a Court Martial, which tries only criminal charges formally preferred, is a purely investigatory body whose one and only function is to inquire into and report upon aspersions or other derogatory matter respecting a person in the military service, with a view to establishing facts; and if so directed, it recommends the action, if any, that should be taken in the premises.

The Court of Inquiry authorized by the President on the 25th day of November 1878, convened at Chicago, Illinois, 13 January 1879, and adjourned 11 February 1879, after an extended hearing, with daily sessions excluding Sundays only. The testimony of 23 witnesses was taken, all of whom were subjected to cross examination under oath, and eleven documentary exhibits were received in evidence. The inquiry quickly developed into a broad investigation of the manner in which the battle was fought, and competent historians and students consider the record of its proceedings to be the chief and most important respository of authentic detailed information on the subject. The original official record, some 1300 pages in length, was held in the confidential files of the Judge Advocate General's Office until

1941, when it was turned over to the National Archives. In 1951 a verbatim edition of the official record, limited to 125 copies, complete and unexpurgated, with every question, answer, objection and argument set out in full, was published by me. *This volume is an abstract of that record.*

An abstract is a condensed version of the *substance* of the evidence in a given case, its method being to restate in narrative form, and as nearly as may be in the language of the witnesses, the material testimony, and to note significant procedural steps.

It necessarily follows that paraphrase, rather than quotation, must frequently be employed in thus condensing the testimony. Repetitious matter should, so far as possible, be deleted and details of minor consequence omitted. Any other method would result in as bulky a document as the complete question and answer record itself. This abstract was made by me in 1921, and, with some revisional additions, is the identical abstract of which copies were furnished to former Secretary of War Newton D. Baker, to General E. S. Godfrey, to General Nelson A. Miles, to General H. L. Scott, to E. A. Brininstool of Los Angeles, and W. M. Camp of Chicago; and during the early 30's, to Frederic Van de Water, then engaged in writing his famed biography of Custer, *"Glory Hunter."* Copies were furnished also to the libraries of the Army War College, and The Judge Advocate General of the Army. It has been extensively used and/or quoted by most of the better writers of Custeriana, and is the principal basis of my own work *"The Story of the Little Big Horn,"* first published in 1926, and now in its fourth edition. It contains the *meat* or *gist* of the evidence, summarizing the testimony of each witness with especial emphasis upon its bearing on the progress of the battle, *its first objective being to present to readers a word picture of the combat,* as told by the only persons, aside from the Indians, who possessed first hand knowledge of the facts.

All Exhibits are reproduced *verbatim,* as are also the finding and recommendation of the Court, The Judge Advocate General's review of the record, and the President's approval. Illuminating excerpts from the arguments of the Recorder and the Defense Counsel are likewise included.

As the testimony of particular witnesses was seldom concluded on the days they were called to the stand, no attempt has been made to divide the proceedings into daily sessions.

The record of the Reno Court of Inquiry is the only official document in existence that contains the sworn testimony of officers and enlisted men; and of scouts, guides, interpreters and other civilian participants in the Battle of the Little Big Horn—"Custer's Last Fight."

POLITICS; YES—WHITEWASH; NO
[W.A.G.]

There was a political angle to the Reno case that should neither be overlooked nor ignored. In 1876 Grant, a Republican president, had summarily removed from his command a prominent Democrat—Custer. The Democratic press bitterly assailed the President, first for removing him, and later for permitting him to go out with his regiment, and not only to be killed, but to be blamed by the President for the disaster. Grant's views permeated the entire high command—there is no record of any dissent from them, nor any intimation that anyone in authority believed that Reno rather than Custer was at fault. Came 1878; Grant was out of office, and another Republican president occupied the White House, who had another and different kind of smear campaign to meet. The high command of the Army remained as it had been under Grant, and the Major's demand for a Court of Inquiry was approved as a matter of course. The sentiments of the General of the Army and the Lieutenant General were well known, and though the Army took no pride in the Little Big Horn, where a crack regiment of cavalry had been soundly drubbed by Indians, it had nothing to hide.

The Inquiry was duly held; the witnesses testified under oath. In the main they told the truth as they saw it, though a more expert interrogator than was Lt. Lee could doubtless have gotten more information from them than Lee was able to do. But he did his best, and all in all, it was a job well done. Benteen's hatred of Custer was but thinly disguised, if indeed it was disguised at all; and we find him, soon after the hearing was over, writing to his friend Price in Philadelphia: "I was close mouthed as I could be * * * I almost regretted I was not allowed to turn loose on Custer, tho Qui Bono?" (See "The Custer Myth, p. 325). That his attitude toward Custer colored his testimony there can be no doubt. But from the evidence as it developed, the vindication of Major Reno was inevitable. The gist of the charge against him was cowardice in the face of the enemy. No one can read this record and reasonably do otherwise than agree that the charge failed of proof. The finding was not a whitewash; it was based, as it needs must be based, upon the overwhelming preponderance of the evidence and upon that alone. Had Reno's personal conduct thereafter been above reproach, he would probably have ended his military career with honor; even with distinction.

MAGUIRE'S MAP, ET AL.

Had Lt. Edward Maguire of the Army Engineers been gifted in 1876 with the power of second sight, and thus to visualize the minute and critical examinations in store for his product, there can be little doubt that the sketch map he prepared of the Little Big Horn battlefields would have been made accurate and correct down to the tiniest clump of sagebrush—the last blade of grass; and both chain and transit (if he had them), would have been employed to plot exactly each and every twist and turn of the river, the height at close intervals of every cut bank, the position of every tree, the depth of every depression and the altitude of every rising contour of the terrain. But neither he nor anyone who visited or observed those fields in 1876, and least of all the

xiv

officers and men who temporarily held them during combat, had then the faintest notion that as time went on, every feature of the ground would become a matter of wide interest, and the subject of controversy and dispute as well.

Every witness before the Reno Court of Inquiry whose testimony involved Maguire's map criticized it severely. They said it was inaccurate: that it did not show "the lay of the land" as they recalled it; that it did not correctly place Reno's skirmish line, nor did it show the timber, the river, or the Indian village as they remembered them. Even Maguire himself damned it with faint praise, saying only what was true, that it was merely a sketch, made to illustrate his report to the Chief of Engineers, and did not purport to be anything more than that. Distances between marked points, however, he said were accurate, and that in general, the map correctly represented the terrain. He admitted freely that the Indian village was not properly placed, for it was no longer there when the odometer measurements were made, and the ground was so strewn with abandoned Indian impedimenta, that the location of the village could not be precisely plotted. So also with the Reno skirmish line. He had put it where some officer whose name he could not recall, had located its position. Admittedly, it too was incorrect as drawn. It was far too long, nor did it clearly appear whether intended to indicate the skirmish line at the point of its farthest advance, or at the place where the troops dismounted, though it was probably the former.

The landscape sketch of the field made in 1877 by an artist representing the New York *Graphic,* which appeared at page 40 of the fourth edition of *"The Story of the Little Big Horn,"* and is reproduced in this volume at page 134, shows a heavily inked line, dotted in by Benteen, to indicate Reno's line when first formed at the point of dismounting, and the letter G' purports to show the point of its farthest advance. If one could match up the landscape sketch with

xv

the Maguire map, he might have an answer to the problem, assuming Benteen's dotted line to have been accurate.

The U. S. Geological Survey's 1891 Contour map affords little assistance, so far as concerns the terrain of Reno's valley fight. It shows the topography as it was in 1891— *not as it was in 1876;* and during the fifteen year interval, the course of the river had changed, how much or how often nobody knows: but that it differed materially is certain.

My own opinion, offered for whatever it may be worth, is that one wastes time in any prolonged effort to locate accurately Reno's valley positions, for such an endeavor simply cannot be successfully accomplished; and when all is said and done, one is forced to come back to the Maguire map,— the only contemporaneous map extant, and which, as to the more significant landmarks may safely be accepted as reasonably correct. After all, the exact location of Reno's skirmish line and/or his position along the edge of the timber is of relatively small importance, so long as its general features and approximate location can be established.

The timber is no longer there, nor is the river where it was. Indeed, I am told that the Little Big Horn changes its course in greater or less degree nearly every year, depending upon the volume of water that each spring cuts its banks —for the soil is peculiarly subject to granulation and erosion. It matters little whether Reno stopped at the Garryowen loop, above it, or below it; and it matters even less whether he advanced to it or dismounted at its peak, or at some other point. The important thing is to visualize, if possible, the immediate terrain as it existed in 1876.

To do this with any degree of satisfaction, one is forced to scan closely the testimony of Lt. Maguire and of General Gibbon, and to a lesser extent, that of Colonel Sheridan, the only witnesses who observed the valley terrain under circumstances that conduced to accurate description.

For this reason, attempts upon the part of officers and men who passed over the ground but once, and then in the heat of combat, to describe after two and one half years, the terrain over which they fought, has been in large part eliminated. Their descriptions as to all but general features were not only contradictory, but confusing, and in my opinion are of little, if any, value.

The Maguire map, I think, may be assumed correct as to the main channel of the river as it was in 1876, though it probably does not show in detail all its smaller curves and loops. And it indicates, too, the *general* placement of the fringe of timber, though it does not accurately show its width at particular points. It shows, too, the general course of the cut bank that marked the westerly edge of a former river channel, but does not show its height at any given point.

But from the map, and the testimony of Maguire, Gibbon and Sheridan, together with general descriptions by other witnesses, the ground over which Reno advanced, fought on foot, and retreated can be visualized somewhat as follows:

From the Point "A", which marks his initial crossing, to the Point "C", where the skirmish line is shown, the ground over which he passed was nearly level, constituting, as it did, the plain of the Little Big Horn valley. As he advanced, because of the serpentine course of the river, which was to his right, he was sometimes close to the timber that fringed the stream, sometimes distant from it several hundred yards. At Point "C", prior to the moment he took "G" Company off the line and into the timber, his right rested at the edge of the cut bank that marked the westerly side of an old river channel. This cut bank was fringed with timber, for the most part cottonwood. At some points it sloped down to the lower "bench", while at others the descent was abrupt, the bank at some places being almost vertical. The height of the cut bank was far from uniform. At many points its elevation above the "bench" was only a few feet; at many others, it was as much as fifteen to twenty feet, and at a few, even more than that.

The "bench", i.e.,—the lowland that intervened between

the cut bank and the stream, was in the main, flat, and it too, varied greatly in width. Opposite Point "C" it appears to have been about 150 yards wide, while at others it was twice that width, and at its northerly and southerly limits, it narrowed sharply, and finally petered out. The "bench" contained some standing timber, which was small, and a considerable amount of fallen timber which, presumably, had in former years been washed out by freshets; and as a whole, it was covered with thick and tangled underbrush that extended from the base of the cut bank of the old channel, to the river's edge. Across the stream, on the right bank, there was some timber, small and sparse, and more underbrush, which led to the cliff-like border of the hills beyond. It was into the underbrush that covered the "bench" on the left, or westerly side of the river, that Reno took "G" Company, in an effort to dislodge some Indians who had crept into it and were threatening his right flank.

One scans Maguire's map in vain for any trace of the ravine or coulee in which, according to the testimony of several witnesses, hundreds of Indian warriors were concealed, and from which they emerged immediately the skirmish line was formed, to circle Reno's left flank. The Geological Survey map of 1891 shows several draws or coulees that slant toward the river, but none appear to be deep enough to conceal mounted men. Dr. Kuhlman, author of "Legend into History," who has explored the terrain many times and knows it thoroughly, has expressed the opinion that the ravine or coulee referred to is the one shown on the Geological Survey's map to be located slightly to the south and east of the Garryowen loop. If he is right, this coulee must have been deeper in 1876 than it was in 1891, and it would follow that the points of Reno's dismount and his extreme advance were considerably farther up river than has generally been supposed. On the other hand, Fred Dustin, who also has carefully explored the terrain, thinks the placement of the skirmish line as it appears on the Maguire map to be about correct (except as to length), and that the valley terrain as it was in 1876, is represented with reasonable accuracy.

"Who shall decide when doctors disagree?" You, perhaps? Not I. All of which demonstrates, to my satisfaction at least, that exact placement of Reno's position in the valley is not only impossible, but immaterial, and that the student will be best served by using the one and only contemporaneous map extant as a guide to a proper understanding of Reno's movements.

As to Custer's field, the situation is otherwise. Here one need not hesitate to accept Maguire's map and his measurements, without, however, accepting Maguire's theories. That is to say, the map is accurate as to relative positions, and reasonably so as to points where key bodies were found. It is *not* to say that the dotted lines correctly represent the paths followed by Custer's troops *en route* to the battle ridge, for whether he came down Medicine Tail coulee and attempted to cross the river at the middle ford "B", and was driven to the ridge; or whether he came to it after swinging wide to the east, is still a matter of doubt and debate, and is likely to remain so forever.

The same remarks apply to the Geological Survey map also. There are no essential differences between it and the Maguire map so far as Custer's field is concerned. "The everlasting hills" have not changed much, and Custer's field in all material aspects, still remains as it was in 1876.

———————

After the foregoing was in type, a battlefield map, drawn and annotated by Capt. F. W. Benteen shortly after the battle, was discovered, together with other papers as yet unclassified, in an old trunk, for many years hidden away in an outbuilding on the Benteen estate. *This map antedates Maguire's map by*

many months; and by courtesy of Anita Benteen Mitchell, grand-daughter of Benteen of
the Old Seventh, it is reproduced at the back of
this volume. Its importance as an original and
authentic item of Custeriana cannot be over-
stated; and though it should go far to settle
some disputes, it will probably be the cause of
others. Certainly it will be closely scanned by
students of the 1876 campaign.

INTRODUCTION

In the spring of 1926, plans were well underway for a grand fiftieth anniversary celebration of the Battle of the Little Big Horn. From June 24 to 26 thousands of visitors and a detachment of horse soldiers from the Seventh U.S. Cavalry would join a handful of aged veterans—both white and Native American—on the ground where George Armstrong Custer had waged his "Last Stand" against Sitting Bull's Sioux and Cheyenne warriors.

One of the most zealous members of the commemorative organization was eighty-two-year-old retired General Edward S. Godfrey, who had fought at Little Big Horn as a company commander in Captain Frederick Benteen's battalion. Godfrey had reason to be proud of his service half-a-century earlier. His leadership had contributed to the successful defense that enabled seven of the regiment's twelve companies to stave off the disaster that befell Custer's 210-man contingent. In 1892 Godfrey had authored a widely read account of the battle for *Century Magazine,* and he continued to maintain a voluminous correspondence with latter-day historians drawn to the enigma and controversy of Custer's Last Stand.

As preparations for the celebration progressed, Godfrey was informed of a proposal to erect a monument on the site where he and his comrades had withstood a grueling two-day siege by the warriors who vanquished Custer's battalion. The memorial would be a fitting counterpart to the granite shaft that already marked the mass grave of Custer's men some four miles to the north. At first glance the proposal seemed far from controversial, but Godfrey was adamant on one salient point. In no way, shape or form could that monument be allowed to bear the name of Major Marcus A. Reno.

As Custer's second-in-command, Major Reno had been allotted a key role in the Seventh Cavalry's assault on the vast Indian encampment gathered in the valley of the Little Big

Horn. While Captain Benteen's battalion scouted to the south, and Captain Thomas McDougall's company escorted the mule-borne pack train on the back trail, Reno's three companies were ordered to cross the river and charge the southern end of the village, which Custer believed to be in the process of decamping. Reno attacked as ordered, but halted when confronted by hundreds of mounted warriors who sallied out to meet him.

After fifteen minutes of skirmishing, Reno withdrew his vastly outnumbered battalion into a stretch of timber that skirted the Little Big Horn. Some thirty-five minutes later, with casualties mounting and no sign of the support that Custer had promised, Reno made the most controversial decision of his military career—to cut his way through the Indians and seek a better defensive position atop the bluffs on the river's east bank. The maneuver was poorly executed, with many soldiers unaware of the move until they saw their fellow troopers bolting out of the woods in a virtual stampede. Some came to believe Reno had been unnerved when the scout Bloody Knife was shot in the head, the bullet spattering Reno with blood and brains. In any event, by the time Reno gained the bluffs and met with Benteen's battalion, a third of his force had been killed, wounded, or left behind in the timber.

With the sound of Custer's fatal battle echoing in the distance, Reno and his officers patched together a defensive perimeter, brought up the lagging pack train, and finally made a poorly coordinated move downstream, toward the sound of the guns. By that time Custer's fate was sealed, and for the next two days Reno's seven companies underwent their own grim battle for survival. Unable to breach the soldiers' defenses, the Indians melted away on the evening of June 26. The next day the arrival of reinforcements led by General Alfred Terry and Colonel John Gibbon rescued the exhausted troopers and brought word of the horrible scene a few miles northward, where the missing battalion had been found in its entirety—stripped, scalped, and mutilated.

Fifty years later, with the frontier tamed and the events of

June 25, 1876, having long since faded into the realm of history and myth, Edward S. Godfrey was fully convinced of one incontrovertible fact: Major Marcus Reno's performance in the Battle of the Little Big Horn had been incompetent, insubordinate, and cowardly.

Godfrey hastened to inform General Custer's widow, Elizabeth, of the monument proposed for the Reno/Benteen defense site. In a rare entrance into controversy, the octogenarian Libbie Custer—whose entire life had been dedicated to perpetuating the heroic legacy of her dashing husband—penned an anguished appeal to J. A. Shoemaker, events coordinator for the fiftieth anniversary celebration. Mrs. Custer implored Shoemaker "not to permit any memorial of any kind to be placed on that sacred battlefield to so great a coward." Asserting that Reno "seemed not to *try* to hide his cowardice," she urged the commemorative organization "not to *single out* for honor, the one coward of the regiment."

Faced with such significant opposition, it was nearly three years after the fiftieth anniversary before another effort was mounted to memorialize the Reno/Benteen site. Again Godfrey expressed his indignation that anyone would consider placing Reno's name on the marker. "Major Reno utterly failed in his part in the valley attack," Godfrey stated in a letter to one official; "he *could* and *should* have held that position." Godfrey derided Reno's characterization of the move from the timber as a "charge." In Godfrey's opinion, Reno "in person led a panic, straggling retreat, thereby sacrificing many lives and the morale of his command." As for the siege, Godfrey claimed his commander "seemed resigned to inactivity except when urged by Captain Benteen," and went on to charge Reno with proposing a withdrawal from the field altogether—a movement, under cover of darkness, that would have necessitated the abandonment of the severely wounded to certain death.

A granite memorial honoring the seven companies was finally erected in the summer of 1929, but nowhere upon it appears the name of their commanding officer.

The ill-starred life of Marcus Albert Reno began November 15, 1834, in Carrollton, Green County, Illinois. He was the fourth of six children born to James and Charlotte Miller Reno, both of whom were dead by the time Marcus reached his sixteenth birthday. Having been adopted as a ward by one of his father's former business partners, in October 1850 Reno composed a letter to Secretary of War C. M. Conrad:

> I desire to receive an appointment as cadet at the Military Academy & as my Father and Mother are both dead and it is not within any power to obtain an education at my own expense, I can give the required recommendation in regard to moral character and intellectual capacity.

As it was, Reno's congressman, W. A. Richardson, nominated another candidate for admission to West Point. But that appointee declined, and on May 30, 1851, Richardson replaced him with Reno, characterizing him to Secretary Conrad as "a suitable young Gent for the place."

Marcus Reno commenced his studies at the Military Academy in September, one of sixty-six original members of the class of 1855. Of the thirty-four who ultimately graduated, nine would go on to serve as generals during the Civil War, while non-graduate James Abbott McNeill Whistler would attain lasting artistic fame. Reno himself was not destined to graduate until 1857. Although he maintained a solid if mediocre academic standing, Reno's penchant for amassing demerits resulted in his being forced to repeat two years at the academy and gained him the dubious honor of having one of the worst records for conduct in the history of West Point.

Reno's conduct roll indicates that his behavior was consistently poor throughout his six-year tenure at the academy. He was repeatedly late to formations, and he sometimes skipped them altogether. He smoked cigars in his room, chewed tobacco at drill, used "profane language," talked and "gazed about" in ranks, and was prone to singing at inappropriate times. He was frequently caught "trifling" in the classroom or "laughing at [the] blackboard," and on August 10, 1856, Reno received four demerits for "imitating a drunken man on the company parade ground by singing and staggering."

Undeniably much of Reno's conduct can be ascribed to immaturity, or to a high-spirited nature, and he was far from the only cadet caught at youthful high jinks. But Reno evinced an ambivalence to military regulations and a tendency to disregard his superiors that was decidedly atypical of those young men who pursued careers as officers in the U.S. Army.

At times he sat down while on guard duty, or strolled away from his post—both gross infractions of the rigidly defined army regulations. On one occasion he received eight demerits for "wantonly destroying a shade tree" that lay alongside his sentinel's beat. In a written apology to the commandant of cadets, Reno sought to explain his action by stating, "Thoughtlessness in regard to the safety of anything entrusted to my care is a defect in my character which I cannot correct." This was a disturbing admission indeed for one who aspired to be a military officer!

Some insight into Reno's standing with his fellow cadets is revealed in the diary of Cyrus Comstock, a graduate of the class of 1855 who went on to a distinguished career as a military engineer. In his entry for March 13, 1855, Comstock recounted a brawl between Reno and Cadet Edward L. Hartz, who had put Reno on report for walking about in the mess hall:

> Reno went to Hartz room last night and told Hartz that he thought him a d—d pusillanimous coward, or something of that kind, and Hartz rushed at him. Reno got the worst of it & got his thumb bitten badly, as he put it in H[artz's] face apparently for the purpose of gouging. Reno is not very popular.

Two weeks after this altercation, Reno received his first

suspension. His second, which very nearly cost him his military career and resulted in his being dropped back to the class of 1857, stemmed from a February 14, 1856, court-martial for disrespect to a superior officer. When an infantry lieutenant ordered Reno to stop singing at his post in the cadet barracks, Reno "replied in a contemptuous and disrespectful manner . . . that he had a right to sing on post." The Military Academy authorities obviously did not agree.

The West Point Cadet Hospital records indicate that with one significant exception Marcus Reno generally enjoyed good health during his six years at the Academy. He suffered from corns and occasional stomach problems and once had a bout with tonsillitis. But shortly after his return from summer furlough in 1856, Reno was treated for a very serious ailment indeed — syphilis.

The hospital records make plain the fact that venereal disease was rampant at West Point in the decade preceding the Civil War (one of the many treated for gonorrhea was George Armstrong Custer). Most of the cases appeared within a week or two of the cadets' return from furlough, probably a result of the young men having sampled the delights of New York City's soiled doves during their passage through the metropolis. The fact that Reno was treated for syphilis on July 5, 1856, and again on October 28, indicates that the disease may have progressed to its secondary stage. Although there was no effective cure for syphilis in Reno's day, in only one-third of cases did the illness progress to its tertiary — and often fatal — stage. Lacking additional medical documentation, historians can only speculate what, if any, role the disease may have played in Reno's later life.

Marcus Reno finally graduated from West Point on July 1, 1857, placing twentieth of thirty-eight cadets. His fellow graduates included future Union generals George C. Strong and Charles H. Morgan, and Confederate generals E. Porter Alexander, Robert H. Anderson, Samuel W. Ferguson, and John S. Marmaduke. Another classmate, Henry M. Robert, would later author *Robert's Rules of Order.*

Though he stood only slightly above the middle of the class in cavalry tactics, Reno found himself assigned to a mounted regiment, the First U.S. Dragoons. After a brief spell at Carlisle Barracks, Pennsylvania, he was posted to the Pacific Northwest, where he got his first taste of Indian campaigning in Oregon and Washington Territories. The outbreak of the Civil War brought Reno promotion to first lieutenant and a transfer to the First Cavalry. By fall 1861 he was a captain, but he did not arrive at the seat of war until early in 1862, when his unit joined General George McClellan's Army of the Potomac in the defenses of Washington.

During McClellan's abortive campaign on the Virginia Peninsula, and through the battles of the Seven Days, Reno conducted himself well and rose to command of a cavalry squadron. While the Federal mounted arm was still largely outclassed by J. E. B. Stuart's Confederate troopers, Captain Reno continued to win recognition from his superiors through the Maryland campaign and at the Battle of Fredericksburg, where he commanded General Burnside's headquarters escort.

On March 17, 1863, Reno led eight hundred men of the First and Fifth U.S. Cavalry into action at Kelly's Ford — one of the first clashes in which Yankee horsemen gave indication that they were finally coming on a par with their Rebel counterparts. Reno's horse was shot from under him during the fight, and the captain sustained a painful hernia when the animal rolled atop him. Brevetted major for his gallantry, Reno recuperated from his injuries in Harrisburg, Pennsylvania, where he courted the young woman who was destined to become his wife.

Reno had met eighteen-year-old Mary Hannah Ross at a social function while he was on horse purchasing duty in Harrisburg the previous year. During his convalescence the two pursued their acquaintance, and by early summer 1863 they were engaged to be married. But Robert E. Lee's great invasion of the North intervened, and Reno was called to duty as acting chief of staff to General William F. "Baldy" Smith, commander of the local defense forces in southern Pennsylvania. Despite the military emergency, Smith granted Reno a brief leave, and on July 1, 1863, as the great battle commenced at Gettysburg, the captain married Mary Hannah Ross at New York City's Astor House Hotel. Following the wedding he hastened back to Pennsylvania, where he served with credit during the remainder of the campaign.

Reno passed the next two months on recruiting service in Harrisburg, leaving his pregnant wife and returning to the front in October 1863. He commanded two squadrons of the First U.S. during the Bristoe campaign, and in March 1864, he was ordered to the Cavalry Bureau in Washington. Robert Ross Reno was born in April, and in May the captain was appointed acting assistant inspector general on the staff of General Alfred Torbert, commanding a division under U. S. Grant's newly installed chief of cavalry, General Philip Sheridan.

By all accounts Reno excelled during the bloody summer fighting and in Sheridan's epic Shenandoah Valley Campaign. His service at the Battle of Cedar Creek brought him the brevet rank of lieutenant colonel for "gallant and meritorious" conduct, and both Torbert and Sheridan recommended Reno for promotion to the rank of brigadier general. Torbert, who had assumed command of Sheridan's cavalry, praised Reno's "coolness, bravery and good judgement," and Sheridan commented that Reno was "full of energy and ability."

Though promotion to general's rank was not forthcoming, early in 1865 Reno was given the colonelcy of the 12th Pennsylvania Cavalry—a hard luck outfit that was on the verge of disbandment. Colonel Reno did what he could to whip the Pennsylvanians into shape, though the unit frequently found itself bested by the intrepid Confederate partisan leader John S. Mosby. Bemoaning what he termed the "utter helplessness" of his regiment, Reno commented, "with such men as Mosby's I could go anywhere."

April 1865 found Reno commanding a brigade in the Department of the Shenandoah, far removed from the glorious

victories of Five Forks, Sayler's Creek, and Appomattox—
battles in which Custer played a notable part. While Reno did
finally receive the brevet rank of brigadier general of Volunteers—along with a brevet as colonel in the Regular Army—
peace required him to revert to his Regular Army rank of
captain in the First U.S. Cavalry.

For three years following the cessation of hostilities Reno
served in a variety of staff positions in New Orleans and on
the Pacific coast. On December 26, 1868, he received the fate-
ful promotion to the rank of major in the Seventh U.S. Cavalry, but detached service prevented him from joining his unit
in the field until early in 1870. That summer, while his wife
and son remained in garrison at Fort Hays, Kansas, Major
Reno had his first taste of active campaigning since the
Civil War as commander of a three-company detachment in
Colorado.

In the summer of 1871 Reno was posted to South Carolina,
where elements of the Seventh Cavalry were stationed as
peacekeepers during the turbulent period of Reconstruction.
Just over a year later, he was honored with an appointment to
a board that was studying improvements to Army small arms
in New York City, following which, in June 1873, he took
command of two companies of the Seventh assigned to Fort
Totten, Dakota Territory.

In the summer of 1873, and again in 1874, Reno functioned
as escort commander to a group of engineers surveying the
boundary of the United States and Canada. This meant that
Reno, with Companies D and I of the Seventh, was not on
hand when the bulk of the regiment—under Custer's command—took part in the Yellowstone campaign of 1873 and the
controversial 1874 expedition into the Black Hills.

While Custer's men saw a fair share of Indian fighting in
1873 and traversed the natural and geological wonders of the
Black Hills the following year, Reno's troops went about their
mundane and largely uneventful task on the northern border.
Reno's only clash in 1873 came not with Indians but with an

xxix

army surgeon, whom he sought to dismiss for incompetency. The surgeon in turn accused Reno of drunkenness, caused by what the doctor called "an over stimulated brain." In fact Reno's fondness for alcohol had yet to reach serious proportions. One of his subordinates on the boundary survey, young Lieutenant Winfield Scott Edgerly, recalled Reno as "a moderate drinker," and noted, "I never saw him drunk."

Reno was en route to the 1874 border survey when he received the shocking news that his wife, Mary Hannah, had died suddenly at her home in Harrisburg. Already having missed her funeral, and anxious to see to the welfare of his ten-year-old son, Reno requested one month's leave of absence, but the Army refused to grant him the leave until his contingent completed and returned from their duties on the border, two months later.

The death of his wife, and his enforced absence at such a time, can in retrospect be seen to have been a watershed not only in Marcus Reno's private life, but in his military career as well. When he finally did start east, Reno was able to extend his leave to include a visit to Europe, and he would ultimately be absent from the Seventh Cavalry for thirteen months. He rejoined the regiment at Fort Lincoln, Dakota Territory, on October 24, 1875, and exercised command of that post until Custer returned from his own extended leave just prior to the campaign of 1876.

By all accounts Reno's tenure as commanding officer was marked by a strict and martinet-like adherence to military regulations, his once ebullient nature having long since turned taciturn, even sullen. Though Reno was nowise a member of the so-called "Custer clique," and in fact had seen very little of his flamboyant commander during the post-war years, he was on cordial terms with many officers. Lieutenant Benjamin Hodgson, a diminutive Philadelphian who was one of George and Libbie Custer's favorites, was also "a great favorite and friend" of Reno's, and would serve as the major's adjutant when the regiment took the field on May 17, 1876.

The chain of events that ultimately led the Seventh Cavalry to Little Big Horn was in large part the result of a strenuous six-company scouting expedition conducted by Reno from June 10 to 19. Both Custer and General Alfred Terry—whose command included the Seventh Cavalry—felt that Reno, by following a well-defined Indian trail, had exceeded his orders and risked discovery by the so-called "hostiles." But the major's exhausting trek had indicated that at least eight hundred Indians were headed for the valley of the Little Big Horn. Ever fearful that the elusive foe would scatter, Terry determined to catch the Indians between his own force and Custer's regiment. The Seventh departed the Yellowstone River on June 22, and three days later rode to death and disaster at Little Big Horn.

Grief, shame, and simmering recriminations clouded the remainder of that summer's failed campaign. Reno was one of several surviving officers who increasingly sought solace in alcohol, and the major's abrasive style of command prompted Lieutenant Godfrey to note in his diary that "Reno's self important rudeness makes him unbearable." Within a month of the battle Reno was drawn into an acrimonious correspondence with former Confederate general Thomas Rosser—one of Custer's West Point chums—who publicly charged Reno with having "abandoned Custer and his gallant comrades to their fate."

Soon after returning to garrison at Fort Lincoln, Reno became involved in an altercation with a lieutenant of the 20th Infantry, the two men grappling on the floor of the post Officer's Club. When Lieutenant Charles Varnum attempted to separate them, Reno snapped, "I will make it a personal matter with you," and challenged Varnum to a duel. Other officers intervened, and urged Varnum to shake hands with Reno. The major slapped Varnum's gesture aside, saying "Don't you touch my hands." A witness to the affair drew up court-martial charges against Reno, but Army authorities chose not to press the matter.

In December 1876 Reno was assigned to Fort Abercrombie, Dakota, where he served as post commander. He soon struck up a relationship with Mrs. Emily Bell, wife of Seventh Cavalry Captain James Bell, who was temporarily absent from the post. Captain Benteen later characterized Emily Bell as a "musky fox" who was "doubtless a nymphomaniac." Be that as it may, Mrs. Bell rebuffed Reno's advances—he had taken her by the hands and put his arm about her waist—and his drinking increased still further. Reno's pique found expression in a number of statements that implied Mrs. Bell was paying inappropriate attention to a visiting cleric. "Mrs. Bell's reputation is like a spoiled egg," Reno allegedly commented, "you cannot hurt it. She is notorious in the regiment as a loose character."

When Captain Bell returned to Fort Lincoln and got word of these goings-on, he instigated court-martial proceedings against Reno. Found guilty of "conduct unbecoming an officer and a gentleman . . . to the scandal and disgrace of the military service," Reno was sentenced to be dismissed. President Rutherford B. Hayes approved the sentence, but commuted the punishment to suspension from rank and pay for two years to commence May 1, 1877.

Reno had been boarding at a hotel in Harrisburg for just over a year, presumably to be near his son Ross, when the bitter legacy of Little Big Horn again cast its shadow upon him. Frederic Whittaker, author of a hero-worshipping paean to Custer, wrote a letter to Congressman W. W. Corlett of Wyoming Territory that was widely published in the press. In it, Whittaker urged a congressional investigation of Little Big Horn in order to "prove or disprove" the veracity of the major's official report. It was Whittaker's professed opinion that Reno's "gross cowardice" and "incompetency" had been the root cause of the debacle.

On June 17, 1878, Reno wrote to the chairman of the House Military Committee asking for an official inquiry to clear his name of "various malignant reports." Five days later he repeated the request in a letter to President Hayes, "that the many rumors started by camp gossip may be set at rest, and the truth made fully known." On November 25, a Special Order from Army Headquarters acceded to Reno's demand, appointing a military Court of Inquiry to assemble in Chicago on January 13, 1879.

For twenty-six days three senior officers, including Reno's former Civil War commander, Colonel Wesley Merritt, listened to a complex and disturbing recounting of the Army's humiliating defeat at Little Big Horn. The court recorder, Lieutenant Jesse M. Lee, was by his own admission "not a prosecutor" and professed to be striving for "the whole truth of the matter." Lee decidedly lacked the legal acumen of Reno's civilian counsel, the former Deputy Attorney General of Pennsylvania Lyman Gilbert, though he did elicit testimony that cast doubt on Reno's decision to abandon the timber and the chaotic manner in which the movement was conducted.

One disturbing revelation that emerged in testimony was Reno's foray back down the bluffs to ascertain the fate of his good friend, Lieutenant Hodgson. That officer had in fact been killed, and while the major managed to recover a ring, watch clasp, and set of keys from the body, it hardly justified his absence from the decimated command at a time when there were decisions to be made, wounded to be secured, and the sound of Custer's battle could be heard in the distance!

Several witnesses described the state of Reno's battalion as "demoralized," and "stampeded," while others spoke of the major's "excitement." When Gilbert asked Captain Edward Godfrey to characterize Reno's "courage, coolness and efficiency," that officer responded, "I was not particularly impressed with any of the qualifications." While stopping short of accusing Reno of cowardice, Godfrey stated that his commander had shown "nervous timidity."

The most strongly worded criticism came not from Reno's subordinate officers, but rather from civilians—Acting Assistant Surgeon Henry Porter, interpreter Frederic Gerard, scout

George Herendeen, and mule packers B. F. Churchill and John Frett, the latter two claiming Reno was intoxicated on the evening of June 25. Drawing upon the prevalent notion that the word of an Army officer was inherently more trustworthy than that of a civilian or enlisted man — and decidedly superior to that of a mule packer — Lyman Gilbert skillfully weakened the impact of this testimony.

While falling short of charging Reno with outright cowardice, most witnesses' descriptions of his conduct were at best lukewarm. Captain Frederick Benteen said that Reno "was doing the best he could, I suppose," and that the major's conduct atop the bluffs was "all right." Captain Thomas McDougall claimed that Reno "was as brave as any man there," but qualified his assessment by stating, "He had no enthusiasm . . . I don't think he could encourage the men like others." These were hardly ringing endorsements of Reno's valor, and it emerged in the course of the inquiry that Captain Benteen had in fact exercised *de facto* command of the besieged troopers for much of the battle.

Given the vapid nature of the testimony, it became inevitable that while stopping short of an official sanction of Reno's conduct, the Army was clearly in no position to censure him. Following the court's adjournment on February 11, Colonel Merritt is said to have grumbled, "Well, the officers wouldn't tell us anything, and we could do nothing more than damn Reno with faint praise." For all the accumulated paperwork, and the close attention the inquiry had generated in the press, Merritt's quip was as succinct a summation as any.

In May 1879, at the conclusion of his two-year suspension from duty, Reno was ordered to Fort Meade, Dakota Territory. There the downhill slide of his blighted military career entered its final stage.

Reno spent an inordinate amount of time in the Officer's Club Room, laying wages at the billiard table, and consuming a substantial amount of liquor. In August he threw a chair through a clubroom window — hardly appropriate conduct for a man of his rank and responsibilities. On October 25, Reno began arguing with twenty-three-year-old Second Lieutenant William J. Nicholson over an overdue gambling debt. The shouting match soon escalated into fisticuffs, and when Reno struck at Nicholas with a billiard cue, the younger man wrestled Reno to the floor.

That Nicholson bore no love for Reno as an officer or a man is made strikingly evident in a letter written by Custer Battlefield Superintendent Edward S. Luce (who served under Nicholson in the early twentieth century) to the noted Little Big Horn scholar, Dr. Charles Kuhlman:

> Old Slicker Bill Nicholson, who Reno tried to crown with a billiard cue told me plenty about Reno. . . . A lot of the stuff, and I believe it, could never be put in print even among friends. . . . The most peculiar thing about his 'proclivities' were, that when he was drunk he was normal, and when he was sober he was abnormal. He was a composite pervert. Both men and women, and I may add animals.

According to Luce, Nicholson also implied that Reno had molested a fellow officer's daughters, and that he had been discovered embracing an enlisted man in the post hay corral. On another occasion Luce claimed that Winfield Scott Edgerly had said Reno "always smelled of urine."

Whether these accusations contained a germ of truth or were scurrilous lies — and it is virtually impossible to tell at this late date — in the wake of his brawl with Nicholson the hapless major was placed under arrest by order of the Seventh Cavalry commander, Colonel Samuel D. Sturgis. The colonel cherished little regard for the tainted major of Little Big Horn — his son Jack had perished with Custer's battalion a few months after graduating from West Point.

Given Sturgis's animosity, Reno's actions on the evening of November 10 were almost incredibly foolhardy. Strolling down an alleyway alongside the commanding officer's quarters, Reno rapped on a parlor window, startling the colonel's comely daughter Ella, who alarmed the household with her cries of alarm. Sturgis came pounding downstairs from his bedroom, clad in a nightshirt and brandishing a cane. By then Reno had wandered off to his own quarters, where he was soon confronted by the regimental adjutant and placed under arrest.

On December 8, a second court-martial for "conduct unbecoming" dismissed Reno from the service. This time he was not to escape the consequences: On March 16, 1880, President Hayes confirmed the sentence.

The last nine years of Reno's life were consumed in an ultimately futile effort to win reinstatement. He repeatedly petitioned Congress, citing "prejudice," "personal spite," and "malice" as the root causes of his dismissal. He moved to Washington, where he obtained employment as a clerk in the Pension Bureau, living in a succession of boarding houses. He married a woman named Isabella Ray in 1884, but this union ended in separation three years later, following which—according to the Union Army veterans' paper *The National Tribune*—Reno made an unsuccessful attempt at suicide.

In the spring of 1889 Reno, a longtime smoker, was diagnosed with cancer of the mouth and tongue and admitted to Washington's Providence Hospital. He underwent an operation, but contracted pneumonia, and succumbed to his illness on March 30. Reno was laid to rest without ceremony in an unmarked grave at Glenwood Cemetery.

Colonel William Alexander Graham began his study of the Battle of the Little Big Horn during a tour of duty in Washington, D.C., following his return from the First World War. As an experienced military lawyer attached to the Army's Judge Advocate General's Corps, it was not surprising that the forty-six-year-old Iowan would seek out a transcript of the Reno Court of Inquiry. Recognizing that the court record was a veritable gold mine of information on the Custer Fight, Graham transcribed the lengthy document in 1921, and drew upon it heavily in his 1926 book, *The Story of the Little Big Horn.* In 1951 Graham, by then a respected dean of "Custeriana," printed his transcription of the Court of Inquiry in an over-sized edition of 125 copies. Three years later, in 1954, following publication of Graham's highly regarded sourcebook *The Custer Myth,* the Telegraph Press of Harrisburg (the Stackpole Company) issued Graham's abstract, or condensed version of the inquiry. It was to be his last book, for he died later that year.

Ever confident in the sanctity of the military justice system, Graham rejected assertions that the Reno Court had been a "whitewash" of the controversial major. Granted, "the Army took no pride in the Little Big Horn," he wrote, but "it had nothing to hide." This may be a bit of an overstatement, as even Graham conceded that a number of officer witnesses did not tell "the whole truth." In any event, debate over the intentions and integrity of the Reno Court of Inquiry is still a potent topic in the field of Custeriana.

While far from exonerating Reno's behavior, Graham refused to brand him a coward, and to that extent he fell in line with more fervent Reno partisans like E. A. Brininstool and Fred Dustin, the latter of whom did not feel Graham went far enough in his defense of the major. While Dustin agreed that Reno's "personality was not attractive," he was determined to defend Reno's name: "He was an underdog, a goat, a dead man that could be kicked about without fear of comeback from him."

In 1967, this revisionist view of Reno as the persecuted victim of Little Big Horn rather than the battle's villain was manifested in dramatic fashion. Acting on the petition of Charles A. Reno, the major's great-grand-nephew, the U.S. Army Board for Correction of Military Records rejected the findings of Reno's second court-martial and posthumously tendered him an honorable discharge. Secretary of the Army Stanley R. Resor confirmed the action, and on September 9, 1967, the bones of Marcus A. Reno were reinterred, with full military honors, in the Custer Battlefield National Cemetery. There, perhaps sadly but most surely, he does not rest in peace.

Brian C. Pohanka
Alexandria, Virginia

TABLE OF CONTENTS

The following analytic table will enable the student-reader to locate the more crucial testimony. Other topics might have been added, but these, such as times and distances, can best be tabulated by the student himself to meet his individual needs.

xliv

xlviii

xlix

1

lii

THE CONVENING ORDER

The Court of Inquiry, of whose proceedings the following pages constitute an Abstract of its record, was convened at Chicago, Illinois, on the 13th day of January, 1879, by virtue of the following Special Orders:

Headquarters of the Army
Adjutant General's Office
Washington, November 25, 1878.

EXTRACT

Special Orders
No. 255

* * *

2. By direction of the President, and on the application of Major Marcus A. Reno, 7th Cavalry, a Court of Inquiry is hereby appointed to assemble at Chicago, Illinois, on Monday the 13th day of January, 1879, or as soon thereafter as practicable for the purpose of inquiring into Major Reno's conduct at the battle of the Little Big Horn River on the 25th and 26th days of June, 1876.

The Court will report the facts and its opinion as to whether from all the circumstances in the case, any further proceedings are necessary.

DETAIL FOR THE COURT

Colonel John H. King, 9th Infantry
Colonel Wesley Merritt, 5th Cavalry
Lieutenant-Colonel W. B. Royall, 3d Cavalry

1st Lieutenant Jesse M. Lee, Adjutant—9th Infantry, is appointed Recorder of the Court.

* * *

By Command of General Sherman.

E. D. TOWNSEND
Adjutant General.

1

ABSTRACT OF THE RECORD

THE Court convened at the Palmer House, Chicago, 13 January 1879, Colonel John H. King of the 9th Infantry, the senior officer, sitting as President. Major Reno, present in person, was asked whether he objected to any member of the Court, and upon his negative reply, the Court was sworn by the Recorder, who in turn, was sworn by the President. The Recorder then introduced the Reporter, H. C. Hollister, who was also sworn.

The Recorder, after some preliminary remarks, produced an official copy of Major Reno's application for the Court of Inquiry, which was thereupon read and introduced as "Exhibit 1." He then adverted to the presence of Mr. Whittaker, the accuser of Major Reno, and desired the Court's ruling whether he should be notified, and/or invited to suggest the names of witnesses or other evidence that would illuminate the investigation.

Major Reno was not ready to proceed, his counsel not having arrived; and stated that he believed himself entitled to the affirmative, to which the Recorder replied that as one is presumed innocent until proven guilty, it was not for Major Reno to prove his conduct good until the contrary was shown. The Court ruled affirmatively as to Mr. Whittaker, and reserved decision upon the question raised by Major Reno. No testimony was taken the first day.

When the Court re-convened, Major Reno introduced as his counsel, Mr. Lyman D. Gilbert of Harrisburg, Pennsylvania, who after apologizing for his belated arrival, at once launched into argument against the admission of a letter of Frederick Whittaker addressed to Hon. W. W. Corlett, Delegate to Congress from Wyoming, a copy of which Reno had attached to his letter to the President. The Court decided that since Major Reno had both attached and re-

3

ferred to it in his application, the Whittaker letter should be considered a part thereof, and it was thereupon read as an addendum to "Exhibit 1."

Major Reno's application, including the Whittaker letter, in the form of a press release, was as follows:

EXHIBIT NO. 1

Harrisburg, Pa., June 22, 1878.

His Excellency,
    The President.

A letter addressed to Hon. W. W. Corlett, Delegate to Congress from Wyoming Terr'y., and by him referred to the House Committee on Mil. Affairs, and thus made semi-official, appeared in the press of the 13th inst. As the object of this letter was to request an investigation of my conduct at the battle of the Little Big Horn river, and was also the first time various reports and rumors had been put into definite shape, I addressed a communication to the same Committee, through its chairman, urging that the investigation be resolved upon. The Congress adjourned without taking any action, and I now respectfully appeal to the Executive for a "Court of Inquiry" to investigate the affair, that the many rumors started by camp gossip may be set at rest and the truth made fully known.

The letter to Mr. Corlett which is referred to, is hereto attached.

I am, Sir

Very respectfully, Your Obed't. Serv't.,
    M. A. RENO, *Maj., 7th Cavalry.*

THE CUSTER MASSACRE

MAJOR RENO ACCUSED OF COWARDICE

An Investigation probable

Washington, June 12. The House Committee on Military Affairs decided today to report favorably to the House a resolution directing an investigation into the Custer Massacre. Mr. Bragg will present a resolution for a subcommittee to sit in recess and send for persons and papers. The basis of this action is embraced in a letter addressed by Frederick Whittaker of Mount Vernon, N. Y., to Mr. Corlett, representing Wyoming Territory, and by him turned over to the Committee on Military Affairs, on whom it seems to have made a very decided impression. Whittaker's letter is as follows:

Mount Vernon, N. Y., May 18, 1878

Hon. W. W. Corlett, M.C.

Dear Sir:

Having been called upon to prepare the biography of the late Brevet Major General George A. Custer, U.S.A., a great amount of evidence, oral and written, came into my hands tending to prove that the sacrifice of his life and the lives of his immediate command at the battle of the Little Big Horn was useless, and owing to the cowardice of his subordinates. I desire, therefore, to call your attention, and that of Congress, through you, to the necessity of ordering an official investigation by a committee of your honorable body into the conduct of the United States troops engaged in the battle of the Little Big Horn, fought June 25, 1876, otherwise known as the Custer Massacre, in which Lieut. Col. Custer, Seventh United States Cavalry, perished, with five companies of the Seventh Cavalry, at the hands of the Indians. The reasons on which I found my request are as follows:

First: Information coming to me from participants in the battle, written and oral, is to the effect that gross cowardice was displayed therein by Major Marcus A. Reno, Seventh United States Cavalry, second in command that day: and that owing to such cowardice, the orders of Lieut. Col. Custer, commanding officer, to said Reno, to execute a certain attack, were not made.

That the failure of this movement, owing to his cowardice and disobedience, caused the defeat of the United States forces on the day in question; and that had Custer's orders been obeyed, the troops would probably have defeated the Indians.

That after Major Reno's cowardly flight, he was joined by Captain F. W. Benteen, Seventh United States Cavalry, with reinforcements, which were placed under his orders, and that he remained idle with this force while his superior officer was fighting against the whole force of the Indians, the battle being within his knowledge, the sound of firing audible from his position, and his forces out of immediate danger from the enemy.

That the consequences of this second exhibition of cowardice and incompetency was the massacre of Lieut. Col. Custer and five companies of the Seventh United States Cavalry.

Second: The proof of these facts lies in the evidence of persons in the service of the United States Government, chiefly in the Army, and no power short of Congress can compel their attendance and protect them from annoyance and persecution if they openly testify to the cowardice exhibited on the above occasion.

Third: The only official record of the battle now extant is the report written by Major Reno, above named, and is, in the main, false and libelous to the memory of the late Lieut. Col. Custer, in that it represents the defeat of the United States forces on that occasion as owing to the division by Custer of his forces into three detachments, to overmanning his forces, and to ignorance of the enemy's force,—all serious charges against the capacity of said Custer as an officer; whereas the defeat was really owing to the cowardice and disobedience of said Reno and to the wilful neglect of said Reno and Capt. Benteen to join battle with the Indians in support of their commanding officer when they might have done it, and it was their plain duty to do so.

Fourth: The welfare of the United States Army demands that in case of a massacre of a large party of troops, under circumstances covered with suspicion, it should be officially established where the blame belongs, to the end that the service may not deteriorate by the retention of cowards.

Fifth: Justice to an officer of the previously unstained record of Lieut. Col. Custer, demands that the accusation under which his memory now rests, in the only official account of the battle of the Little Big Horn now extant, should be proved or disproved.

I have thus given you, as briefly as I can, my reasons for asking this investigation, and the facts I am confident of being able to prove. My witnesses will be all the living officers of the Seventh United States Cavalry who were present at the battle of June 25, including Major Reno and Capt. Benteen;—myself to prove statements of an officer since deceased, made to me a few days before his death; F. T. Girard, Indian Interpreter to the United States forces; Dr. Porter of Bismarck, D. T., contract surgeon at the battle in question; Lieut. Carland, Sixth Infantry; Sergeant Godman, now of the Signal Service, and others whose names I can find in time for the committee's session, should the same be ordered.

Trusting, dear Sir, that this letter may result in an investigation which shall decide the whole truth about the battle of the 25th June 1876, and the purgation of the Service.

I am your obedient servant,
Frederick Whittaker.

The Court ruled that press reporters would not be permitted to make notes of the proceedings.

The President of the Court having stated, "We are not to be confined to that letter. We expect to go over the whole ground"; it was then agreed that "Exhibit 1" should be accepted as the basis of the investigation, and that the Recorder should "proceed in his own way to prove whatever matters he chooses to allege against Major Reno." The taking of testimony then began.

THE FIRST WITNESS CALLED WAS

FIRST LIEUTENANT EDWARD MAGUIRE,
Engineer Corps

WHO TESTIFIED AS FOLLOWS:

DIRECT EXAMINATION, BY THE RECORDER

I was Gen. Terry's Staff Engineer. Gen. Gibbon commanded the column moving to join Gen. Custer. We arrived at Reno's hill position about 10 A.M. June 27, 1876. In my official capacity as Engineer, I had measurements of the Little Big Horn battlefield made by a Sergeant who accom-

[THE BATTLEFIELD MAP]

panied me. Exhibit 2 is the map of which the original was attached to my report to the Chief of Engineers.

The general features of the country were a river bottom

"THE LAST STAND"

The upper left-quarter of Maguire's map enlarged to show lettered and numbered positions of bodies as found:

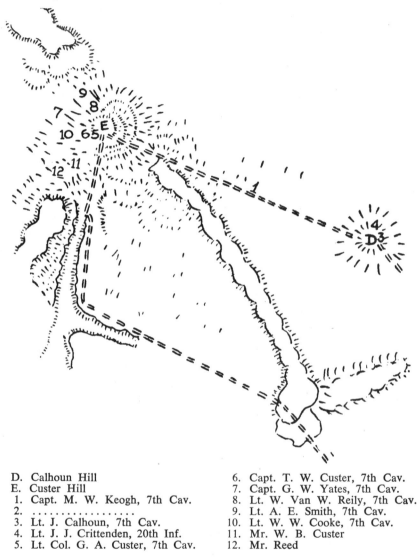

D. Calhoun Hill	6. Capt. T. W. Custer, 7th Cav.
E. Custer Hill	7. Capt. G. W. Yates, 7th Cav.
1. Capt. M. W. Keogh, 7th Cav.	8. Lt. W. Van W. Reily, 7th Cav.
2.	9. Lt. A. E. Smith, 7th Cav.
3. Lt. J. Calhoun, 7th Cav.	10. Lt. W. W. Cooke, 7th Cav.
4. Lt. J. J. Crittenden, 20th Inf.	11. Mr. W. B. Custer
5. Lt. Col. G. A. Custer, 7th Cav.	12. Mr. Reed

proper, timbered and narrow: then a treeless first bench, an open grassy plain, back of which is a rise, and prairie beyond.

I instructed the Sergeant who had the odometer cart and instruments to pace off the whole of the bottom land down to the Indian village, taking compass bearings, to make a plat. The position occupied by Maj. Reno was across the river on bluffs 80 to 90 feet high. The troops were not in position when I arrived and I plotted their positions on the map as I was told. Except for relative points, it is a mere sketch, not like a transit and chain survey. The dotted lines illustrate my report, and are what I supposed were the troop

[RENO'S SKIRMISH LINE]

trails. The skirmish line was placed for me by some officer I don't remember. The line indicates direction and is not intended to show troops stretched across the bottom. The odometer was run across the part from point "B". It is full of ravines and hillocks, covered with gravel and sand, and little grass. Views were taken with prismatic compass and intersection lines taken, and the map filled in by eye. The distance between "Reno's command" and "E" where Gen. Custer's body was found, is correct, as are the ravine's location and general direction of the battlefield. I can't tell the position or arrangement of the Indian village, as the ground was strewn with things they had left. I put in tepees to give a general idea of its location.

[RENO TO CUSTER, 4½ MILES]

The distance from Reno's position to point "E" is 4½ miles. Point "B" is a ford where it was supposed Custer attempted to cross, and the line indicates tracks of men and horses. No well defined trail was found; the ground being covered with tracks.

[THE SIGNS OF BATTLE]

Near point "B" there were empty shells and marks of ponies and horses, and as we advanced we found bodies

and more shells on the crest of a hill. There were bodies
all the way from "D" to "E", and in ravine "H", 28 bodies
were found. We found Government and Winchester shells
and one peculiar brass shell supposed to belong to Gen.
Custer's pistol.

[THE VALLEY BATTLEFIELD]

From Reno's position to point "B" is 2 4/10 miles by
dotted line, 2 2/10 in a straight line. Point "A" is Reno's
crossing, and between it and the skirmish line is open bottom
with cottonwood timber around the stream, and between
the bottom and first bench, underbrush. To Reno's right the
timber was 150 yards wide, and the blank space was sup-

[SITTING BULL'S LODGE]

posed to be where Sitting Bull's lodge stood. The timber was
continuous from Reno's right to point "B", 1 8/10 miles.
The right bank, above point "B", is the highest ground in
the vicinity, being 150′ above the bottom. Precipitous
bluffs bordered the river near "B", and back of them was

[THE FIRST DEAD SOLDIER]

a valley. The first dead soldier we found was all alone,
6/10 of a mile from point "B". Reno's hill position was
1 2/10 miles from the river. The distance from point "C"
to the [re?] crossing was 9/10 of a mile.

Lts. Wallace and Hare were the first officers I saw. They
rode rapidly toward us and did not seem excited.

[EMOTIONS OF THE RESCUED]

On going upon the hill Gen. Terry and the rest rode up
and there were shouts and some enlisted men and officers
were crying, the tears rolling down their cheeks; and others
showed it in their voices. They talked rapidly and excitedly
about the affair. I stopped with the younger officers, and
Gen. Terry rode on to confer with Reno and Gen. Gibbon.
I did not see Maj. Reno till we'd been there over an hour.
He was not then at all excited. Also saw Benteen and French
—they were perfectly calm and quiet.

CROSS EXAMINATION, BY COUNSEL FOR MAJOR RENO

We came up the morning of the 27th; no Indians there except bodies in two standing lodges. The representation of Indian lodges on the map is not correct, being put in to give an idea of the camp, which was not there when I arrived. In the little space opposite point "C" we found evidences of an old camp, set apart as if for a particular chief. No evidence of lodges in the woods; but between the timber

[RENO'S POSITIONS UNCERTAIN]

and the bluffs there was. I cannot fix the location of Reno's position in the timber except as it was told me by some officer I don't remember. The dotted line does not accurately show the length of Reno's skirmish line and was not so intended; and I do not know whether or not point "C" correctly indicates the extreme of Reno's advance. The distance from "A" to "C" is 1 6/10 miles; between "C" and the square space in the timber is 1/6 mile. The timber on the right bank was sparse.

The first dead man was found on the second plateau near

[CUSTER'S ROUTE?]

point "B". The dotted lines represent only my idea of the paths taken to reach "E". I was not over it. From "D" to "E" there was a heavy trail. My theory was that Gen. Custer went to the ford and was met there and driven back, and they separated into two bodies to concentrate at the hill "E", and the lines represent my idea of the routes they took. Capt. Benteen was sent over to hill "E" before I was there and the tracks there and at "B" may have been made by his troops. It was at least an hour after we arrived that I saw Maj. Reno. He was then cool. I understood that he changed position during the night of the 25th, but have only hearsay knowledge.

RE-DIRECT EXAMINATION

The map (Exhibit 2) was made in my official capacity, and I regard it as reasonably accurate as to relative troop

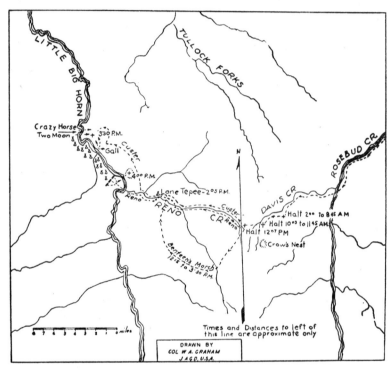

Map showing movements of the several columns of the Seventh Cavalry, June 25, 1876, with times and distances.

positions, the village, the stream and other prominent points. The data first was obtained on the 27th and 28th of

[THE LINES DISTINCT]

June 1876. The lines on the right side of the river were more distinct than any others. From "D" to "E" bodies were found at intervals, and it was my idea that Capt. Calhoun had stopped at "D" and the other companies had formed some sort of skirmish line from "D" to "E". We found Calhoun and Crittenden and some men at "D".

EXAMINATION BY THE COURT

The dotted lines indicate practicable trails. The river was fordable all the way from "A" to where Reno [re?] crossed. Above "B" it was not fordable because of the bluffs, except at the dotted line, where there was a large ravine. I think Capts. Benteen and Weir went there with their troops.

RECROSS EXAMINATION

The river is 30 to 40 yards wide to the right of point "C"; it varied from 30 to 75 yards along there. Its average depth was about to the stirrups of a horseman.

THE SECOND WITNESS WAS

LT. GEORGE D. WALLACE,
7th Cavalry

DIRECT EXAMINATION

Gen. Custer's command consisted of the entire 12 troops of the 7th Cav. Maj. Reno was second in command. There were while the command was all together on the 25th of June, all signs of the proximity of hostile Indians, and the reports of Indian Scouts indicated that they were within 25 miles.

[THE COMMAND DIVIDED]

At about 12:15 P. M. the command was halted; 3 companies were given to Maj. Reno; 3 to Capt. Benteen, and

1 to Capt. McDougall, who was placed in charge of the pack train and Gen. Custer took the other 5 with him.

[BENTEEN DEPARTS]

At the time of the division I don't know what orders were given. Capt. Benteen moved to the left. Gen. Custer moved down the right bank of a little stream and Maj. Reno down the left bank. Maj. Reno had 110 to 115 men, including Indian Scouts. Benteen had more. Custer had about 225.

[CUSTER AND RENO ADVANCE]

After Benteen started to the left Gen. Custer and Maj. Reno moved down this little stream. Custer on the right and Reno on the left. They moved from 100 to 200 yards apart. After going 10 or 12 miles, Maj. Reno was called over to the right bank where Gen. Custer was. The two

[RENO ORDERED FORWARD]

battalions then moved parallel for some distance. We passed a tepee which had some dead bodies in it and soon after that the Adjutant came to Maj. Reno and said that the Indians were about 2½ miles ahead and Maj. Reno was ordered forward as fast as he could go to charge them and the others would support him. I was riding near Maj. Reno and with his battalion. The little stream I spoke of is a tributary of the Little Big Horn and runs into it a mile or two above where the Indian village was.

The first I saw of the village was after we were dismounted and were forming skirmish line. Others may have seen it before, but I did not; there was some timber between us and the village. Gen. Custer's order to charge was, I think, promulgated to Maj. Reno's command by the Adjutant. The two columns were then parallel, 25 to 50 yards apart. I don't know where Benteen was then; he had moved to the left over broken ground and was not in sight.

[THE ATTACK ORDER]

Gen. Custer's order was about this: "The Indians are about

2½ miles ahead on the jump. Follow them as fast as you can and charge them wherever you find them, and we will support you." I think those were the words. I am not positive as to "we".

The length and width of the village I could not tell, because the timber hid it.

[THE INDIAN VILLAGE]

Of the exact size at that time I could form no estimate, but I saw plenty of Indians. Afterwards, when we passed over it, the village was found to be over 3 miles long and varying in width from a few hundred yards to a ½ mile where the tepees had stood.

[RENO'S BATTALION]

When Reno received the order to charge he had 22 Indian Scouts and 3 companies of cavalry; average 35 to 40 men. They had been marching for 3 or 4 days, making long marches; up all the night before and moved that morning with little or no breakfast. The men were tired and the horses worn out.

[RENO'S ADVANCE]

At the time the order was given we were moving along the right bank of the little tributary to the Little Big Horn, at a gallop. After going some distance the trail led to the left and we re-crossed this little stream. A few hundred yards further we came to a ford on the Little Big Horn that had been used by the Indians. It was about belly deep to the horses. We crossed and halted to reform. Companies A and M were formed in line with the Indian Scouts under Varnum and Hare ahead; and my company in rear in line as a reserve. There were 22 scouts. We moved forward first at a trot and then at a gallop. The Indians when the order was given were apparently running. There was a big dust; but as that cleared we saw them coming back. After moving some distance my company was brought to the left of the line and the command moved in that way until near the timber. There the command was halted, dismounted and prepared to fight on foot. The horses were put in the timber

[RENO DISMOUNTS TO FIGHT ON FOOT]

and the men deployed, with the right on the timber and the left extending toward the bluff. The line was only a few hundred yards long. The Indians, instead of pressing our front, passed to our left and opened a flank fire. When we went on the skirmish line I for the first time saw the village and the Indians were thick on our front and were passing to our left and rear. After a short time it was reported that they were coming to the opposite bank and were trying to get our horses. Company G was taken off the line and put

[THE SKIRMISH LINE FALLS BACK]

in the timber. The skirmish line soon had to fall back into the timber on account of exhaustion of ammunition and Indians on left and rear. After being there some time the Indians commenced firing from across the stream 50 yards from us and in our rear in the timber. There was no protection where we were and on the other side was a bank.

["WE WILL HAVE TO CHARGE THEM!"]

Word was passed that we would have to charge them, as we were being surrounded and no assistance had come, and we must get to a better defensive position. The companies were mounted and commenced getting out. I could not find Lt. McIntosh commanding Company "G", and so I

[RENO'S RETREAT]

mounted what men I could find and started. When I got out I saw the troops in column of fours at a gallop. I followed along with my men. The command did not follow its own track, but crossed lower down and were making towards the bluff. The Indians were in the bottom and we rode through them. They would ride along beside the column and fire into it. At the creek they halted and fired at the men as they crossed. They came over with the rear of the column and one or two men were killed there. After getting to the top of the hill we halted and prepared to stand them off. Soon afterwards it was reported that Benteen was

[OUT OF AMMUNITION]

coming up, and he joined us. We were out of ammunition, had several wounded, and I could find but seven of my company. We waited then for the packtrain to come up. Then we got ammunition and attempted to move on, but Capt. Moylan could not move his wounded. It took 6 to carry one and the Indians were coming up thicker, and we had to fall back and take position. The men worked all night the 25th. There were only 3 spades and with these and tin cups

[INDIANS ATTACK AT DAYLIGHT]

they scraped and dug rifle pits. On the morning of the 26th the Indians opened at daylight. After 12 the fire was not so heavy, except from prominent points, where they located sharpshooters. Some time near sunset we saw the village moving off.

[THE VALLEY FIGHT]

After Reno received the order to charge we moved a mile and a half or two miles at a gallop to the crossing in about 15 minutes. The crossing was not opposed. The fight commenced two miles further on. The crossing was over two miles from the nearest part of the Indian village; broad bottom all the way—first a belt of timber and after that a broad level prairie that had been covered with grass, but that had been grazed off and the ground cut up by pony hoofs. It was similar to an ash bed a mile or two wide to the foothills, and beyond that came the bluff. The stream (Little Big Horn) on our right was very crooked and we were sometimes close to the bank and sometimes away from it on account of the turns and twists. The first shot was fired about 1¾ miles from the crossing. We had seen lots of Indians, and after the skirmish line was formed and moved forward about 100 yards it got within 75 to 100 yards of the tepees. I had looked at my watch when Gen. Custer

[BEGAN AFTER 2:30]

called Maj. Reno over the little tributary and it was then 2 o'clock (that was before we had the order to charge), and estimating the distance we passed over, I should say it was after 2:30 when the fight commenced. The command "charge" was not given. We were moving at a gallop till we halted. We had been fired on and were being fired on when we halted, but had not returned the fire.

When we were first engaged, there was a loop of the Little Big Horn to the front of our right wing; to the left was open prairie and in front of that some hundreds of yards away, we could see a ravine, out of which were coming many Indians. When we formed skirmish line, there were two or three hundred Indians and these increased till we got out of the bottom.

[INDIAN STYLE FIGHTING]

They were fighting in regular Indian style—riding up and down—a few on foot, and some on the hills to the left passing around and coming on our rear, filling the whole space in our rear, a mile or two; not a solid mass, but riding around, yelling and hooting, and those in range were shooting.

My opinion is that the Indians knew what we were doing and exactly what our movements were from the time we left the mouth of the Rosebud the 22nd. Our scouts saw their scouts that morning (i.e., 25th) watching us and saw them riding back into the village. They knew of our approach and were ready. After we crossed the stream their running was only a sham. They ran and then turned back to meet us. They probably did not notice Reno's command until it crossed, but they knew we were coming and could see the dust for miles.

After dismounting and forming skirmish line, Maj. Reno went back with Lt. McIntosh and Company "G" to the timber and I did not see him again until we were driven

[THE RETREAT DESCRIBED]

into the timber; and I could not see him then on account of brush, but I heard his order to get ready to charge. Exactly what the orders were I don't know, but I heard his voice and recognized it. The engagement lasted, I estimate, about three quarters of an hour. Up to the time we left the timber to go on the hill, only two men were killed or disabled, and I heard of one other. As I rode out of the woods, the Indians were scattered all over the country. They were thick as trees in an orchard, or thicker. The men were in column of fours and as they came up the Indians would give way and let them pass them and then fire at them. After the men had passed, if they saw that a man was not using his pistol they would ride close and fire. One came within ten feet of me.

I did not see the first formation. When I got out I saw the other companies moving at a gallop. If the Indians had closed in they could have made short work of us, but I had no fear of it then. It was about one half or three quarters of a mile from the timber to the hill to which we retreated; took us about 15 minutes. I did not see Reno during the retreat. Where we re-crossed the Little Big Horn was about 25 feet wide and belly deep to a horse. The left bank was four or five feet high and the right bank probably 8 feet. There was a narrow place on the right bank to get up on and consequently the men could not get out as fast as they got in. But they crossed in three to five minutes, I think. The hill was about a quarter of a mile from the stream. In my opinion there was no defensible position on the left side of the Little Big Horn. On the other side the hills were high and broken, and furnished a better position in which to defend yourself, but from that side the village was not threatened.

[CUSTER LAST SEEN: HIS TRAIL]

The last I saw of Gen. Custer was soon after the order

to move forward. He was moving to our right at a slow trot. I did not see him again and supposed he was following. He must have been to our right and rear when we first engaged the Indians.

I don't know where Custer's trail passed, but suppose it passed near where we took our stand. On June 28th, when we moved out to bury the dead, I was told we followed his trail, but have since been told we did not. We moved down to a point about two and a half miles below our position and then back up on a hill on the bank of a large ravine. After going two or three hundred yards we found the first man and some distance further on found others. From then on they were scattered all over the country for about a square mile.

We followed his supposed trail down to the Little Big Horn. There or near there was a gray horse; then back almost on a line perpendicular to the creek two or three hundred yards was a dead man on top of a hill, his body filled with arrows. Then to the left and down the creek were found some of the men. Further on they became thicker, till we crossed over two ravines where we found more men and horses; then we came apparently to where the last stand had been made; there were the killed in a kind of circle, the bodies lying around thick. The evidences were of a retreating and running fight. This was about three miles from Reno's position. From the place the first bodies were found to the place of the last stand was about a mile. Where we found the first horse was a ravine, making a little valley running to the river; on a knoll was the first man and then another ravine running into the first; then a ridge and over to a second ridge. It was on this second ridge the last stand was made; a sort of T shaped ridge; not the highest point, for there was a higher one between it and the river and back of it two hundred yards a still higher one.

Custer's command could not have been seen from Reno's

position. Whether their firing could have been heard I don't know. I heard none; though others will testify that they did. I heard scattering shots in the bottom on the left but no heavy firing. It was apparently in the village; it did not sound like fighting.

[CUSTER ENGAGED BEFORE RENO REACHED HILL]

By the time Reno occupied the hill Custer must have been engaged beyond the point we found the first body. Capt. Benteen with about 120 men arrived about 10 minutes after Reno got on the hill; it was well on to an hour before the pack train got up, guarded by McDougall, and probably 140 men.

When we first occupied the hill (after moving down the river and back again), the Indians commenced firing—they were coming back from Custer. They occupied several high points down the river, and others passed round up stream to a little knoll.

[THE FIGHT ON RENO HILL]

In front of us was a long ridge and they occupied that and poured in a heavy fire until dark; it was a continuous roar. There would be lulls and then it would start again with a volley.

[NO SOLICITUDE ABOUT CUSTER]

Soon after Benteen came up, while we waited for the packs, most of the Indians left the bottom, some occupying points between us and where Custer fought; the remainder went back to the village. There was a high hill which hid the upper part of the village from us. After going through the valley they crossed and engaged Custer, but we could not see them on account of high ground between. After we occupied the hill there was no uneasiness or solicitude about Custer; but there was a great deal of swearing about Gen. Custer's running off and leaving us.

[ADVANCE AND RETREAT]

Capt. Weir moved his company in the direction of what proved to be Custer's field, and after the packs came and ammunition was distributed, the whole command moved in that direction. We were going to find out where Custer had gone to. I went to a point where I could see the place where Custer's battle occurred. Indians were all over the country, but no firing. All was quiet. Capt. Moylan could not keep up on account of his wounded and as the Indians were coming back in heavy force we had to go back to him. That was about five or six o'clock. Reno's losses in the valley fight that day were 27 killed and 7 wounded. After Benteen came, one in Weir's company was wounded and left; two in "K" killed, and one or two killed in Benteen's and several wounded. Of the companies in the bottom, "A" lost 8 killed and 5 wounded; "G", 11 killed; "M", 8 killed, 2 wounded. The other companies lost some also.

[2000 INDIANS]

I estimate the number of Indians around us about two thousand. They did not bother us much till we started forward. Then they commenced their second attack and took up every piece of ground that they could shoot from. Whether these were the same Indians who fought Custer I don't know. They had enough to have fought both commands; but I have no doubt that many came back from Custer to fight us. They all left our front after we left the bottom, and went in that direction but whether they took part in the Custer fight I don't know.

It was a cloudy day; not much wind. The sun went down as a red ball; the next day was cloudy and rainy. The spirit of the men was good the night of the 25th. No grumbling— worked all night, though tired and hungry and in need of water.

At this point in the proceedings, the Court, upon Maj. Reno's suggestion, announced that reporters would be permitted to make notes, reversing its former ruling.

CROSS EXAMINATION

The regiment was broken up shortly after noon, and divided into battalions, companies D, K and H to Benteen;

[NO BATTLE PLAN]

A, G and M to Reno; C, E, F, I and L remained with Custer; B company, Capt. McDougall, was packtrain guard.

There was no announcement made to Reno as to junction with Benteen that I know of. There was no plan for the reuniting of the 3 battalions that I ever heard of. Reno and Custer moved on from where Benteen diverged to the left, 9 to 12 miles, when Reno was called across the little tributary. Custer motioned with his hat. When Reno crossed there was no communication with Custer that I saw. They marched about a mile that way parallel. I was riding to the left of Lt. Hodgson, Reno's adjutant, and he to the left of Reno.

[THE ATTACK ORDER REPEATED]

After the two columns had marched about a mile Lt. Cook, the Regimental Adjutant, came over from Custer to Reno and said: "The Indians are about 2½ miles ahead; they are on the jump. Go forward as fast as you think proper and charge them wherever you find them and he will support you." I am in doubt as to the pronoun; but I understood and it was the understanding of all the other officers to whom I talked, that Gen. Custer was to support Reno. That was the only order I heard given. I went on with Reno till after we crossed. Reno moved off at a gallop till we came to the crossing; there we came to a walk and the horses scattered. The command crossed in column of twos, passed through the timber and halted and closed up and after entering open ground formed line. There was not a saber in the command. They had revolvers and carbines; revolvers loaded and two additional loadings, 18 rounds, 50 carbine cartridges in belt and 50 in saddle bags.

"A" Company was commanded by Capt. Moylan, "G" Company by Lt. McIntosh, and "M" Company by Capt.

French. After forming a line they moved at a trot and then at a gallop. "A" and "M" in front; "G" in reserve. While moving at a gallop "G" went up on the line at an increased gait.

[COOKE AND KEOGH START WITH RENO]

Lt. Cook and Capt. Keogh went with us toward the ford. I heard them talking as we rode along. I thought at the time they went into the fight with us.

While some of our men had been in service from two to four years, a great many of them were recruits who had never been on a horse till that campaign, and lost control of their horses when galloping in line. Reno was in front, to the right of the center. The command was halted and dismounted to fight and the horses taken into the timber. At this time about two hundred Indians were in sight. There was a heavy dust, indicating the presence of mounted men further down the valley. The first shots were fired at us after we had moved down a mile and a half or so, and before we dismounted. The Indians were then riding around and shooting and passing around us, between us and the place we crossed. The skirmish line advanced till the right struck the loop in the river and then halted, below the point "C". The line stayed there till the left was enveloped and then had to fall back into the woods. The map (Exhibit 2) does not correctly place the skirmish line; the angle and length are wrong. The map does not represent the ground.

Maj. Reno went to the woods with Lt. McIntosh and Company "G". Lt. McIntosh was killed during the retreat from the bottom.

[RENO'S CONDUCT GOOD]

Maj. Reno's conduct was all that could be expected from any one. The troops could not have been handled any better. We were in the bottom about three quarters of an hour and about two thirds of that time on the line. The troops used up most of their 50 rounds. One company had to get ammunition from the saddle bags.

The Indians were at our ford long before we went into the timber and in large numbers, and they were moving down the opposite side of the river in large numbers also. Some few of them were getting into the timber.

[CUSTER DID NOT SUPPORT]

While on the line, when I first saw the village, I looked back and did not see Gen. Custer coming. The first officer I saw was Capt. Moylan and I asked him if we could not communicate with Gen. Custer. There was a half-breed scout named Jackson and we asked him if he could not go. He waved his hand to the rear and said there were too many for one man to go through. That was the first time I had seen the Indians to our rear. Up to that time I had expected Custer and his men to support us.

[RENO DID THE RIGHT THING]

I think Reno did the only thing possible under the circumstances. If we had remained in the timber all would have been killed. It was his duty to take care of his command and to use his best judgment and discretion. I think his conduct as to courage was good, I saw no evidence of fear then or at any time. Before we retired from the timber, Indians were crossing the river on our right and firing on us from the right bank. The map shows timber there, but there was

[TIME OF VALLEY FIGHT AND RETREAT]

none. It was about 2:20 when we first crossed the river; 2:30 to reach the timber and about 3:15 to 3:30 when we reached the hill in retreat. There were many Indians ahead of us on the hilltop over there, and Lt. Hodgson was killed about 50 yards after crossing the stream by a shot from the bluffs, and Dr. DeWolf by the Indians on that side. We lost about 27 killed and 7 wounded in the bottom. I don't know how many in the timber. The troops were first dismounted and deployed on the crest and then mounted and moved back about the time we heard that Benteen was coming. He was close to us, about 200 yards, not coming over our trail, but to the right of it. The packtrain was then about 3 miles to our rear.

[NO WORD FROM CUSTER]

No communication of any sort had been received from Custer, except that a trumpeter (Martin) had been sent back to Capt. Benteen. I heard no firing when on the hill from the direction of Custer's field; only some scattering shots to the left.

[THE FIGHT ON THE HILL]

When the whole command started in the direction Custer had gone, we got only about a mile. The movement was by Maj. Reno's order, after the pack train was up and ammunition replenished. Moylan couldn't keep up on account of wounded and there was heavy firing on Company "D." I was on the right from where I could see all over the Custer field. There were lots of Indians riding around quietly, no firing going on. They seemed to be moving back our way in large numbers; several thousand Indians. Weir fell back to Moylan—the head of the column was nearly up to Weir—and then there was a general movement back to the position we occupied on the night of the 25th and the 26th. The men were dismounted, and formed in as near a circle as the ground would permit. Horses in a swale. The ravine was like a saucer with one side out. The wounded were placed behind the horses. The Indians followed and surrounded us about 5 to 6 P.M. Deep twilight came about 9 P.M. Firing till then, very heavy. Commenced again on the 26th before 3 in the morning and continued till after 10. Between 10 and 12 there was considerable, but the afternoon was comparatively quiet. Later, none at all and at sunset the village was moving away. It took a long time. We estimated that it was two and a half to three miles long and one half mile wide. I thought then there were four to five thousand—now from what I've heard from the Indians, I think about nine thousand.

HOW MANY INJUNS?
[W.A.G.]

The fighting strength of the Indians and the population of their village at the Little Big Horn pose questions that have puzzled many people, myself frankly included. Like some other questions that inevitably arise when studying this battle, each is capable of an easy answer, or a hard one. The easy answer is, of course, that nobody knows, nor ever will, how many Indians were there; the one certainty is that there were enough of them to win their greatest victory. The easy answer is true, but it begs the questions. The hard answer cannot build on certainties, but by marshalling available information, one may arrive at fairly reasonable estimates.

We know that the Indian village comprised at least six tribal circles, five of which pertained to segments of the Sioux Nation. The sixth was composed of Northern Cheyennes. The Sioux tribes represented were the Uncpapas, Blackfeet, Sans Arc, Minneconjou and Ogalalla. Augmenting the six circles, the village contained also a smattering of young men of other tribes, for the most part Siouan septs such as the Brulé, Yanktonnais and Santee, some stray Arapahoes and probably a few Gros Ventres.

Each tribe camped by itself, in a great circle of tepees and/or lodges, and between the circles stood numerous wickiups, most of which were occupied by "strays" and young unattached men, and some of which were used for sanitary and other purposes.

No actual count of the tepees and/or lodges was made; nor of the wickiups. While the village was standing, there was neither time nor opportunity to make one. Officers who examined its location after the Indians withdrew, basing their estimates upon the number of sites distinguishable in limited areas by abandoned lodge poles and other evidences of occupancy, generally agreed that the standing village had contained from 1500 to 2000 tepees and/or lodges, and from four to five hundred wickiups.

Dr. Marquis, author of "A warrior who fought Custer," learned from Wooden Leg and other Cheyenne elders that their own tribal circle contained some 300 lodges, with a population of about 1600, of whom more than 500 were warriors. They told him also that the Blackfeet Sioux circle was of equal size, the Sans Arc's larger, while those of both Minneconjou and Ogalalla were larger than the Sans Arc's. The Uncpapa circle, they said, was twice the size of their own circle. If one accepts this Indian statement as the basis for a computation, and assumes the proportions constant, he can estimate both the population and the warrior strength of the six circles. It adds up about as follows: Cheyennes 1600, warriors 500 plus; Blackfeet Sioux, 1600, warriors 500 plus; Sans Arc (larger), say 1700, warriors 530; Minneconjou and Ogalallas (both larger than Sans Arc), 1800 each (or 3600), warriors 1125; Uncpapas (double the Cheyenne) 3200, warriors 1,000 plus. Total population 11,700—warriors, 3,655 plus. Add to these figures the probable number of occupants of the wickiups, most of whom presumably were young men, and we may safely add another 400 to 500, making a grand total of fighting men in excess of 4,000.

How nearly accurate these figures are can never be known; but if the Cheyenne story is even reasonably near the truth, they are not far from correct. Dr. Marquis estimated the population of the village at 12,000, which would account for some 3,750 warriors. But he did not take into account the occupants of the wickiups, who were numerous.

The estimates made by various witnesses at the Inquiry run from 1,800 to 9,000; the latter figure being based, however, upon what the witness (Lt. Wallace), understood the Indians to have reported. His own estimate was far lower. It is not unlikely that the 9,000 figure was just another instance of bad interpreting, a principal cause of misunderstanding during the Indian War period, and that his Indian informants were probably trying to tell Wallace the population of the village—not its fighting strength. And that such was the case is indicated by the testimony of Edgerly, who quoted Indian sources for his estimate of 4,000 warriors, and a village population of six to seven thousand, the high proportion of warriors being due to the presence of war parties which in Indian custom, had no women or families with them.

As the reader scans the Inquiry testimony, he will find many differing estimates of the population, and of the number of warriors also. If the many differences prove anything, they prove that the witnesses did not know, and therefore gave their best judgment with little but guesswork to rely upon.

Immediately after the battle, and before any Seventh survivor had an opportunity to ride over the ground where the village had stood, General Terry interrogated various officers as to the size of the hostile force. According to Capt. E. W. Smith, his Adjutant, their estimates then pivoted around the figure 1,800. After they observed the immensity of the village, however, these estimates increased, and properly so. Thus we find Benteen in a letter to his wife dated 4 July 1876, stating the fighting force of the Indians as 3,000; and 3,000 will be found the average figure around which pivots the estimates of most of the Inquiry witnesses, both military and civilian. But these were estimates only (perhaps guesstimates would be a better word), and it is unquestionably true that because of the impracticability of counting them during the action, there may have been many more, or many less. The Indians were individual fighters who moved about when, where and as they pleased; they neither moved nor fought by organizations, for they had none. Several of the witnesses make clear that it was practically impossible to do more than guess at their numbers at any given time.

In Reno's valley fight, for example, the estimates vary widely— from two to four hundred at the beginning to eight hundred or a thousand at the end. This means only that the force of Indians increased as the fight progressed. When Reno broke from the woods and gained the hills on the east bank, these Indians followed until they saw Benteen approaching. Then a large part of them, nobody knows how many, rode down river under Gall's leadership to take part in the attack on Custer, which had already begun. The rest remained to watch Reno.

Against Custer were first arrayed the Cheyennes, Minneconjous, Sans Arcs and Ogalallas, and these were augmented by the larger part of the Uncpapas and Blackfeet under Gall. If Marquis' figures are correct, Custer had at least 3,500 Indians to fight, providing all were there except those who had stayed to watch Reno. If Marquis' figures are not correct, one can scale the number that opposed Custer up or down accordingly. If one uses the 3,000 estimate, there were some 2,750 against Custer; if one uses the 1,800 estimate, Custer was wiped out by some 1,600 warriors, and so on.

The fight on Reno hill was participated in, *probably,* by more warriors than were arrayed against Custer; at least this was so during the late afternoon of the 25th. But at dawn on the 26th after an all night's carousal, fewer warriors felt the urge to turn out, and as the day wore on, Reno's opponents gradually decreased until all finally withdrew. It is probable, however, that during the late afternoon of the 25th, the whole fighting force of the Indians was pitted against Reno, and that all got into it at one time or another, though it is not likely that all were engaged at any one time.

During the 20's I discussed with a number of Reno's men, then at the Soldiers Home in Washington, D. C., the number of Indians who opposed them in the valley and on the hill. I got all kinds of estimates. Finally one of them, I think it was Sgt. Fremont Kipp, remarked: "Frankly, we haven't any idea how many Injuns there were; we do know there was a hell of a lot of 'em,—more than we ever saw before or since. I'll tell you why all we can do is guess. You take a stick and stir up a big ant hill; stir it up good and get the ants excited and mad. Then try to count 'em. The Injuns were like that at the Little Big Horn."

I gave up. I quit figuring because it was getting me nowhere fast. So I "estimated" too, and took the higher figure because it seemed to me the most reasonable in view of all the evidence. I thought the warrior strength exceeded 4,000 and still do. But don't let my belief deter *you* from figuring. The solution of indeterminate equations is excellent mathematical exercise.

[GENERAL TERRY BRINGS RELIEF]

At 9 A.M., on the 27th, we saw dust; and scouts sent out reported it was Gen. Terry. I was sent by Reno to Terry. I reported to him that I had been sent to show him how to get to our position. He asked me who was there and I told him Reno and 7 companies. He asked me in detail what occurred; how the fight commenced and the result. When I got time I asked him where Gen. Custer was, and received

reply that they had all been killed. This was the first intimation; we were looking for him back the first night and didn't
understand why we hadn't seen him. The command thought
Custer had sent us in and then gone off and left us to look
out for ourselves—that he had made an attack and probably
been defeated and had gone off down the river to meet Gen.
Terry.

[THE CUSTER BATTLEFIELD]

I can form no estimate of Custer's route except from the
bodies found. I saw no evidence of fighting at ford "B," and
I am unable to state how many dead we found on the field.
The companies were formed in column of fours and moved
parallel and each would bury the dead it found; and the
number each company commander had buried was reported
to me and the total made up.

The body of Capt. Calhoun was on the top of the last
ridge—not the one on which Gen. Custer was found, but
that ran at right angles to it, marked "D" on the map. There
was some indication of a line there. There were none up to
that point. I afterwards saw some men in the bottom of a
deep ravine in skirmish order; they were of "E" Company.
After Calhoun's we found Keogh's men; they were half way
down the northern slope, between Custer and Calhoun and
they appeared to have been killed running in file, but not in
skirmish line. These men occupied most of the ground well
in toward Custer. Custer's body was found at point "E." The
men around him (4 or 5) were piled in a heap beside a
horse, and the body of Custer was lying rather across one
of them. They had struggled but not for long; they had apparently tried to lead the horses in a circle on the point of
the ridge and had killed them there and made an effort for
a final stand. There were twenty or thirty men, not all right
around Custer. I saw no indication (except as to Calhoun)
of any lines; they were not killed in order but were scattered
irregularly all over the hill, south and east of Custer.

At one or two places I saw little piles of cartridge shells, twenty-five or thirty. This was near where Calhoun was killed. Very few elsewhere.

[CUSTER'S FIGHT DID NOT LAST LONG]

I do not think the fight lasted long. I think the Indians met Custer as he came down to cross and did not give him time to make a stand. The country was not one in which a prolonged resistance was possible; his position was on a ridge; there was no way to protect himself. I do not think it lasted above one half hour.

From the point I last saw Custer to where his body was found was six or seven miles. It would have taken him more than an hour from the time we separated to get there. All his men were killed so far as I know.

[STRENGTH OF CUSTER'S AND RENO'S COLUMNS]

Custer had about 225 men; Reno, after the union with Benteen and McDougall, about 280. Reno's was the only command that crossed the Little Big Horn.

I can recall no act of Maj. Reno during those two days that exhibited any lack of courage as an officer and soldier, or that I can find fault with; nor any lack of military skill.

[HORSES EXHAUSTED]

The horses of the command were exhausted. We had left the mouth of the Rosebud the 22nd of June and made a march of twelve miles that day. The next day (23rd), 33 to 35; there was not much grazing and little grain, not more than a pound or two. The next day (24th) we made 30 miles and camped. There was little grass. The ponies had eaten it up. We started again at 11 o'clock that night and moved till daylight (25th). The horses were stopped again without anything to eat. We moved again at 8 or 8:45, having gone about 10 miles during the night. From that point we moved on into the fight. On the 24th we moved 30 miles during the day and during the night 8 or 10. The 25th, anywhere from 25 to 35 miles. There was hardly any grazing; the ponies had clipped the grass almost like a lawn mower.

Reno lost no time after the packs came up in moving in the direction Custer had gone. Ammunition had first to be distributed and he moved as soon as practicable.

RE-DIRECT EXAMINATION

Reno received the order to charge about 2:15 P.M. I had looked at my watch when Custer called Reno to his side of the little stream. It was then about two o'clock; taking the distance we passed over I estimate it as 2:15 when Reno

[JUNCTION WITH BENTEEN 4:00 P.M. OR LATER]

received the charge order. It was about one and a half hours later that we were joined by Benteen on the hill or at 4 P.M. or later. Custer's fight must have been going on at that time, if it was not after. My watch may have been fast or it may have been slow. I never claimed it was the local time of the place.

When we crossed, Custer must have been to our right and rear. Benteen to our left and rear, but I knew nothing as to his orders and expected no assistance from him. I supposed from what Lt. Cook said that our support would come from Custer, not Benteen. I don't know where Lt. Cook and Capt. Keogh turned back. I saw them within a half mile of the ford "A."

[MAGUIRE'S MAP NOT ACCURATE]

I do not think the Maguire map accurately represents the principal and important features of the battlefield, except as to relative positions. The points "D" and "E" are the best part of the map.

When we moved downstream in Custer's direction, Maj. Reno was at the head of the column; the men were in column of twos, 150 to 200 yards long. We went about three quarters to a mile. I was toward the rear. We moved to within 200 yards of Capt. Weir's position on the high point he had gotten to. They were then skirmishing in front and we prepared to take part in it. My company was sent to a high point on the right and another came up on my left. The command then occupied two almost parallel ridges and had no way of defending the space between; it was in two lines and the end toward the Indians open, and it was ordered to fall back to a better position; by whom I don't know. There was heavy firing on Weir's company, and Godfrey's company acted as rear guard when we fell back, and received a heavy fire. The only casualty I heard of there was one of Weir's company who was wounded and left.

[INDIANS ESTIMATE 9000 WARRIORS]

When the Indian village moved off several officers were together and we tried to make an estimate. It was the largest body of Indians I ever saw. My estimate of 9000 warriors is based on information received from the Indians. They state that they had 1800 lodges and counted 5 to 7 warriors to a lodge. There were also wickiups occupied by visiting bucks. I don't know what proportion of the Indians were women and children.

The firing I heard to the left came from the opposite side of the river and nearer than Custer's field. I heard not over a dozen shots, and they were not in quick succession.

EXAMINATION BY THE COURT

Gen. Custer, I think, after we moved forward, followed our trail for about one half mile and then swung to the right at almost a right angle; then owing to the nature of the country the two trails would tend toward the same point several miles down river.

RE-CROSS EXAMINATION

The position we took was nearer the water and better adapted to defense than the advanced point Capt. Weir got to.

THE THIRD WITNESS CALLED BY THE RECORDER WAS

F. F. GIRARD
Citizen and Interpreter

DIRECT EXAMINATION

I was ahead of the command till about 11 o'clock. Was present when Reno was ordered off. A few minutes before I had ridden up on a little knoll near where was a lodge with some dead Indians in it, and from this knoll I could see the town; the tepees and ponies. I turned my horse sideways, and

["HERE ARE YOUR INDIANS"]

waved my hat and hallooed to Gen. Custer "Here are your Indians, running like devils." This knoll was on a tributary to the Little Big Horn, about 50 yards to the right of a lodge that contained some dead Indians, and about one and a quarter miles from the river at nearest point. Reno was ordered forward almost at once.

About eleven o'clock on the evening of the 24th Gen. Custer sent for me and ordered me to take the Indians named Half Yellow Face and Bloody Knife and ride at the head of the column with him. He said to be sure to take the left-hand trail; he didn't want any Sioux to escape; he wanted to get them all together and drive them to the Yellowstone. While the two Indians were locating the trail, Gen. Custer and I sat and talked. He asked me how many Indians I thought he would have to fight and I told him not less than 2500.

[CUSTER CONFERS WITH SCOUTS]

Custer asked the two Indians if he could cross the divide before daylight. They said "No." Then he asked if he could cross after daylight without being discovered. They said "No." Then he asked where there was ary timber where they could be concealed during the day.

I heard Gen. Custer give the order to Reno.

The General hallooed to Reno and beckoned him over. Maj. Reno rode over and Custer said "You will take your battalion and try to bring them to battle and I will support you"; and as the Major was going off he said "And take the scouts with you."

I joined Reno; having heard the order, that's where my duty was. It was about noon. We lost sight of Custer's column after going about a mile, when we arrived near a knoll, right at the river bank.

THE TIME PUZZLE
[W.A.G.]

Nearly everyone who has made a serious study of the Little Big Horn has emerged from it puzzled and bewildered by the differences in the times he finds assigned by persons whose veracity he has no reason to doubt, as the very hours at which particular events occurred,—differences that in many instances approximate as much as two hours, and sometimes more.

Early reports of the battle, it is interesting to note, invariably put the crossing of the divide at about 10 a.m., the division of the regiment into battalions at about 10:30 a.m., and so on. When we scan the time periods of the official intinerist, however, we find that the divide was crossed about 12:000 noon, the battalion division made at 12:05; and that the regiment marched at 12:12 p.m.

Throughout the record of proceedings of the Court of Inquiry, these differences in time, relating to the same and identical indidents, persist to confuse the reader and confound the student, both of whom are prone to throw down the book in dismayed disgust, and curse all witnesses as liars and dissemblers. There is, however, a reasonable and logical explanation of these discrepancies, which, if understood, should cool the fevered brows of outraged readers, and bring smiles in place of scowls and frowns to the countenances of worried students.

When I was a youngster in the grand old state of Iowa, I recall distinctly that our town operated everything on "Chicago time": but some communities in the northwest part of the state, operated on what was known as "railroad time," which was set by the Chicago and Northwestern Railroad. "Chicago time" and "railroad time," however, were to all intents and purposes, identical in that part of the country. Time zones, which prescribed what we know as Standard Time, were not established until 1884, when I was between 9 and 10 years old, and I have reasonably clear recollection of conditions that existed prior to their estab-lishment.

It was the habit and custom, before the establishment of legal time zones, for communities to adopt the time standard in use in a nearby city, and local telegraph offices in many towns each day received a "noon flash" by which local clocks were set. To what extent this custom prevailed throughout the entire country I do not know; but it is my belief that it was quite general. However, as it was not obligatory, any community or individual was at liberty to use sun time if he chose.

Fort Abraham Lincoln in Dakota Territory, operated on Chicago time, and it was *Chicago time* that was meant by those of the Seventh's officers who testified to *watch time* at the Inquiry. Lt. Wallace, the official itinerist, made it clear that his time entries *did not represent local sun time*, but were *the readings of his watch;* and Lt. Godfrey made it equally clear that the watches of the officers *had not been changed* since leaving Ft. Lincoln.

On the other hand, if the same custom prevailed in the west that was in vogue in the central part of the country, the far west probably operated on San Francisco time, between which and Chicago time there was a difference roughly of 2¼ hours.

It is advisable, however, to ignore the time periods fixed by various witnesses as much as possible, and to pin one's faith to the official periods designated by Lt. Wallace. It is possible, by using his time periods, to approximate closely the time that key incidents occurred; and by using the times of these key incidents as they relate to other events, to approximate the time of those events also.

It is unfortunate, surely, that one cannot be definite and certain, but it is a condition and not a theory that confronts the student here, which may best be met by not meeting it at all, but by avoiding a maze of conflict and confusion to which entry is all too easy, but from which, once in, there is, unhappily, no door of egress.

Before crossing the river the scouts on my left called attention to all the Indians coming up the valley. I called Reno's attention to it, and thought Gen. Custer should know about it and rode back toward the knoll, meeting Col. Cook; I told him and he said "All right, I'll go back and report."

After Custer gave the command to Reno, I called out to the scouts "We are ordered to go with this party and join them." When we came to the creek skirting the knoll I halted some time and when I told Reno about the Indians coming up the valley he halted a second or two and gave the command "Forward."

As I came back from reporting to Col. Cook I could see Reno's command going down to where they dismounted and threw out the skirmish line. [*Here the witness referred to the map, Exhibit* 2.]

[CHARLIE REYNOLDS WAS DEPRESSED]

From this ford, marked "A," the march was not made in a direct line. It was made around skirting the edge of the timber, and the point where the skirmish line was drawn, was approached. I halted 45 or 50 yards back from the edge of the timber and there were Charlie Reynolds, Dr. Porter, George Hunbein (Herendeen) and Bloody Knife, and myself, and Reynolds asked if I had any whiskey. He said he never felt so depressed and discouraged in his life and needed something to stimulate him, so I gave him some, and offered it to the others, who refused it. I took some myself and told Reynolds not to take too much; that he needed a cool head; that we had plenty of business on our hands for that day.

We dismounted and just then the skirmish line was being drawn up, and the Indians were coming up. They were about 1000 yards distant from the left flank of the line, and in front. We fired a few shots at them.

[THE FIGHT IN THE VALLEY]

The firing had started with some of our scouts that had gone into a little valley after some ponies, and more Indians were coming up here and riding around the command. Charlie Reynolds and I fired a few shots at long range and then put our horses in the timber, and as we started up to get to the brow of the hill, a soldier hallooed, "Boys, I've got it; I'm hit." I told him to ride down to the timber, that the Doctor was there and would attend to him. Reynolds and I turned into the timber and we tied our horses 8 or 10 feet from the foot of the hill, and then the left flank of the skirmish line on the brow of the hill had been swung around and made the right flank. I didn't see the movement made. I was at the extreme right, Reynolds next, and then Lt. Varnum. We stayed there 4 or 5 minutes and fired about seven shots, when somebody gave the order "Men, to your horses: the Indians are in our rear."

The timber was here (pointing to the map) and we were facing the brow of the hill. Charlie Reynolds looked at me and I said: "What damn fool move is this?" Says he: "I don't know: we will have to go. We will have to get out of this," and went after his horse. I looked for mine, but the Indians had got on the brow of the hill and were firing on the troops, and the Indians on this side—

[*Here Major Reno interrupted the witness, who had been pointing to the map throughout the foregoing testimony, and was apparently confused. The Major stated: "The stream runs east and west in front of our position. I determined it with a compass."*]

[GIRARD CRITICISES MAGUIRE'S MAP]

The witness then continued—I think this map is wrong.

My remembrance of the lay of the country and the course of the stream and where the skirmish line was makes me think this map is wrong.

The Indians that were firing at that time were north of where we struck the woods. Reynolds had mounted. I was leading my horse and told him he had better dismount or he would get hit, as the Indians were firing at him. At the foot of the hill I saw him whip up and start on a run up the hill and I hurried up there, but could not see any men or

[CHARLIE REYNOLDS KILLED]

troops. I saw some Indians cut Reynolds off and shoot him down. He seemed to be pinned under his horse and had lost his gun, and in the meantime, I knew I had been discovered, so I turned my horse down the hill and hunted a place where I could defend myself.

When we left the brow of the hill, the troops were mounted and going by very fast—pell mell. I asked an officer "What are you going to do?" and says he, "Charge the Indians." Says I, "We'll go out slow; we don't understand bugle calls, and they will undoubtedly come back to the point of timber." The Indians set fire to the timber after the troops left.

From the time that Reno crossed the river it was not more than 10 minutes until he halted and deployed as skirmishers. From the ford the march was in a column skirting the edge of the timber, making a circuit and the skirmish line was drawn up, out from the outward edge of the bend of the timber. There were no Indians then within 1000 yards. The Indians were firing at our scouts and the scouts at them. They came closer, about 200 yards away. There were only about 50 or 75 of them.

[RENO'S LINE CHANGES FRONT]

I did not see that the skirmish line advanced any, and after a few minutes, while I was in the timber with Reynolds, it pivoted around so that the left flank became the right. The village at that time was a mile or half mile away. The timber was about 75 yards at the widest portion, narrowing to about 30 yards.

["EVERY MAN FOR HIMSELF"]

After leaving the skirmish line the troops stayed in the timber about ten minutes. They went diagonally across from the village. They were in a great hurry to get out—no order at all; every man was for himself. There were no Indians in the timber.

Lt. DeRudio, Pvt. O'Neill and Scout Wm. Jackson were left in the woods. This was about one o'clock in the afternoon. We left the timber at 9 P.M.; it had been dark only a few seconds. It was twilight; you could see, but not far. I looked at my watch both times: it was a very good time keeper.

The timber was a sheltered position. The Indians could not sight us from the rear; the underbrush was very thick.

[CONTINUOUS FIRING HEARD]

Ten or fifteen minutes after Reno left the timber I heard firing to the left of where he was: it was on my right and on the right bank. I could see the Indians going up the ravines on that side, and the firing was as if they were shooting at passing troops. I had seen troops back of that.

I heard continuous firing clear on down as if there was a general engagement, down to where I afterwards went to Gen. Custer's battlefield. And I heard firing to the left of the village; 3 or 4 volleys as if there were 50 to 100 guns at a volley. Lt. DeRudio was with me and he said "By God, there's Custer coming; let's go and join him." I told him to wait—that we had plenty of time—that when the firing got opposite we could go out and join him; that he was now too far away. I heard the volleys during the firing down there; after the heavy firing that sounded like a general engagement.

There was a continuous scattered fire all the time until it got down below where Custer's battlefield was and then it became heavy. There was a skirmish fire all the way down from where I first heard it.

When we went to bury the dead we found a wounded horse standing in the stream on the left side, a gray horse.

[HEAVY FIRING LASTED TWO HOURS]

The whole firing, from the time I heard it on the bluff to my right—on the right bank—they were firing till dark. But the firing along the line of march I first heard lasted twenty or twenty-five minutes. The heavy firing down at Custer's battlefield lasted about two hours.

The night of the 25th we left the timber and attempted to join Reno—got lost and ran into several parties of Indians, and we did not get to him until 11:30 o'clock on the night of the 26th.

[2500 TO 3000 WARRIORS]

My estimate of the fighting strength of the Indians is between 2500 and 3000.

The last I saw of Custer's column it was moving downstream very fast; this was about 15 minutes before Reno left the timber. No other command passed beyond the point

["I SAW CUSTER HALF WAY TO FORD "B"]

Reno was. It must have been Custer I saw about half way between Reno's position and the middle ford "B."

When I first came to the ford where Reno crossed and turned the knoll, I had a full view down the valley. The bottom was alive with Indians, at least 1500 of them. When we got in the woods I was astonished that there were not more around and having seen Custer down there and no more attacking us, I think they had discovered him and went to intercept him.

[MOST OF THE INDIANS ATTACKED CUSTER]

All the Indians I saw go to Reno's left and rear were about 200. The line was moved into the timber by the time they got within 300 yards. The bulk of those I first saw went to intercept Custer before he reached the village. The party I was firing at numbered only 20 or 30.

I think Reno could have held out against all the Indians as long as his ammunition and provisions held out if he were determined and resolute.

When I went to the Custer field, I found a ford. The marks around it indicated to me that Gen. Custer had attempted to cross, but was delayed and left it. I saw two dead bodies of white men on the north side, a half mile from the ford. I saw several dead horses in the village marked "U.S., 7th Cav."; they were to the right of some lodges. One of the dead men had on blue pants; the other was stark naked. There were several dead between Custer's body and the ford.

[AT THE CROW'S NEST]

At dawn, the 25th, the command was halted and ordered to make coffee with small fires, fires to be put out—horses to remain saddled and we would camp until after daylight. I laid down and slept and Gen. Custer woke me up to take two scouts that had come in from Lt. Varnum, and accompany him to the mountain. Lt. Cook or Tom Custer asked if the command would follow. He said "No, you will remain here until I return." We rode to the foot of the mountain and then walked to the top, where we found Lt. Varnum, Boyer and Bloody Knife. I returned with the General and met the command which in the meantime had moved after us about 3 miles. No orders had been sent back to move. Who ordered the troops to move on I can't say.

The horses of the command did not seem fatigued; they were on the bit; mine was; and comparatively fresh. I rode the same horse all the time.

CROSS EXAMINATION

From the mountain top where Lt. Varnum was, I could see a black mass moving which I took to be Indians and ponies.

When I saw them from the knoll by the dead warrior tepee, they were about 3 miles away, on the left in the bottoms; we were then about a mile from Reno's crossing. It was then I told Gen. Custer "Here are your Indians, etc."

[CUSTER IN PERSON ORDERED ATTACK]

The order I heard was given by Gen. Custer in person to Reno. I do not pretend to say that the Adjutant (Cook) did not deliver it first. I can't help what Lt. Wallace says.

When we got to the ford, and I saw the Indians I said "Major Reno, the Indians are coming up the valley to meet us." He looked at me, looked at the valley and gave the order "Forward." The Indians were two and a half miles away and in large numbers coming.

[CUSTER BELIEVED INDIANS WERE RUNNING]

I knew that Gen. Custer was laboring under the impression that the Indians were running away and it was important for him to know that they were not, but were coming to meet us. I thought the information might change his plans. He might have called in parties, or re-called Reno. I did not think it likely he would cross to support Reno.

[THE WARNING TO COOK]

When I got back to the ford the troops had crossed and gone on about 500 yards. They were crossing when I rode back to report, and met Lt. Cook about 75 yards from the crossing. He said "Hello, Girard, what is the matter?" I said I had come back to report that the Indians were coming to meet us and I thought Custer should know it. He said "All right, go on: I will go back and report." After the line was formed, I kept in rear of the command about 75 yards. I had galloped to overtake them and then fell in the rear on the left. When the skirmish line was formed, Reynolds, Dr. Porter, Herndine (Herendeen) and myself went to point 1 and dismounted. As I was about to go down into the timber at Point C, I looked up and saw what I took to be General Custer's column. It was at about the letter *D* in the word

COMMAND on the map; and at the rate it was moving, I think it would have travelled about 5½ miles by the time Major Reno reached the top of the hill. [The witness here indicated the point of advance by the figure 2].

The reason I said "What is this damn move" was because I thought that to move out into the prairie was like running into certain death. I didn't know what the intentions were, but when I understood the troops were to charge I supposed that they would then return.

The advance of Capt. Weir's company would not account for the heavy firing I heard in the direction of the Custer field. I do not suppose that it would be audible to Maj. Reno while the firing was going on right around him. But there was a couple of hours when there was no firing.

Reynolds was killed while trying to overtake Reno's troops when they left the timber at point 3. Major Reno dismissed me from my position of interpreter and Gen. Custer re-instated me, but I have no unkind feeling toward Maj. Reno.

The bodies I saw on the left side of the river were scalped.

RE-DIRECT EXAMINATION

[WHO MOVED THE COMMAND?]

The reason I say the command was moved forward without his orders when Gen. Custer was up on the mountain is that when he saw the command coming he put spurs to his horse saying "Now, who in the mischief moved that command"; and started at a fast lope. The first man we met was Col. Tom Custer and the first question the General asked him was "Tom, who moved the command?" His reply was "I don't know; the orders were to march and we marched."

I think it was the whole fighting force of the village that I saw coming up the valley to meet us, the time I reported back to Lt. Cook. The firing I heard on the right bank became general 15 to 25 minutes after the first shots, and lasted about 2 hours.

The wind's direction when I heard the firing was from that point. I know that from the smoke when the Indians set fire to the timber. It had ceased for about ½ an hour before the firing around Reno's hill position began.

EXAMINATION BY THE COURT

The middle ford [Point B] was not a crossing. The left side was miry. It was a watering place for the opposite side.

THE FOURTH WITNESS CALLED BY THE RECORDER WAS

LT. CHARLES A. VARNUM
7th Cavalry

DIRECT EXAMINATION

I was in command of the Indian Scouts. They reported on the morning of the 25th that they could see the village. I was not present when the battalion division was made. Reno's command was passing Gen. Custer and staff when I reported to Gen. Custer. That was about a mile from where Reno crossed. I joined him—one company had already crossed the river when I reached it. I had seen the village from the high bluffs an hour or more before the commands separated, but because of the bends of the stream and the timber, it was impossible to see much of it.

[THE INDIAN DUST SCREEN]

Eight or ten Indian Scouts were with me and as soon as the column passed I was joined by Lt. Hare who had been detailed to assist me. We started down the valley 50 or 75 yards ahead of the column. The bottom opened wider as we advanced down stream. There was a large body of Indians some distance off, running toward us and back and across the prairie in every direction, kicking up all the dust they could, so it was impossible to tell their number. At times they were apparently running away; then circling back and making a heavy dust. All of a sudden they stopped and turned back and as they did so I glanced back and saw the column deploying into line. It moved forward and we rode on, working to the left of Reno's line.

The Indians let us come closer, and we could see about one half way to where the final halt was made. We could see quite a number of tepees. The Indians didn't uncover the village much. We went down about two miles and the line halted and dismounted. I did not hear any of the orders. The Indian scouts disappeared and were gone; I didn't know where and so Hare and I rode to the line, and I reported to my company commander, Capt. Moylan.

The line was then deployed perpendicular to the general direction of the river and skirmishing at once commenced.

["G" COMPANY ENTERS THE TIMBER]

When I had been there ten or fifteen minutes I heard some of the men calling out that Company "G" was going to charge a portion of the village down thru the woods or something to that effect. I rode into the timber where there is a little glade or opening from which I could see the river and supposed we were going across. I saw Col. Reno there, deploying "G" Company, and I said "I'm going to charge." I rode to where Col. Reno was, and he said to me "I wish you would go back to the line and see how things are going on and come back and report to me."

On my way back I met Lt. Hodgson who had just come from the line and asked him to report to Reno how things were. When I got to the line, it had fallen back to the edge of the timber and was lying along the edge instead of perpendicular to it. I could not see all the men.

[THE HORSES MOVED]

Capt. Moylan called to me that the Indians were circling to the left and into the timber and our horses and ammunition would be cut off and something must be done. I told him I would bring them up and went back. I rode thru the timber to the left of the line and called for "A" Company to follow with their horses and I guess all the others followed. We went

to the rear of Capt. Moylan's company. I dismounted and
returned to the line, when I heard Capt. Moylan say that he
was out of ammunition and had ordered every alternate man
back to get ammunition out of the saddle bags.

[CHARGE OR RETREAT?]

When I got to the right of the line I met Girard and
Reynolds, and talked with them about 3 minutes, when I
heard cries: "Charge! Charge!; we are going to charge!"
There was confusion, and I jumped up and said "What's
that" and started down the woods and grabbed my horse.
Everybody was mounted. I didn't hear any orders. The men
passed and I followed out and let my horse race to the head
of the column which was then half-way to the place we
crossed soon after. I came up on the left side of the column,
and saw no officer at the head and supposed the column had
met some Indians and had wheeled and started for them
and the others had followed. I yelled to them to stop. I then
saw Maj. Reno and Capt. Moylan and they went on then to
the crossing. Immediately on the other side there is a high
bluff and they climbed that. The horses were tired and pant-
ing and could hardly make it.

My orderly was shot and I stopped to help him, so don't
know what happened at the head of the column. When I
arrived at the top of the hill I found several wounded there.
A few minutes after a column of troops was in sight coming
down stream toward us and we stopped ten or fifteen minutes
'till they came up. It was Benteen and his three companies.

I don't recall seeing Maj. Reno there until he came up
from the river and spoke about Lt. Hodgson's body at the
foot of the bluffs; that his watch was gone, etc. At this time
McDougall's company and the packs were not in sight and
Lt. Hare started to hurry them up.

[RENO ADVANCES TOWARD CUSTER AND RETREATS]

Reno then ordered me to take some men and bury
Hodgson's body. When the packs arrived three quarters of

an hour later, I got two spades and started. About two thirds of the way down, I saw some men coming out of the woods. There was one citizen and some soldiers dismounted, climbing the bluffs. Then Lt. Wallace called to me to come back and when I got there most of the command, except Moylan's company, had started down stream along the bluffs. He was hampered by his wounded, and moved very slowly. I started ahead, and in about one and a half miles found Weir's company. They were on the far point of a long range of high bluffs and were firing at Indians who seemed to be coming out from the prairie and turning back. A great many shots were fired at him. All the Indians in the country seemed to be coming a little distance off, as fast as they could come, and soon after we turned and gradually dropped back. I didn't see the troops leave the point, as I went back to Capt. Moylan to help with the wounded.

The troops fell back to a point a little further up stream than where we first touched the bluffs. It was a slow movement. The firing was kept up. The entire Indian force seemed to have turned back against us and we had to fight dismounted to cover the retreat to the position we occupied.

The firing kept up as long as we could see and the men fortified as well as they could with tin cups. On the 26th the fight continued nearly all day and the next day we were joined by Gen. Terry.

[THE VALLEY FIGHT DESCRIBED]

Our skirmish line was about two miles from the first crossing and about 800 yards from the nearest part of the village; the tepees in the bend of the river. After we crossed, it was about 15 to 20 minutes before the troops were halted and deployed. Moved at a fast trot, I think. I think it was about 2:30 P.M. when the skirmish line was formed.

To the right of the line was the thick timber, and then dense underbrush clear to the river, which may have been 100 yards away. I could not see it and don't know.

I don't know whether the line was ordered to charge before it was dismounted. I was not near enough to hear commands. A few shots had been fired by the Indians before the deployment. There was a sort of an engagement between the scouts and the Indians. I don't know who began it; there were some stray shots. Except for those few shots there was no firing on the line; these shots were at the left, toward the bluff. Lt. Hare fired a few, I think.

As soon as the line was formed, firing commenced from both troops and Indians. No further advance was made that I know of.

[IMPOSSIBLE TO COUNT INDIANS]

It is almost impossible to estimate the strength of mounted Indians. There was a large force there soon after the command was dismounted, and a large force circling around all the time and passing to the left and rear. The heaviest force was toward the right of the line, as that covered the village. There they came within three or four hundred yards.

I don't think there were less than three or four hundred Indians in Reno's immediate front, and there may have been a great many more. The number actually firing I can't say: a heavy fire was coming from there, and up the valley the whole country seemed to be covered with them. How many the dust concealed it is impossible to estimate. The dust more or less covered their main force. As a rule they fired from their horses, scampering around and pumping their Winchester rifles into us. The heavy dust was eight hundred or a thousand yards away. I would estimate that the fight lasted half an hour before the command went into the woods. Up to the time we left, I know of only two casualties, the 1st Sergeant of my company and my orderly.

[NO BUGLE CALLS]

I do not recollect hearing any bugle calls till the evening of the 26th. I don't know how the orders were given during the valley fight. I was on the line and heard the men yelling

"They are going to charge," and I made for my horse and mounted.

The timber was not a very safe place. At the time the move was made a great many bullets were dropping into the woods from the rear. I did not see any Indians there, and whether the bullets came from the bluffs above or from below I don't know. The bottom near the stream was heavy underbrush.

When the command retreated from the timber no rally point was designated that I know of. We stopped about four hundred yards from the point where we crossed in retreat, up a steep hill.

[INDIANS HAD WINCHESTERS]

When I came out of the timber there were a great many Indians riding along the column with Winchester rifles across saddles, firing into the column. A great many were in the bend next to the river. By the time I got to the head of the column those in front had run off. I saw fifteen or twenty to our left and near some clumps of bushes were others. Several bodies were found there.

HOW THE INDIANS WERE ARMED
[W.A.G.]

Of late years a persistent effort has been made to minimize the armament of the Indians at the Little Big Horn and to magnify the errors committed by the Seventh Cavalry.

In the face of the testimony of the men who were there, the claim now made in some quarters that but two or three warriors out of several hundred were possessed of repeating rifles, seems to me somewhat absurd. It is based largely upon the fact that when in 1877, the surrendering hostiles were disarmed, they turned in few repeating rifles, and handed over a collection of ancient and obsolete weapons whose appropriate place was a curio shop. Hence, it is argued, it is clear that they owned no Winchesters or Henrys, for, had they possessed such deadly tools, these "honest Injuns" would have produced them instanter. As the French are wont to say—"c'est rire."

I do not contend, nor have I ever believed, that the *majority* of the warriors at the Little Big Horn were possessed of repeating rifles; but that nearer ten percent than one percent were so equipped, I think established. In my opinion nearly all who were members of war parties were so armed. During Reno's retreat from the timber to the hills across the river, they swarmed along his flank, pumping shot after shot into his column from repeating rifles held across the withers of their ponies. Not only does the Inquiry testimony establish this as a fact, but the oral statement of every man I was able to contact throughout the years 1920-25, and who was in that column, confirmed it. It is probable that not less than two score of repeating rifles were used by the Indians during the dash for the river and at the crossing. Those men who met the Indians in action did not imagine their armament; they saw it at close range; they saw its deadly effect; and they saw of what it consisted.

These same men took part the following year in the disarming of the hostiles. They looked in vain for the repeating rifles that were used against them at the Little Big Horn; the rifles that they knew the Indians possessed. They could not find them. 1st Sgt. John Ryan of "M" Company has described the thorough searches that were made and expressed the conviction held by all of them that the Indians had concealed their best weapons miles away from their camps. They knew the troops were coming—they had plenty of time to prepare for their reception, and they did. (Hardin *Tribune,* June 22, 1923).

When Custer was disposed of, the warriors gained possession of more than two hundred Springfield carbines and Colt revolvers, and much ammunition beside. These weapons they distributed among the warriors who were poorly armed, and these same weapons, together with those used against Reno in the valley, were combined against him on the hill.

The price the Indians had to pay for modern weapons and for ammunition did not deter them. Despite the oracular pronunciamentos of present day pundits who appear to think that "Lo the poor Indian" refers to Lo's financial status rather than to his morals and education, the officers of the Old Army knew what was going on, and of the fortunes being made by traders in firearms. Gen. Charles King, then Adjutant of the 5th Cavalry, was on the ground, engaged in the effort made by the government "too little and too late," to stop that trade. King was no romancer when it came to treating facts of which he had personal knowledge; and in the introduction he was kind enough to write for my work "The Story of the Little Big Horn," he discussed as follows, this very matter.

"Only muzzle loaders had either white or red warriors in that bitter December of 1866; but in the famous 'Wagon Box battle' some months thereafter, * * * the first issue of Springfield breech loaders had given the Sioux their first lesson in the possibilities of warfare with the paleface. Then came the decade in which all over the wide Indian frontier, with the full knowledge if not connivance of the servants of one department of our paternal government, the red wards of the nation were gradually supplied with the latest model repeating arms and ammunition * * *. In plain words, * * the red warriors of the most famous tribes became possessors, not only of the single shooting rifle or carbine as issued to our infantry and cavalry, but, far more effective, the Henry or Winchester magazine rifle * * *.

"Summer after summer, loading up with these modern arms of the best make, enterprising fellow citizens steamed away up the Missouri, meeting their Indian customers at well known rendevous, and there bartering their weapons at standard rates—one hundred dollars worth of robes, hides or furs * * * the price demanded for either Henry or Winchester; and according to distance, ten, fifteen or twenty cents worth, as the price of a single cartridge, * * *.

"Deny these statements as some at least of the officials of the Indian Bureau occasionally did, the fact remains that between the date of the Wagon Box battle early in '67, and the triumphant summer of '76, nine out of ten of the warriors known to be on the warpath, had not only the magazine rifle with abundant supply of copper cartridges, but as a rule, two revolvers, Colt's Navy preferred. The very few dead that fell into the hands of our troopers fairly bristled with deadly weapons."

As the command rode out and across, the men were using revolvers—they had to jump the horses into the river; it was a straight bank four or five feet high; the other side was a little better; but my horse nearly threw me as he jumped on the other side; the water was about four and a half feet deep.

When I got across I started up a ridge to the left but some men called me back. Evidently they saw some Indians there, because Dr. DeWolf started up that ridge and was shot.

There were Indians on the hill we went to. The command started its retreat in column of fours at a fast gallop. The crossing was not covered.

[THE COMMAND EXCITED AND DEMORALIZED]

Everybody I saw was considerably excited when they got on the hill. They were excited when they went in, for that matter. The command was demoralized to a certain degree. They left a great many behind—the organization was not as good as when it went in. A great many men were missing.

The point to which we retreated was quite near the one we afterwards took. I think it was a very good defensive position. It was about one hundred feet above the level of the water.

I don't know who stopped the command, but I think Maj. Reno said the side of the hill was no place to form and that we better go to the top. It may have been Capt. Moylan. I'm not sure.

The position in the timber was as good as any place on the left bank, but I don't think we had enough men to hold it and keep the Indians out of it. The front was good; but I don't know about the rear. Of course, the position threatened the village to some extent and kept a containing force of Indians there. These were withdrawn when we left and I think that the attack made elsewhere was made about the time we left the timber,—but I don't think the entire force was at any time attacking us, because we could see parties a long way off, after we got on the hill. But I think the main force was against us when we were dismounted.

On the hill we did not threaten the village, nor was the command in any condition to create a diversion.

[CUSTER'S GRAY HORSE COMPANY SIGHTED]

The last time I saw Custer's command was about the time we dismounted in the bottom. I then saw the gray horse company moving down along the bluffs. I only saw it momentarily. It was back from the edge of the bluffs and the head and rear of the column were behind the edge of the bluffs. They were further down stream than the point we struck in crossing, and not quite so far down as Point 2 on the map. They were probably three quarters of a mile from where we then were in the bottom; they were moving at a trot. This was about an hour before Capt. Benteen joined us after we got on the hill. Gen. Custer must have been in action before Benteen joined Reno.

The first evidences of Custer's fight I saw on the 28th were some bodies about one thousand yards from the watering place or middle ford "B," about two miles from Reno's position on the hill.

["A HEAVY FIRE—CRASH—CRASH"]

About the time, or a few minutes after Benteen came up, I heard firing away down stream and spoke of it to Lt. Wallace. I don't recollect any except that one time. I had borrowed a rifle and fired a couple of long range shots when I heard it. I said "Jesus Christ, Wallace, hear that—and that." It was not like volley firing but a heavy fire—a sort of crash—crash—I heard it only for a few minutes. It must have pertained to Custer's command at the other end of the village. It was from the end of the village where Custer's body was found. I thought he was having a warm time down there.

When I saw a battalion going down the bluffs, of course I thought that it was going to attack the lower end of the village, either from the bluffs or into the village.

When I went afterwards to Capt. Weir's advance position,

the plain that proved to be Custer's field was in plain view, and it was just covered with Indians in all directions coming back toward us. This was about two hours after Reno first got on the hill. From the time I was with Weir on that point, back to the time the position was taken on the hill and the line formed where we remained that night, was an hour and a half.

[WHERE IS CUSTER?]

I suppose everybody felt as I did—wondering what had become of Custer and where he was. I don't know that there was any special worry—he had 5 companies with him. I don't think there was any idea or thought in the command that he was in the fix he was. The command felt in doubt—wondering if he was corralled as we were, or had been driven away to Terry; but that he had been wiped out—there was no such thought. I had no such idea, because when Gen. Terry came up, the first thing I and others asked was "Where is Custer; do you know what has become of Custer," and I supposed the cavalry of Terry's command was Custer.

I thought from the firing I heard that he had got to the other end of the village and struck this force of Indians we had been fighting and was having a siege of it too. But the idea of Custer's command being killed never entered my mind, and as much as I thought of it was that they had got rid of him and were coming back after us. They first caught us and then him; they had thrown us back and driven him off and now they were coming back to give us another dose. That was my thought.

[TO UNITE WITH CUSTER]

The object of our move down stream, as I suppose, was to unite with Custer. I don't know of any other reason there could have been for a move in that direction. The entire command did not come up to where Capt. Weir was. One other company was there, and the two were dismounted. The others came very near there, but did not dismount, and then the orders were to go back. Capt. Weir started to withdraw his company and the others turned their horses around and went back as he withdrew his line. The others did not deploy at all. They did not move up in a solid column, but separately. The Indians that engaged us in the bottom turned back and went to the other end of the village. As Custer was there and fought there, they probably were in that fight. I have no doubt of it, though it is only supposition.

[THE NIGHT OF THE 25TH]

I remember no wind on the 25th, but it was a little cloudy, and it sprinkled during the night. I laid down on the line with the men while the firing was going on and then went to sleep, being exhausted, and did not waken till the bullets were flying the next morning. The men had fortified during the night, digging little holes. Maj. Reno was on Weir's line to the right. I laid with Capt. French two or three hours, while the Indians fired very rapidly. We made no reply until they stopped to make a rush, when we would get up and open on them. I persuaded two or three Crows to go out with a despatch, provided the Rees would go too. Maj. Reno wrote four copies, but the scouts did not get through the lines. I don't think they even attempted it.

[SURROUNDED BY INDIANS]

The Indians lay behind ridges from 200 to 500 yards off; in one place they were less than 100 yards away; and there was one continuous line of smoke around our whole line. Then when they thought they had hurt us, they would charge us. They would sit back on their horses and ride up and then we would pour it into them and they would fall back. That was kept up all day long.

Capt. Benteen came over and said he had extended his line further and would have to charge to drive them from the other end of his knoll. "That cuss up there," he said, "is shooting right into you. We want to skip them out." And everybody said "Is it a go?" "It's a go," and we got up and made a rush for 15 or 20 yards, and the Indians scattered. We could see them skipping out to the hills.

I don't know how many wounded we had; there may have been 20. The horses and pack animals were corralled in a circle by tying the reins of a dozen together and fastening them to the legs of dead horses. Capt. Moylan's company covered the corral from behind pack saddles. On his left were Weir and Godfrey; then French and Wallace and Mc-Dougall. The latter's left rested on the river. On the up-stream side is a higher knoll and Benteen had his line there. The command was in no condition for hard work, or more than circumstances forced, and probably the majority slept that night.

I think there was plenty of courage with the officers and troops and everybody. There were no signs of fear or anything of that sort.

[RENO AND BENTEEN COULD NOT HAVE JOINED CUSTER]

I don't know whether Benteen could have joined Reno in the timber or not, if the Indians had seen him. It would depend on how much they opposed him. They might have driven him into the timber and prevented him from joining us. As it turned out, he could have done so when the Indians turned back and left us and went the other way.

Such a junction would have kept a large containing force of Indians there, but we could not have united with Custer, except by going through the village to him or his coming through to us. I do not think either force could have done that.

As to Col. Reno's conduct, I have nothing to say against him and nothing in particular for him, either one way or another. Certainly there was no sign of cowardice or anything of that sort and nothing especial the other way. I didn't see anything special to say on either side.

The retreat from the woods was hasty and the rear of the column disorganized. It was a movement to get out of there and get to higher ground. When I got on the prairie they were getting away from the Indians as fast as they could. The reason I went to the head of the column was because I thought there was no officer there, and I intended to take command, but found Reno there. I don't know how the command felt when we got to the hill, but I felt personally that we had been badly licked.

CROSS EXAMINATION

I think that at the time Reno left the woods Custer's column had about time to reach the watering place, the middle ford (Point B); and this was about the time the bulk of the Indians left us and went toward the village. Gen. Custer, if he looked down from the point where I saw the gray horse troop, could have seen Reno's command dismounting in the bottom.

[CUSTER COULD HAVE SEEN RENO]

If he rode at the head of the column, he was in a position to see what we were doing. The men of the gray horse troop were certainly able to see that we were not charging, but were dismounting and deploying. I believe that Gen. Custer must have been satisfied to proceed after seeing what we were doing there. There was no communication between Reno and Custer after that time that I know of. It is my belief that not less than 4000 warriors were in that fight. We did not have enough men to hold the timber.

I do not see how Maj. Reno could depend on Capt. Benteen or Capt. McDougall. I don't know whether he knew or could have known what orders they had. I do not know that he knew the plan of the fight. I did not.

[RENO'S DUTY TO USE OWN JUDGMENT]

If Reno thought he could not hold the timber, and saw no troops coming, it was for him to use his own judgment and leave it for a place he could defend better. Capt. Benteen united with Reno 20 to 25 minutes after he left the timber, and the command moved down river in about an hour or an hour and a half.

It is possible that the command could have gone further downstream, than the point made by Capt. Weir; but I doubt whether any one would have gone further at that time, because the Indians were all coming as fast as they could in our direction.

It was not a general fight as we retired; but we had to fire to keep them back and it got warmer and warmer all the way till we got back and then the fire became very heavy. We made a stand about 5:30 P.M.

On the 26th Reno tried to get a letter thru to Gen. Terry. The scouts returned the letter to him. It described our position and the fight, stated that he did not know where Custer was, and asked for medical aid and assistance, and that he was holding the Indians in check. The longest range guns the Indians had were, I think, those they took from Custer's command.

RE-DIRECT EXAMINATION

I do not think the Winchester will shoot accurately over 600 yards. The Springfield carbine is accurate at 1000 yards. Indians would not be likely to charge mounted into timber; they would take advantage of cover and crawl up on the line; but I saw no Indians in the timber.

Many casualties must have occurred in the rear of the column as it left the timber; the majority of ours were killed and wounded in the retreat from the woods to the bluff.

[INDIAN RIFLES ACROSS POMMELS]

The Indians did not charge into the column, but rode its flank, 50 to 100 yards away, with rifles across the pommels of their saddles. As we neared the river they veered off. I do not consider Maj. Reno's retreat a disorganized rout so far as the head of the column is concerned, but the rear I think was. Column of fours was a good formation to go through the Indians; platoons would have caused delay. There was no danger of enfilading fire, as Indians would ride the flanks. I do not know whether any wounded were left in the woods; there were men left there and they were dead when we saw them. If a man was so disabled he could not mount, he would be left, and probably killed at once.

[THE INDIAN VILLAGE]

A village containing 4000 warriors would have a population of about 15,000 if they all had families with them, but I don't think all did. I saw many wickiups which probably contained bucks only. 15,000 Indians would require about 20,000 ponies, and there was an immense pony herd there. My Indian scouts, I think, started for Powder River. I found them there afterwards. If 1000 Indians had closed in on Reno's column as it crossed and was going up the hill, it would never have got on the hill. It would have been stopped at the creek.

RE-CROSS EXAMINATION

Indians are individual fighters; each one has his own way of doing it. It would make no difference whether a ford was narrow or wide so far as troop formation was concerned. In such a movement, the troops must be kept well closed up, and if there is any delay in crossing, some disposition must be made to cover it.

RE-DIRECT EXAMINATION

The Indians did not get away with Gen. Forsythe at the Republican River in 1869.

RE-CROSS EXAMINATION

And they did not get away with Maj. Reno at the Little Big Horn.

THE FIFTH WITNESS CALLED BY THE RECORDER WAS

DR. H. R. PORTER

On June 25th and 26th, 1876, I was acting Assistant Surgeon under Gen. Custer.

[CUSTER PROMISED TO SUPPORT]

I heard the Adjutant give an order to Maj. Reno about 1 o'clock, June 25th. The Adjutant told him the Indians were just ahead and Gen. Custer directed him to charge them. Reno asked whether Custer was going to support him. The Adjutant answered that Custer would support him. Reno asked if the General was coming along and he said "Yes, the General would support him." I heard no other order.

This was by the tepee with the dead Indian in it, about one or one and one-half miles from the crossing of the Little Big Horn.

Reno started down to the crossing at a trot. Some horses were galloping. We crossed and halted, and some horses were watered. The watering generally was done passing through. The horses generally were in good condition. High spirited—some wanted to run.

Going to the crossing, Reno asked me if I didn't want his gun. He had a fiery horse and had trouble managing him, and the gun was in his way. I said "no."

After we crossed I heard him command "Forward!" and they went on down to the woods, about two miles, at a lope or trot.

I saw a few Indians and a great many ponies. They seemed to be driving the ponies down the river. There was no opposition.

When we got to the woods the men dismounted and formed a skirmish line. I was right where I could see them. The horses were led into the woods.

["WE HAVE GOT TO GET OUT OF HERE"]

I watched the fight a few minutes and then led my horse

into the woods, looking for my orderly who had the bandages and medicines. I had been there only a few minutes when the men on the left and right came in and then I saw Maj. Reno and heard him say that we had got to get out of there. He rode out.

One man had been wounded up to that time: the only one I know of, wounded in the breast.

["DON'T RUN: WE'VE GOT TO GO BACK"]

At the time I heard Reno say we would have to get out and charge them, he moved out and the men followed from all directions. They had a great deal of trouble finding their horses, but as soon as they mounted they went out. I stayed a few minutes with the wounded man and when I got out the men were all running and the Indians too, within a few yards of me. There were a few Indians between me and the command. I went out expecting to see the command charging the Indians, but instead the Indians were charging the command. They were all on the run. I let my horse out and got to the edge of the river and he jumped in and crossed with the rest. There was a great deal of dust, hallooing and confusion. The wounded man was left in the timber.

The first officer I saw on the bluffs was Lt. Varnum. He had his hat off and said "For God's sake, men; don't run. There are a good many officers and men killed and wounded and we have got to go back and get them."

When I saw Major Reno I said to him "Major, the men were pretty well demoralized, weren't they?" He replied "No, that was a charge, Sir."

The command was demoralized. They seemed to think they had been whipped.

In a few minutes I saw some troops coming and some of the men shouted "Here comes Custer"; but it was Benteen and his battalion.

Then the command felt pretty good; they thought they were going to have some help.

We hadn't been there long till I heard firing down the stream and to the left. Pretty heavy and sharp for a few minutes and then scattering shots, that grew less and less.

After Benteen joined we went further up the river and in a little hollow made a hospital.

I saw Capt. Weir go downstream, Lt. Edgerly with him. That was before the packs came up. He went about half a mile or farther, perhaps.

After we got in position the Indians came back and fired into us pretty sharp and it kept up till after dark. The next day it was the same from daylight until some time in the evening. I attended many wounded.

No wounded were brought from the bottom, but I know that some were left there. Seven or eight, however, had hung to their horses and dropped off when they got to the top of the hill.

[BENTEEN EXERCISED COMMAND]

I did not see Reno exercising command, but did see Benteen. He came down several times to order skulkers out from the horses, and asked about the wounded. Reno was the ranking officer, but Benteen appeared to be the officer actually in command.

It was about 1 P.M. when Reno got his order. I just guess at the time, as I did not look at my watch. It took 10 or 15 minutes to get to the crossing and 5 or 10 more to cross and reform, and 15 or 20 more to go to the place the command halted. The Indians were then eight or nine hundred yards away. It was hard to reach them with the guns at that time.

I do not remember any firing until the men dismounted. Then a few shots were fired. The Indians were circling back and forth and coming nearer in squads and firing more rapidly as they came. I did not see the village till I got in the woods and then saw it through a clearing. I would judge there were about one thousand lodges. The nearest tepee was one quarter of a mile away.

[ONLY ABOUT 50 INDIANS]

There were only about fifty Indians who were engaging Reno when he halted. They increased to seventy five or a hundred. There were many more down the river, but I could not see how many. Reno's command, while in the timber, was about a mile from the main village; perhaps more. I heard no bugle calls at any time. The way I knew the command was leaving was that I heard Maj. Reno say "We have got to get out of here. We have got to charge them."

When I got to the river I saw that there were a dozen cavalrymen in the water and Indians on the right bank firing at them. I don't remember seeing an officer till I got across. There was no order at all in the rear of the column; every man seemed to be running on his own hook.

[VALLEY FIGHT LASTED ABOUT 20 MINUTES]

I judge it was fifteen or twenty minutes from the time of deployment when they left the woods; possibly longer. I don't think the run to the hills lasted over four or five minutes; it was between a half mile and a mile.

The river was forty or fifty feet wide and the water up to the saddle pockets; the left bank was straight, four or five feet high, but after some of the horses had caved it in, it made a pretty good crossing. On the other side it was about the same. When I got there everybody was rushing in, trying to get across as fast as possible, and the Indians were firing into them. It was every man for himself.

It was about an hour from the time Reno left Custer that Benteen joined Reno. The packs came in from half an hour to an hour later.

[RENO EMBARRASSED AND FLURRIED]

I saw nothing in the conduct of Maj. Reno particularly heroic or the reverse. I think he was a little embarrassed and flurried. The bullets were coming thick and fast and he did not know whether it was best to stay there or leave. That was my impression at the time.

CROSS EXAMINATION

I was at Maj. Reno's side when he received the attack order and heard his conversation with the Adjutant. He was at the head of his command and Lt. Hodgson, I think, was with him. Do not remember seeing Lt. Wallace. The Adjutant rode back and Reno went on to the crossing. I do not recall seeing Girard there. I crossed the river with Reno and halted on the other side in the timber. Reno formed the command into line and charged on through the valley. I was within speaking distance of him till we reached the woods, where the command dismounted, near point "C" on the map. I left him there and went into the timber. After the horses were taken into the woods, I rode out and met Girard and the others. I was there a minute or so and then rode back into the woods and stayed there.

I first saw the village from the woods, though I saw many Indian ponies when about half way down to point "C." The first Indians I saw were the few who were herding the ponies, gathering them up. It raised a thick dust. I saw no Indians coming toward us. I thought they were running away. I did not see Reno at Point "C"; and suppose he was up on the skirmish line; but I did see him in the woods just before he said we had to get out of there. I know nothing about his going into the woods with part of "G" company. He rode out in the direction we came in and I next saw him across the river. I left the woods several minutes after the command started, and passed some of them on the way to the river; crossed it with some of them and went up the hill. I reached the ford just as the last were going in. Lt. Varnum was on the hill and his remarks about the wounded were made before we reached the top, and while some of the men were still coming up, before Benteen's command was in sight.

[STAMPEDED?]

The tendency of the men was to keep on running, and

Lt. Varnum tried to halt them. His remark applied to all the wounded who had been left:—he said "Go back."

I saw Maj. Reno only once during the night of the 25th, and do not remember him coming to the hospital at all. I don't know how far Capt. Weir advanced: he might have gone 2 or 3 miles.

I was moderately cool during the fight, a little excited, most all were; but I was not so much so that my judgment was much out of the way. While on the run I was frightened —I found that I was alone, and I let my horse go. I was frightened at other times during those two days.

I think there were two or three hundred Indians mixed up with the troops to the right and rear during the run to the river.

RE-DIRECT EXAMINATION

About four o'clock in the afternoon of the 26th firing ceased; it had been growing less and less. The village moved away. There was a large body of Indians and ponies. It seemed a mile or two long and a quarter mile wide. I judge there were from two to five thousand Indians; men, women, and children.

RE-CROSS EXAMINATION

There may have been seven or eight thousand; that would represent 500 bucks or warriors.

"Q. That would not be a very formidable array?

"A. They proved pretty formidable to us.

Maj. Reno knew as well as I did that there were officers and men killed and wounded in that stampede. Everybody knew it.*

---

*Note: Dr. Porter, at a later session, corrected his testimony by stating that "the idea I wish to convey as to the number of Indians is that there were 2 or 3 thousand warriors and 3 or 4 times, perhaps 5 times, as many people."

THE SIXTH WITNESS CALLED BY THE RECORDER WAS

CAPT. MYLES MOYLAN
7th Cavalry

During the morning of June 25, battalion assignments were made. Maj. Reno, Capt. Benteen, Capt. Keogh and Capt. Yates each had one. They consisted of three companies except Yates', which was two companies. Capt. McDougall, absent with the pack train, accounted for the other company.

[A NIGHT MARCH BEFORE THE BATTLE]

On the 24th the command made a night march, leaving camp about 11 P.M., and marching 2½ hours; it then bivouacked without unsaddling. The men were ordered to lie down and sleep if possible; and to make coffee in the morning if water could be found. The order was brought to me by one of Gen. Custer's staff. We remained there till about 8 A.M. of the 25th and then moved forward; by whose orders I don't know. We halted about 10:30 to 11 o'clock. There was a fresh trail visible only a day or two old; and while at this halt at the foot of the divide between the Little Big Horn and the Rosebud, a sergeant of one of the companies returned on the trail some miles to recover some clothing of his that had been lost from a pack mule the night before. He had gone back several miles and in going over a knoll saw two or three Indians four or five hundred yards in front of him, one of them sitting on a box of hard bread and examining the contents of a bag. He returned at once and reported it to Capt. Yates, his company commander. Capt. Yates talked it over with Capt. Keogh, and Keogh hunted up Col. Cook to notify him in order that Gen. Custer might be informed.

Gen. Custer was at that time some distance ahead at the point where the Indian ponies were visible.

[BENTEEN TO THE LEFT: CUSTER AND RENO ADVANCE]

The separation was made into battalions, a mile or so the other side of the divide. It was about 12:30. Benteen's battalion first left. He went off at almost a right angle. Our course was almost due north and he went a little north of west. It was at that time the command pulled ahead of the packs.

Benteen pulled out within a few minutes after the organization of battalions; Reno diverged a little to the left and Custer a little to the right, with the heads of Reno's and Custer's columns nearly on a line. They traveled in that manner several miles. Sometimes 150 to 200 yards apart. They continued that way till they reached the dead warrior tepee when Reno was sent for and received orders to move forward, as the Indians were supposed to be a few miles ahead and retreating. I know nothing of the orders save by hearsay.

[RENO TO THE ATTACK]

After Reno moved forward the command "Trot" was given and we moved three to three and a half miles to the Little Big Horn and crossed it. A slight pause was made to close up. Then we moved forward again at a trot, the head at a very fast trot and the rear companies galloping. They moved a third of a mile when the companies were formed in line on a little high ground. An immense dust was seen down the valley, with a little opening in it occasionally when we could see figures moving. After the line was formed the command moved again in line and the dust seemed to recede until the command passed a mile further when it stopped. Then we could see Indians coming out of the dust, mounted.

[RENO HALTS TO FIGHT ON FOOT]

They were so numerous that I suppose Maj. Reno thought it was more force than he could attack mounted. Consequently he dismounted his command. At that time we had reached the point of timber and the command was given to halt and to fight on foot.

[THE VALLEY FIGHT]

The horses were led into the timber for protection and

the men deployed as skirmishers, "G" on the right, mine in the center, and "M" on the left. In about 10 minutes I understood that Maj. Reno had information that the Indians were turning his right—coming up the left bank of the river, and threatening the horses, and the greater portion of "G" was withdrawn and taken into the woods, leaving an open space between the right of my company and the timber. I extended to the right to cover that.

We remained there twenty five to thirty minutes under heavy fire till the Indians seemed to be withdrawing from our front and working around to the left. Fearing that they would turn our left, I called Maj. Reno out of the woods to see, and he ordered the line withdrawn. The movement was executed by a flank movement to the right. About a half of "M" had to face to the left again to change front in the direction of the hills, as the attack came from that direction.

[RENO RETREATS TO THE HILLS]

The order was then given to mount. Being mounted and unable to form in the timber, I ordered my men to move out and form outside. When half of them were mounted, I went out and formed them in column of fours. "M" came up soon and formed on my left; "G" did not mount so soon nor get up as fast, but they were in the column before it reached the river. Maj. Reno was on his horse overlooking the formation. He asked my opinion as to the point we better retreat to, as it had been evident we would be entirely on the defensive, on account of the force of Indians in sight and coming. He designated a high point on the opposite side where we would go and establish ourselves and await developments. The command moved forward at the trot and then at the gallop. At gallop, the heads of the companies were almost in line, and the Indians closed in on both flanks and fired into the columns. There were many Indians in the woods. The firing into the rear was very severe. A good many men were wounded and some killed. When I reached the river I found it full of horses and men. I stopped at the head of my people and tried to get them together. Many were missing, nine or ten hit and four or five killed. Then we rode to the top of the hill and dismounted and while having my wounded attended by Dr. Porter, I heard some one say there was cavalry

[BENTEEN JOINS—RENO ADVANCES]

approaching, which proved to be Benteen, as I supposed it must be from the direction from which he was coming. In a half to three quarters of an hour the packs came up. I saw Capt. Weir's company move out down stream; I don't know by whose orders or with what intention. Soon after the packs came; ammunition was distributed and the order given to prepare to move forward.

I stripped some of my horses of blankets to carry my wounded. It took nearly all my men, four to a wounded man, to carry them. The command moved forward. I couldn't keep up and sent word to Reno. I rode forward and told Capt. McDougall, and he sent half of his company to help me. Then I rode forward and told Reno. He was at the head and told me it would not be necessary to go further in that direction as he thought the whole force of Indians was in front of Weir's company. So I returned and awaited the return of the rest. A point was selected near where we came to the top of the hill the first time, and the companies assigned positions. The wounded were placed inside a barricade behind my company and among the animals.

[THE FIGHT ON RENO HILL]

We had been there but a short time when the action commenced—very heavy all along the line. It continued till after dark and opened again about 3 A.M., and continued till mid-afternoon of the 26th.

On the 26th the attack was very heavy on the right, held by Benteen. I was next and Weir next to me. Some of my company went to help Benteen and strengthen his line. Any movement was attended with great danger. There was a great deal of shooting over my line at the animals, and they succeeded in killing many of them. After firing ceased the night of the 25th, by direction of Maj. Reno we fortified with dead animals and packs. We pulled them out to the line and covered them with dirt as well as we could. We had only 3 spades. We were occupied all night at this work. On the 26th my casualties were light, only 2 wounded. I understood Benteen had 20 wounded and 2 killed. I estimate that no less than 900 to 1000 Indians were in that attack at all times; they relieved each other at intervals, coming from the village. We could not see them, but if a man showed his head he would very soon find out that there was something there. The men had to shoot at the smoke puffs; the grass was long and they had thrown up works of their own which were visible. The Indian line was two to two and a half miles around, in a circle. In some parts they came very close, within 15 or 20 yards, but for the most part it was long range.

I have no doubt Reno's column was discovered before it crossed the Little Big Horn. The valley was lower than where we crossed and if they didn't see the command they saw the dust. I am perfectly satisfied that the Indians knew about our crossing.

Whether Custer followed us on the trail toward the crossing I don't know. I only knew by what Maj. Reno's Adjutant told me that he was to be supported by Custer.

I saw no movement of Indians toward us before we crossed. It was not until we were close to the point of timber that they advanced. The distance was about a mile and a half. We rode at the gallop and it took about ten minutes to get to it.

[RENO'S HALT JUSTIFIED]

There were, I think, enough Indians within 500 yards to warrant Reno's halting and dismounting; from 200 to 400 yards away there were about 400 Indians. The line advanced about a hundred yards after being deployed. The engagement commenced before the deployment; the Indians firing before we halted or dismounted. There were no casualties up to this time.

The Indian fire was scattering and the companies commenced as they were deployed. The scouts were already firing, and had been for some time at long range. Some of the men were new and it was impossible to regulate their fire, but the fire of the majority was well regulated.

[POINT "C": RENO'S RIGHT]

The right of the line was 200 yards from the river; perhaps not over 150; the first 30 yards, being timber and the rest only a tree here and there and scattering underbrush. In the timber was heavy undergrowth.

At the point where the horses were put in, the timber bent down to the river, but where we made the second crossing there was none. Above that it commenced again and went I don't know how far.

The bottom in which Reno placed his command extended to the river and to the right of my line, and not over 300 yards distant there was quite a number of Indian lodges.

Aside from putting part of "G" company in the timber, between the horses and the river, none of the command was placed in the timber at all.

[WHY THE COMMAND CHANGED FRONT]

The change of front was made to protect against an attack from Indians coming in from the left. The command as a whole was never placed in the timber, which was about 30 feet higher than the bottom, and the banks were precipitous in places. Not less than 200 Indians had turned our flank before it was withdrawn. Before the command left the woods these had come within five or six hundred yards; there were none in our front toward the river as we came out, facing the river, but a good many on our right and rear. They passed along the banks of the stream and there were 30 or 40 near the right of our second crossing who fired on us as we crossed. I had one man wounded there. I don't know how many Indians had got into the timber. I saw 40 or 50; there may have been several times that many. I saw only six or seven hundred Indians while in the valley.

[CASUALTIES AND AMMUNITION]

Up to the time the command was ordered out of the woods I had one killed and two wounded in my company, and another was wounded as we were going out.

The men had a hundred rounds, 50 on the person and 50 in the saddle bags. I had to send men back for saddle bag ammunition. They had fired 40 or 50 rounds apiece while dismounted, which would take about forty minutes. I think two-thirds had been judiciously expended.

The object of leaving the timber was, if possible, to save the command. In going to the river I lost 4 killed and 4 or 5 wounded. I took 38 men into the fight and lost 11 killed and wounded. The loss was about the same in the other companies, I think.

[RETREAT JUSTIFIED AND DESCRIBED]

If we had stayed 30 minutes longer in the timber, unsupported, I doubt whether we would have gotten out with as many as we did. If we reached the other bank there was a possibility of aid coming up. We could not have successfully resisted the force of Indians if they had followed to the river; we had not sufficient ammunition. The command was not, however, actually driven from the timber. It was virtually so, however, and would have been actually, in a very short time.

The Indians in the timber next to the river in the rear were firing—40 or 50 shots or more when we left.

There were no trumpet calls, either during the advance or the retreat. Some men, including Lt. DeRudio, were left behind in the timber, and there were 12 enlisted men who afterwards came out and joined the command about an hour later. Several were killed and wounded at the crossing, among them Lt. Hodgson. The crossing was not covered.

The men were not demoralized or despondent when they reached the hill—neither were they exultant with success. A skirmish line was thrown out in a few minutes.

I think Maj. Reno rode in the interval between two companies at the head of the column during the retreat. I do not know whether any officer was charged with looking after the rear of the column.

[NO DAMAGE TO VILLAGE]

The timber position, of course, threatened the village, but from the timber we could not damage it any, as it was on so much higher ground we would overshoot and the bulk of it was too far away. I think it extended for 3 miles and was two or three hundred yards wide. The Indians estimated it at about 1800 lodges. There were also four hundred wickiups. Our hill position could not threaten the village. It was entirely out of range.

Lt. Hodgson told me that the orders to Reno were that we were to charge the Indians, as it was supposed they were retreating, and we would be supported by Custer's command.

When we got on the hill it was rumored that Custer's command had passed that way. My own idea was that it was in our rear and was coming to our assistance. Benteen's command I did not know much about. McDougall would be on our trail with the packs. His company was about 40 strong, and he had a non-com and six privates from each of the other companies.

An attack lower down or in flank would be a supporting attack to the extent that it would draw off some of the Indians to resist it.

[FAINT FIRING HEARD]

I heard some firing in the direction of the Custer field, about an hour after reaching the hill. It was after the packs came up. The sound was like volley firing, but very faint. I called McDougall's attention to it and asked him what he thought it was. He said he supposed it was Custer at the other end of the village.

[CUSTER'S BATTLEFIELD]

I did not examine Custer's trail at all. The evidences of fighting were a great many dead men lying around. Calhoun's company was killed in regular position of skirmishers. I counted 28 cartridge shells around one man, and between the intervals shells were scattered. In deploying the men to hunt for bodies, my company was on the left next the river and there were but few evidences of fighting there. But as soon as Calhoun's body was found, I was sent for to identify it, as he was my brother-in-law. That's how I happened to see those bodies.

I rode to where Custer's body was found. In the ravine "H" we found 20 odd bodies of "E" company; they were undoubtedly fighting and retreating. The marks were plain where they went down and where they tried to scramble up the other side, but these marks only extended half way up the bank. This was a half or three quarters of a mile from the river. Custer's body was not so far. Three officers and about 18 men were never found. My belief is that these were all buried with the others, but were so disfigured they could not be identified. There were men I had known 12 or 15 years whose bodies were unrecognizable but for certain marks. Some were missing and could not be accounted for. I understand some bodies were found a considerable distance from the field, which might make up the deficiencies.

[3500 TO 5000 WARRIORS]

The fighting force of the Indians I estimate at from 3500 to 5000. There were about 1800 lodges, and they estimated about two men to a lodge. The moving village was two and a half or three miles long and a quarter to a half mile wide. I saw it after sun-down, and it looked like an immense buffalo herd. You could not distinguish men from ponies.

[RENO COOL: NO COWARDICE]

Maj. Reno gave his orders during the advance in the bottom as cooly as any man under the circumstances. He was in front of the command all the time. During the afternoon of the 25th he seemed perfectly cool. I saw nothing indicating cowardice. After dark, the 25th, I laid down beside him, talking with him. I saw very little of him on the 26th and received no orders from him that day.

CROSS EXAMINATION

On the advance to the ford and after crossing, the companies were in column of fours, the heads of the columns with an interval of 15 to 25 yards between until formed in line. Reno's order was "Companies form left front into line." He was in front. He turned in the saddle and told one of my men who had a restive horse to keep it under control; that he would get all the fighting he wanted before the thing was over. The skirmish line was deployed by his command. He ordered the men out of the woods and to form on the plateau.

Dr. Porter rode at my side out of the timber and up to the plain where my company was being formed. He has told me since that he never was so scared in his life.

I saw nothing in Maj. Reno which betrayed evidence of cowardice; there was a certain amount of excitement visible in his face, as well as that of anybody else, but no trace of cowardice.

[RENO'S TACTICS APPROVED]

In my judgment if Reno had continued to charge down the valley he would have been there yet. The purpose of leaving the timber was to save the command, which without assistance, would, in my judgment, have been annihilated in the timber. If the Indians had followed and closed in on the retreat to the bluffs the same result would have followed.

The Indians first became visible in force about the time the companies were formed in line, about a half mile from the crossing. There was a very large dense cloud of dust; you could not see through it; it is Indian tactics to raise dust to conceal their movements. But if there had been no dust

From a photo by Copelin.   A newspaper cut of the Reno Court of Inquiry held at Chicago in 1879. Maj. Reno at center window. Lt. DeRudio testifying.

at all, we could not have seen 1000 lodges from that place.

I have never heard anyone claim that the retreat to the hill was in the nature of a triumph; and I would rather be dejected on the top of the hill than be dead in the timber, or anywhere else.

[EVERYONE'S CONDUCT GOOD: BENTEEN SUPERB]

The conduct of everyone on the hill was all right; things went like clock work. It was not so regular before. The men were well intrenched and felt they could hold it. I think all the officers did their duty, though I had no opportunity to see much of anyone except Benteen. His conduct, for coolness and gallantry, was perfectly superb. No other word could express it. Maj. Reno made mention of it and deservedly so.

[DURATION OF CUSTER'S FIGHT]

In my opinion Custer's fight might have lasted an hour and possibly less than that time.

There was no evidence of organized and sustained resistance on the Custer field except around Calhoun, and in the circle where Gen. Custer lay.

RE-DIRECT EXAMINATION

Dr. Porter did his duty on the hill in a superb manner. Excitement was a pretty general thing that day, and being frightened at a time of great danger does not imply cowardice. I think everybody was a bit shaken up.

"Q. Would it not have been better as a soldier to have been dead in the timber than dishonored on the hill?

"A. I don't know that that is a proper question to put to me. Very few men but would prefer to die in the timber than to be on the hill degraded."

RE-CROSS EXAMINATION

If the command was seen deploying by the column passing down the right bank (Custer's), it would have shown them that the enemy was not retreating and that the cavalry was not charging. The enemy were not fleeing; else there would be no necessity for the skirmish line.

["NO ONE MAN COULD GET THROUGH"]

While the command was in the timber I remember having a conversation with Lt. Wallace about the lodges in the village; not the hostile forces. He asked me if I could not send word back to Gen. Custer of the facts. There was a halfbreed Indian by the name of Jackson there and I asked him if he would take a message back.

He looked around before he made reply, then sweeping his hand as in the manner of Indians, to the left and rear, said "No one man could get through there alive."

THE SEVENTH WITNESS CALLED BY THE RECORDER WAS

GEORGE HERENDEEN
citizen, scout and courier

DIRECT EXAMINATION

The command moved from the camp, about twenty miles from the Little Big Horn at sunrise the 25th. I saw Gen. Custer when I went out to my place on the right flank. The troops were just getting under way. When we got on the divide we went some distance up a dry fork and the command halted. I went off some five or six hundred yards and stayed there while Gen. Custer was on ahead looking for the Indian camp.

["DID YOU SEE THAT INDIAN?"]

A few minutes before he came down, a halfbreed scout named Boyer came to me and asked me if I "had seen that Indian." I had been looking at an object I thought was a deer. Boyer said "It was an Indian and when he saw you he run for camp." He said he had seen 2 others with 3 or 4 loose horses and they had run.

About a mile or a mile and a half from the village I heard Gen. Custer tell Maj. Reno to lead out and he would be with him. Those are about the words I understood him to use. It was about three quarters of a mile from the crossing right beside an Indian lodge. Directly after, Custer said "Take the scouts with you, too." We started at a lope and went to the Little Big Horn.

[RENO'S ADVANCE AND VALLEY FIGHT]

Maj. Reno said "Keep your horses well in hand, boys," and we took a slow lope so as not to wind them. We were 5 or 6 minutes getting to the river.

I had some trouble before I got there, and I did not catch up till Reno and the men were in the creek. There were 6 Crows along, 2 or 3 with me. One of the Crows called out in Crow that the Sioux were coming up to meet us. I did not see any Indians myself, but supposed the Crow had. They kept on crossing and went down through the timber and on at a lope. I kept off to the left and out of the way. As we advanced down the valley, fires commenced springing up in the timber. We kept right on, facing a little point of timber that came out on the prairie. A few shots were fired into it by the soldiers. The command halted then and formed a skirmish line. The horses went down in good shape, I thought. I did not see any Indians oppose the advance, and I was in front. They were sitting still on their horses, and seemed to be awaiting our approach and did not move till we dismounted. Then they commenced making up and skirmishing. I was between the troops and the bluff to the left, about on a line with them. I was about 100 yards to the left of the column. When they deployed I went to the left and rear, in a little swale.

We dismounted and sat down and watched the fire of the troops a few minutes. No Indians were close enough to shoot at, so we sat still. We could see some on the hills, too far away to shoot at. The troops fired rapidly. Reynolds and Girard were with me and all shot at one Indian, but the shots fell short. That was the only shot we fired there. We judged our shots at 7 to 900 yards and saw the balls fall short. At that time I could not see any Indians closer. A little while after those down the valley came up within 3 or 4 hundred yards.

Directly after we fired that shot, we took our horses in the timber and tied them. In coming out I got separated from Reynolds and Girard and was alone after that. When I came out I saw Indians circling around the hills and coming in the valley closer to us. I could not see the troops; I was facing away from them. Presently the soldiers ceased firing and the Indians came within forty or fifty steps of me and ran into the timber. I got in some nice shots and then went to see what the soldiers were doing. I found all the horses gone but mine. I mounted and rode through into a little park or glade in the timber. There I saw some troops, probably a company, drawn up in line, mounted, and facing the creek. When I went from the prairie into the timber, it was at the point I have marked 4.

[INDIANS IN THE TIMBER]

The Indians came around our left and into the timber. As there was no firing on the line they came closer and closer. I saw twenty or twenty five where I fired at them and more coming. They were not firing at the troops. They fired 3 or 4 shots at me. Ten men could have checked them from getting in the timber at that point. I was there 6 or 7 minutes and fired 7 or 8 shots.

["DISMOUNT—MOUNT"]

Maj. Reno was sitting on his horse in the park. The troops were in line, in close order, their left toward the river. I heard him order "Dismount," and there was a volley fired by the Indians; I judge the ones I had seen coming in and had fired at. There was an Indian named "Bloody Knife" standing in front of Maj. Reno, within eight feet from him and he and a soldier were hit. The soldier halloed and then Maj. Reno gave the order to dismount, and the soldiers had just struck the ground when he gave the order "Mount" and then everything left the timber on the run.

["AS FAST AS SPURS WILL MAKE A HORSE GO"]

Major Reno started out and the line broke to get out as far as I could see; they were getting out at any place they could find. There was dense underbrush and not more than one man could pass at a time, so they had to go single file on a trail that had been made by buffalo or some animals.

That volley and the man hollering seemed to startle everybody and they ran. I followed. I was not frightened at first, till after I got dismounted. I was not in the timber and thought I had a good position, and there was nothing to get frightened at.

I started and got to the edge of the timber. The men were passing me and all going as fast as spurs will make a horse go; and I started my horse. There was a dense dust and I could not see where I was going. I got about 150 yards and my horse went down and I went off. Men were passing me all the time and everybody running for his life. Some Indians almost ran over me as I fell, about twenty of them. I got up and turned and went right back into the timber.

["FOR GOD'S SAKE, DON'T RUN"]

As I got near the timber, the men were still coming out, and from the other side of the timber I could hear an officer trying to halt his men. I think he said "Company A men, halt! let us fight them. For God's sake don't run."

I saw no shots fired by the men as they ran. I saw one man throw his gun away as he left the timber. He was left behind and I don't suppose he knew what he was doing.

I found a few mounted and a few dismounted men left back in the timber. I advised them to go into the timber and stand the Indians off; there was no use trying to get away by running, as I had tried that. So they turned back and stayed. We found no Indians there.

[LEFT IN THE TIMBER]

We had plenty of ammunition and seven or eight horses. About half of us were mounted. We were not molested by the Indians. We stayed in there about two hours.

When I first went in everybody was a good deal frightened, but had plenty of time to cool off as nobody was molesting us. We considered we were in a desperate situation and had to do something, so we commenced cleaning our guns and getting our ammunition ready for a fight.

[VOLLEYS FROM DOWNSTREAM]

After we had been in there some time, a half hour or less, I heard firing. It began in volleys. I heard a great many volleys and between them, and after they had ceased, scattering shots. It came from down the stream, from the direction of Custer's battlefield. It lasted about an hour, not more than that. I heard no firing on the right bank after that.

At the time Reno and his command left the timber Custer, in my judgment, was about half way from where he and Reno separated to where he had his fight, i.e., about opposite us. I should say about two miles from the place he was found.

[REJOINS RENO]

I left the timber late in the afternoon. Eleven enlisted men were with me, 3 of them wounded; one of them told me he got it outside the timber while dismounted. We joined Reno at the other side on the hill. I have heard that there were two men who did not go with us. I didn't see them. We crossed right in the bend of the river. When we started up the hill Lt. Varnum and 4 or 5 men came to meet us. When we came out of the timber we encountered only 5 Indians; they fired one shot and we returned it.

Reno's command was not engaged when we joined; some were marching down the ridge. They became engaged soon after. As I was coming up the hill I could see Indians advancing. The pack train was just up as I arrived.

Directly I got on the hill Major Reno called to me to

interpret for him and Half Yellow Face. He wanted to inquire about the Indian camp. I called the Indian and he went up to where he could look into the valley. Maj. Reno wanted his opinion about what the Indians were going to do, as they had taken their lodges down. Half Yellow Face said he thought they were going away. A short time after Maj. Reno called him back and asked "How is that, the lodges are all up again?" Half Yellow Face said he didn't know. That's all the conversation I had with him the 25th.

[BENTEEN IN COMMAND?]

Capt. Benteen seemed to be in command of the troops I could see; but I was not in a position to see all the line. I saw the village. It was about 1500 lodges. This was the largest camp I ever saw, by a great deal. I also saw it move away. It was too dark to distinguish anything clearly, but it was about 2 miles long and a half mile wide.

I could not judge the number of Indians that attacked Reno the afternoon of the 25th and 26th, except by their fire. You could not see them. There were probably 500 around him at a time. They don't use all their men in a bunch, but in reliefs. They had enough to hold every position.

[3500 WARRIORS]

I estimate their force at 3500 fighting men. I think there was a large number who had no women along.

In my judgment 100 men with 6 or 7 thousand rounds of ammunition could have held that timber against the Indians; and that they couldn't have gotten them out of there at all, if they had water and provisions.

CROSS EXAMINATION

I was not exhausted the morning of the 25th. We had slept until 11 the night of the 24th and then marched till about 2 and then laid down again. We marched again about 7. I was right by the side of the dead warrior lodge when Custer gave the order to Reno. I had helped cut it open to see what was in it. Gen. Custer was within 15 feet of me, coming up, and Major Reno was right in front as I heard the words spoken. I was mounted and I rode out within ten feet of him until my horse fell, about 3 to 4 hundred yards from the ford. He received no other orders from Custer or his Adjutant that I know of.

When the command halted and deployed, I stopped with a Crow Indian, Girard and Reynolds. We dismounted as soon as the troops did, and sat there a short time watching the line firing. I dismounted in the vicinity of the point 4. Point 1 is not the place. I did not see Major Reno while we were there, and do not know what he was doing. I tied my horse between the glade and the prairie. The skirmish line was firing then. I came back to the same position, and my attention was attracted by the Indians coming out on the hills to the left. I don't know how many got into the timber. I sat down on a buffalo trail and waited for them; and when they got close enough to fire at them, there was no fire from the line. It was deployed for about 15 minutes before being withdrawn.

When the Indians came close I went to my horse and untied him and rode into the glade, where I saw Major Reno. The troops I saw were on their horses in the glade; about 50 men. Reno ordered them to dismount and afterwards, to mount; then he started through the timber, rapidly. The soldiers also left the timber.

I did not go out very fast, but as I came out, the men were going across the prairie on a dead run. I don't know where Reno was, and I did not see Moylan. I think the soldiers I saw in the glade were from more than one company.

I did not know of the two men who say they were left in the timber at the time I left it. I did not see Girard there either. I was at the edge of the park and could see into it and into the timber, and also onto the hill on the other side.

[CUSTER COULD HAVE REACHED POINT "B"]

After Reno left, I judge we had been in the timber about 20 minutes when we heard the general firing in the direction of Custer's battlefield. If the gray horse company was at point 2 at the time Reno deployed, Custer would have had time to reach point B by the time we heard that firing, but I do not think there was any fight at point B.

All I saw of Major Reno in the timber was when he gave the two orders and started; probably half a minute, while standing there before that volley was fired by the Indians.

RE-DIRECT EXAMINATION

Lt. Cook might have given an order to Major Reno without my knowledge. I judge it was about 20 minutes from the time Reno halted and deployed before he left the timber.

EXAMINATION BY THE COURT

I did not go over the field immediately after the battle; I was sent with the 2nd Cavalry to destroy what was left of the village. I saw no soldier dead there. We crossed right

[CRAZY HORSE'S CROSSING?]

under the hill that Gen. Custer lay on. There is a crossing there that I should say the Indians used. The reason I do not think there was any fight at Point "B" is because it was so near to where I was that I should have heard the firing very plainly. There was a good ford there that I saw the next year. I think Custer's probable route would come to the river to get around easy. There was a swale that led to the creek and he could follow the creek down.

THE RECORDER'S EIGHTH WITNESS WAS

CAPT. R. S. PAYNE
5th Cavalry

DIRECT EXAMINATION

In August 1878, I measured the distance between Reno's hill position and the spot where Gen. Custer was killed. It is 4 miles, 160 yards.

CROSS EXAMINATION

Extending from the point where Custer's body was found, in a southwesterly direction, is a "backbone" as we call it on the plains, very narrow, and about 600 yards long. To the right, toward the upper part of the "backbone," the country falls away into slight ravines and depressions and more or less little knolls. The knoll where Calhoun's company was found is about the highest point in the vicinity; but it was hardly a good defensive position against Indians.

[THEIR CASE HOPELESS]

A command of two hundred against fifteen hundred Indians —their case would be hopeless. Their resistance could not be continued for any length of time. The ground lies so that the enemy, lying around and encircling the position, could fire into the troops without any danger of firing into each other.

RE-DIRECT EXAMINATION

The length of the resistance would not depend on the troops, but on the enemy. If the enemy pushed them, it would be a matter of only a few minutes; 20 or 30 minutes; to ¾ of an hour.

THE NINTH WITNESS CALLED WAS

LT. L. R. HARE
7th Cavalry
On duty with scouts

DIRECT EXAMINATION

Major Reno's column pushed ahead about 5 miles from where he crossed the Little Big Horn, by Gen. Custer's orders. What gave rise to the orders was that my attention had been called to some Indians ahead by our scouts and I spoke to Gen. Custer about it. He told me to take the Indian scouts

[RENO'S ADVANCE ORDERED BECAUSE SCOUTS REFUSE]

and go ahead and he would follow. The Indians refused to go and he ordered them dismounted, and then turned to Adjutant Cook and told him that as the Indians would not go, to order Maj. Reno ahead with his battalion.

Reno started forward immediately at a fast trot. He was twenty to twenty-five minutes reaching the river. There was a momentary halt at the head of the column. Some of the men were watering their horses as I passed them.

The first Indians I saw were from the knoll near the dead warrior tepee. I saw forty or fifty between us and the Little Big Horn. They evidently discovered us, because they disappeared at once. When I came to the ford, I saw Maj. Reno standing on the right bank.

[RENO HALTS—500 WARRIORS EMERGE FROM COULEE]

I crossed the stream and rode to the edge of the timber. I could see Indians driving ponies down stream and to my left. I was at the edge of the timber long enough to fix my saddle blanket and when I mounted, the head of the column was emerging. Shortly after, the command formed column by trumpet call, and moved down the valley to within a short distance of the point of timber and was there dismounted and a skirmish line formed. Up to this time, there were probably 40 or 50 Indians riding around and firing. As soon as the command dismounted, 4 or 5 hundred came out of a coulee about 400 yards in front of us, and moved to our left and rear.

I was a little in front of the line, about two hundred yards to the left, near the foothills, and could see the upper part of the village, probably four or five hundred tepees. When the command halted, the Indians, who had been riding back and forth stirring up a big dust, were about two to three hundred yards away. As fast as they came out of the coulee they would fire from their horses. They were riding to the left, going out in the foothills and coming down again. During the time we were in the bottom, there were always Indians in our front, downstream, 200 constantly, maybe more.

I did not hear Maj. Reno give any orders in the bottom. The first I knew that we were going to leave was when my man brought me my horse and told me they were leaving. The left of the skirmish line was thrown back near the timber.

I stayed in one place; sat down near the right of the line near the edge of the timber; I had no command. The Indians (i.e. Scouts) had all left me, and I sat there, firing an occasional shot when I got a chance. I was nearer than the troops to the Indians, but did not have as good a view as those farther out on the line.

[1000 WARRIORS AGAINST RENO'S 112.]

There were probably a thousand Indians opposing Reno on the bottom. The constant firing came from only a part of them, probably 200. The command left the timber about 30 to 40 minutes after the skirmish line was formed.

When I rode onto the bench, the three companies were individually together, well closed up, and seemed to be moving independent of each other. They formed three angles of a triangle, and they were going at a fast gallop. I first thought it was a charge; but I soon saw they were making for the bluff on the other side. I caught up at the crossing

where there was considerable confusion and for that reason
I went below and jumped my horse off a bank 6 or 8 feet

[A PRETTY FAST RETREAT]

high. The hostile Indians were all on our right flank, 50
to 100 yards away during the retreat, firing into the column.
The crossing was not covered and no effort was made to hold
the Indians back. After I got on the hill I looked back and
not a great many Indians remained in the bottom, probably
100, until the time Benteen came up. I did not think the
movement from the timber was a run; but it was a pretty fast
retreat.

I heard no bugle calls in the timber; and when I got
on the hill, most of the men had come up and Capt. Moylan
was forming the skirmish line. Maj. Reno was standing there
where he could supervise, but I did not hear him give any
orders. At that time a few shots were being fired by the
Indians on the right bank. Three or four men were killed;
our contract surgeon (DeWolf) was killed near the top of
the hill; my orderly was killed near the edge of the river.
The fire came from Indians on the bluffs on the right bank.

[COMMAND SCATTERED—NOT DEMORALIZED]

The command was scattered, but not demoralized. They
rallied and formed promptly. Before I got to the top I heard
Lt. Varnum calling to the men to halt and when I got there
Capt. Moylan was forming the skirmish line. If the Indians
had followed us in force to the hill-top, they would have
got us all, though not before Benteen came up. The hill
position was much better than the timber. I think the difference in the positions more than balanced the loss sustained in getting there. If the Indians had charged us in the
timber we could not have stood it but a few minutes; but
Indians don't do that. We could have stood them off for
perhaps 30 minutes by using our ammunition judiciously.

At this point in the proceedings, the Recorder presented to the Court a communication from Frederick Whittaker, which was thereupon introduced as Exhibit 3, as follows:

EXHIBIT NO. 3

Questions to be asked the witness HERENDEEN respectfully submitted to the Court by FREDERICK WHITTAKER, accuser of MAJOR RENO.

Submitted January 28, 1879.

1. Did you or did you not observe any evidences of fear on the part of Major Reno on the 25th or 26th June 1876? State the grounds of your opinion.
2. When Bloody Knife was killed by Major Reno's side in the glade or park of which you have spoken, what effect did it have on Major Reno, and how do you know, if you know?
3. Did you ever converse with Major Reno on the subject of the death of Bloody Knife, and what was the conversation, if any?
4. What words were uttered by the cavalry soldier who was shot at the same time as Bloody Knife, if you heard them?
5. Did Major Reno give any other orders than "Dismount" and "Mount" before he started to leave the timber?
6. Did he start before or with the men, and did he exhibit coolness and courage in so doing, or did you then think that he started under the influence of fear for his own personal safety?
7. Have you had cause to change your opinion since that time as to Major Reno's conduct whether cowardly or the reverse?

———————

I further desire leave respectfully to submit to the court that in case these questions should lead to fresh ones by Major Reno's counsel I should be permitted to ask questions if necessary in my own person of this or any other witness, subject to the discretion of the court in the same manner as Major Reno and his counsel.

Respectfully submitted
FREDERICK WHITTAKER.
Accuser of Major Reno.

The Recorder then stated:

"As far as I am concerned as Recorder, I have not considered that I was here as the prosecutor of Major Reno. I have desired to elicit all the facts in the case, whether they are for or against Major Reno; and while I have not a very exalted opinion of my own abilities in the matter, still I feel that I am, if I may be allowed to say so, competent to go on with the matter as I have done heretofore, because if I had not felt so, I should have asked the Court before this time for assistance in this matter."

To which Major Reno replied (referring to Exhibit 3):

"There are many of these questions that I shall not object to; but in regard to the request of Mr. Whittaker to appear as assistant prosecutor, I think that it is evident to the Court that the Recorder does not require it. If the Court then thinks or feels that this man, Mr. Whittaker, can be any addition— any desirable addition, to these proceedings, then of course I withdraw my objection, but as far as I can understand the course of procedure to be, it is that the War Department designates the officer who shall take charge of the eliciting of testimony, and I submit that it is entirely against the spirit of the law, and against the substance of this order to permit the authority given to the Recorder, which is not only that of a prosecutor, but is of a semi-judicial character, to be delegated to anybody else. It is entirely apart from this case."

The court was then cleared and closed, and upon reopening, the following decision was announced.

"The request of Mr. Whittaker to appear before the Court as an accuser or assistant to the Recorder will not be allowed. The Court determines that the matter of all questions proposed by Mr. Whittaker shall be decided by the Recorder, in whose abilities to conduct the case to a thorough investigation, the Court has the utmost confidence."

THE RECORDER THEN RECALLED THE WITNESS

GEORGE HERENDEEN
for further

DIRECT EXAMINATION

At the time that volley was fired and the Indian (Bloody Knife) killed and the man who was struck hollered, everybody left the timber in a great hurry. I don't know whether Maj. Reno was scared or not, but he left there.

[WHAT STAMPEDED THE COMMAND?]

On the 26th or 27th I was near Major Reno and asked him if he remembered Bloody Knife being killed. He said "Yes, and his blood and brains spattered over me."

I thought at the time it demoralized him a great deal when Bloody Knife was killed and the soldier who was hit hollered. The Indians were not over 30 feet from us when they fired that volley. The soldier cried "Oh, my God, I have got it." All I heard Reno say was "dismount" and "mount"; then his horse jumped as if the spurs were put to it. I always judged, and do still, that the volley and the killing of that man was what made him start, and was what stampeded the command in there—that was what made them start.

CROSS EXAMINATION

Maj. Reno left the glade on a run and the men started in no order at all; and that fixed it in my mind that they were running. When I got out a minute later the troops were running across the prairie, but I could not see the head of the column on account of the dust. They were running as fast as they could. There would not have been

[NOT SAYING RENO A COWARD]

time to form outside the timber. I am not saying Maj. Reno is a coward; he was under my observation not more than a minute, and I have given my judgment as to the length of time it took him to get out on the prairie. *(Re-direct and Re-cross examination of the witness developed nothing further.)*

THE TESTIMONY OF LT. HARE WAS THEN RESUMED AS FOL-
LOWS:

The men's firing was continuous from the time they dismounted till they left the timber; they probably expended 40 rounds per man. By judicious use the ammunition might have lasted an hour longer, though that would depend upon the action of the Indians.

Benteen joined on the hill about 15 minutes after we got there, about an hour and a half after Reno left Custer at the tepee.

[RENO SENDS FOR AMMUNITION]

As soon as Benteen joined, Reno ordered me to go and find out where the packs were and get them up as soon as possible. I went back one and a half miles, met them, and told them to hurry; and to cut out the ammunition as soon as possible and send it ahead. I came back ahead of the train and when I reported to Reno he told me to go to Capt. Weir, who had advanced while I was gone for the

[WEIR ORDERED TO COMMUNICATE WITH CUSTER]

packs, and tell him to open communication with Custer and he would follow as soon as the pack train was up. After I delivered the order to Capt. Weir, I returned to the command and met it coming down stream. When they got to a high hill, the highest point around there, the Indians returned and attacked. Maj. Reno said that the position would not do to make his fight in, and he selected a point further up on the bluff, and ordered Weir's and French's companies to cover the retreat back to that point. They did so up to a few hundred yards of the line, when Capt. Godfrey's company was dismounted. I came back with that company. It was put in position on the downstream side and I suppose the others were on the other side. The command was placed in an elliptical form, with the horses coralled in the center. There was little fire that night from the men on my part of the line. The men laid still and took the fire of the Indians.

I was gone after the pack train about 20 minutes. I rode to it and back as fast as I could.

It was fully three quarters of an hour from the time Benteen joined before the command moved down in Custer's direction.

[WHY THE COMMAND ADVANCED]

The supposition was that Custer would support Reno by following. He had not done that; he had plenty of time to follow, and everybody supposed he would attack somewhere, if he did not follow us; and the direction in which Capt. Weir advanced was the only way he could have gone to the village. Also, I heard firing down there just after Benteen came up. My attention was called to it by Capt. Godfrey. He asked if I "heard that volley." I said "Yes, I heard two distinct volleys." That was just before I started for the pack train.

The column could have made a general movement in that direction, but they wanted the pack train up. McDougall had about 45 men of his own, and six from each company, about 120 men all told.

[WHY THEY TURNED BACK]

The command turned back because they could see the Indians coming from downstream in great numbers; and Maj. Reno said he did not think that a good position to make a stand. It was evident he would have to fight for it. The high point he went to was further down stream than where Capt. Weir went. [*Here the witness indicated by the figure 5, Reno's position, and Weir's by the figure 6, on the map Exhibit 2.*]

Whether such an attack on the flank as Custer made would have supported Reno would depend entirely on what disposition the Indians made. As it was, it was no support at all and did not amount to anything. The results of the battle show that.

[HILL FIGHT COMMENCES]

On the retreat Capt. Weir and Capt. French were the only ones engaged until within 3 or 4 hundred yards of the final stand; then Capt. Godfrey engaged them and held them in check till we took position. The general engagement began at once, about an hour and a half after Capt. Weir started on his advance. I heard Capt. Benteen say to Maj. Reno that the position we took was the best place to make a stand and he agreed. Maj. Reno gave no orders that I heard: the captains put the men in position.

Reno was lying down. I saw him the next morning after reveille making dispositions on the line.

[THE TIMBER POSITION]

The timber position contained very few large trees; it was mostly underbrush. The basin or park was about two hundred yards wide and on the north bank, four or five hundred yards long where it runs into the river. There is a cut bank down stream and a bend on the other side continuing to where the river makes this cut bank; in this there is a little park containing ten acres of ground. The bench around the plain runs right into the river downstream; upstream I don't know how it was.

[THE INDIAN VILLAGE]

The village was not visible from down on the bottom. On the bank you might have seen the tops of the tepees. We were about 600 yards from the first tepee. The village extended right down the stream for three or four miles. The timber position threatened it, but I don't think it would have held the bulk of the Indians there. It did not do so—there were at no time more than a thousand Indians around there. It was a very good defensible position; the bench, or 2nd table was 5 or 6 feet above the level of the park and ran

[BENTEEN MIGHT HAVE JOINED—NOT McDOUGALL]

entirely around it, and men in behind there were protected by the edge of the bluffs. I think Capt. Benteen could have joined us there; but not McDougall.

In either case they would have had to charge through to get there and McDougall could not have charged with the pack train, and he had the bulk of the ammunition, 24,000 rounds, besides what his men carried. There were 140 mules in the pack train.

I don't think if Benteen had joined it would have made any difference as to McDougall. The Indians would have closed around again. McDougall could have come along the bluffs on the other side, but he could not have gotten down there; twenty Indians could have kept him back or else have got his pack mules.

[WHY RENO LEFT THE TIMBER]

Maj. Reno stayed in the timber till all hope of rear support from Custer had vanished. I think the reason we left was because if we stayed much longer, say 20 minutes, we could not have gotten out at all. Of course, as soon as the command got to the top of the hill, all the Indians left, but about 100 to 150, and went downstream. Those that stayed in the bottom were taking care of their dead and wounded. They were too far away to tell whether they were warriors or old men and women.

My impression of the retreat from the timber was that Maj. Reno thought we would be shut up there, and the best way to get out was to charge out. I did not think it absolutely necessary at the time.

If the command had been pursued by the 1,000 Indians who were about us, we would all have been killed; it would not have lasted ten minutes.

I was with the battalion that burned the tepee poles after the fight. I counted forty lodges at the place I stood and estimated the whole village from that. I estimated 1,500 lodges and 500 wickiups—4,000 fighting men, and that is a very low estimate. I do not think it very much out of the

[*"YOU CAN'T COUNT INDIANS IN ACTION"*]

way. It is very difficult to estimate the number of Indians in action; they ride around so constantly that it is impossible to tell their numbers.

I saw the village move away on the evening of the 26th. It was two or three miles long—a dark moving mass. I estimated about 20,000 to 25,000 ponies in the herd.

I know of but one instance of gallantry on Reno's part, and none of cowardice. When Capt. Benteen joined, Maj. Reno turned and said in a very inspiriting way to his men, "We have assistance now, and we will go and avenge the loss of our comrades."

[RENO'S RETREAT SAVED REGIMENT]

I can only estimate his conduct by the way it turned out. I think his action saved what was left of the regiment. His conduct was always good. I didn't see anything particularly inspiriting about it, except what I told you. He seemed to be very cool at all times.

I think Gen. Custer must have opened his fight about the time Reno left the woods, or a little before, from the fact that the first dead man was found about half a mile from Point B.

I think the Indians must have been around him all the time; the country was rough and cut up with coulees, and if he ran the Indians from one place, they would get around him again within seventy-five to two hundred yards.

[NO CHANCE FOR CUSTER TO GET OUT]

I don't think there was any chance for him to get out by charging through—not for some distance back, from the looks of the country.

The first evidence I found of Gen. Custer's fight was the dead man near the middle ford, Point B. The only evidences we could find were dead men. I saw no cartridge shells of ours. The bodies were mutilated; and there were evidences of bodies having been dragged off; but I think these were the bodies of dead and wounded Indians.

CROSS EXAMINATION

As I was not present when Benteen departed, I do not know what orders were given him; nor do I know whether Reno knew what his orders were. Of course, Reno could form no estimate of his duties based on any action of Benteen unless he knew these orders. At the time Reno left the timber Benteen's column was not in sight.

From the timber one can see all the way back to Point A where Reno crossed to make his attack. I saw Reno but once in the timber; he was about 50 yards away, going from the park out to the skirmish line. He was coming from where the horses were. The disposition of the troops in the timber was a very good one. I saw no evidences of fear among the men.

[IF RENO HAD KEPT ON, EXTERMINATION CERTAIN]

The cloud of dust hid the tepees, but everybody knew, whether they saw them or not, that there were lots of Indians there. The coulee in which they were concealed was about 300 yards in front of the skirmish line; four or five hundred Indians came from it. If Reno had continued to advance mounted, I don't think he would have got a man through; the column would not have lasted 5 minutes. His dismounting and deploying was the only thing that saved us.

As to the retreat from the timber, there is certainly always more or less disorder about a cavalry column moving at a fast gait; but I don't think that command was much demoralized, because when I got on the hill the men were halted in column and moving into line without any difficulty.

[RENO LOST NO TIME]

I can't think Maj. Reno lost much time in moving in Custer's direction; I went to the pack train and then to

Capt. Weir, who had moved out during my absence; and when returning from Capt. Weir, met Reno advancing. He could not have moved to where I met him if he had lost much time. His column moved altogether and about a mile or maybe a little more.

I reported to Maj. Reno that Capt. Weir had ceased his forward movement because the whole country was covered with Indians; at least 1500 in sight, and the country was favorable for concealment of a larger force. I do not think that Reno's consultation with Benteen as to the best place to make a stand indicated cowardice or indecision.

COULD RENO AND BENTEEN HAVE SAVED CUSTER?
[W.A.G.]

Critics of Reno and Benteen believe that had Reno remained in the valley, and had there been joined by Benteen, the two together might have created a diversion that would have saved Custer. They believe also that had Reno and Benteen at once advanced to Custer's aid after the junction of the two battalions on Reno hill, Custer would have been saved.

The answer to both these propositions is necessarily one of opinion, for Reno did not remain in the valley, nor did the combined battalions at once advance to Custer's aid. Therefore it is necessary to analyze the situation as it had developed in both instances, and ask ourselves whether, in light of the facts, any reasonable prospect of saving Custer was present in either.

Reno went into the valley fight with Custer's assurance that he, Custer, would support him. He found himself opposed by an overwhelming force of Indians, and after waiting in vain for any sign of support, during which time he used up much of his ammunition, he correctly concluded that no support was coming.

He thereupon withdrew to the hills on the east bank of the river, in the hope that he might there connect with the other parts of the regiment. His ammunition, while not exhausted, was so depleted that upon Benteen's unexpected arrival some fifteen minutes after he reached the summit of the hill, he at once dispatched Lt. Hare on the freshest horse to be found, to ride *post haste* to the pack train with orders to cut out the ammunition mules and bring them up as speedily as possible.

While Hare was absent on this mission, Weir marched without orders, advancing about a mile and a half downstream, and toward the sound of heavy firing that some of the command had heard from the direction that later proved to be that of Custer's field. When Hare returned from the pack train, Reno sent him to Weir, with orders to open communication with Custer if possible to do so. By the time Hare caught up with Weir, however, so many Indians had massed in his front, with many more visibly advancing, that Hare took it upon himself to use Reno's authority to order immediate retirement. In the meantime, however, the rest of the command had advanced, Benteen's battalion in the lead, and Reno, upon consultation with Benteen, decided that the entire command must retire or be overwhelmed.

That, in broad outline, is the story. It should be clear to any unbiased mind that Reno, by remaining in the valley, could have accomplished nothing but his own destruction, and that Benteen, who had no information of Reno's position or situation, could have accomplished less than nothing had he tried to cross the river to attack the village. He would, probably, have been cut to pieces long before he reached the village.

When the two joined forces on the hill, Reno's battalion was in no condition to advance. He was short of ammunition, and had many helpless wounded. Obviously, he could not fight without ammunition, nor could he leave his wounded. Benteen, on the other hand, had just completed a hard, forced march. His horses were jaded, his men exhausted. Yet he could have advanced sooner than he did. Had he done so, would it have saved Custer? Or would it merely have destroyed Benteen?

Weir advanced as soon as the heavy firing was heard on the hill. Before that time, no one had any clear idea of Custer's whereabouts, and even this was guessing. All anybody knew was that Custer's messengers, Kanipe and Martin, had come from down stream. Was Custer there? There was no way to find out but to go in that direction.

There was then no anxiety concerning Custer. He had his

favorite five companies with him and could, presumably, take care of himself. Other than Weir, no company commander sensed an exigency; nor is it clear that Weir did, for instead of asking Reno's permission to advance, he made a personal reconnaissance, which Edgerly misinterpreted. But that he believed Custer was engaging the Indians below is undoubtedly true (See "The Custer Myth," p. 217). But even he did not envision a disaster, for that night he conferred with Godfrey, both convinced that the command should move under cover of the darkness, to join forces with Custer if possible.

But on the hill, both afternoon and evening, belief was general, among enlisted men and officers alike, not that they had abandoned Custer, but that Custer had abandoned them. The Washita was still fresh in their memories.

When Weir and his command reached the furthermost point of their advance, they were still more than three miles from Custer's battlefield. They saw Indians rushing toward them *en masse:* and they saw also, other Indians in the far distance, riding about and shooting at objects on the ground. No fighting was going on, the heavy firing had long since ceased; even the scattering and receding fire that followed it had ceased. Only the desultory firing at those objects on the ground continued. What those objects were they could not tell; but they were to see them again three days later, when they went to bury the dead

Weir who had moved promptly, was too late to help Custer. Could Reno and Benteen together have done more? I think the answer is and must be—"No."

The left bank at the middle ford (Point B) was boggy, the right a gravelly bottom; it was easily fordable: just about as good a ford as Point A. There was, however, no evidence of any engagement there. The first body was found a half mile from it.

I saw only Lt. Smith's company; twenty-eight bodies were in a coulee, and in skirmish order. From what I saw I don't think Custer's fight could have lasted over three quarters of an hour.

I saw no evidence of cowardice upon Reno's part. The command was under good control and the disposition as good as possible under the circumstances. We were in the timber between thirty and forty minutes, and the whole time from our crossing at Point A till we left the timber was between forty and fifty-five minutes. A command which passed the point of the bluff (Point 2) at the time we were deploying would have had ample time to reach the middle ford (Point B) before we left the timber.

I was mistaken when I said I did not hear Maj. Reno give any orders on the hill. I did hear him directing the deployment into skirmish line just as I reached the top of the hill. This was immediately after the retreat from the timber.

I did not report to him that I heard firing from Custer's direction.

RE-DIRECT EXAMINATION

Reno could not have seen the Indians in the coulee before he halted and deployed. I could not see them till they came out, and I was in a better position to see than he was. He halted before any of them came out.

The middle ford "B" is right across from the village— the ford "A" where we crossed to attack is not.

The evidence on the Custer field indicated very hard fighting, especially where he fell.

If Gen. Custer saw us deploying, he could also have easily seen that there were five times as many Indians as we had men. If he saw the line after it was deployed, he saw the Indians come out of the coulee.

General Custer would, of course, expect his orders to be obeyed, and would naturally think Maj. Reno would hold his position as long as possible; and in my opinion, if Maj.

Reno could get away as he did, Gen. Custer could, by leaving his dead and wounded, have gotten away also.

RE-CROSS EXAMINATION

The middle ford would not be a good place from which to support Reno.

BY THE COURT

I crossed the river at the ford "B". The command did not.

THE RECORDER NEXT CALLED HIS TENTH WITNESS,

LT. CHAS. DeRUDIO,
7th Cavalry

DIRECT EXAMINATION

On June 25th, I was attached to Company A. After we passed the dead warrior tepee, Gen. Custer diverged to the right, and Maj. Reno went ahead four or five miles to the river, at a trot; it took us about half an hour. I heard no orders from Reno. There was no delay at the crossing, Reno being the first to go into the river. I saw a few Indians before crossing, going down the creek.

[RENO GALLOPS TOWARD VILLAGE AND HALTS]

As soon as we cleared the woods, Reno called the battalion into line and moved at a gallop. He was ahead of me about fifteen yards. He was continually checking the men and keeping the line in good order. The horses on the right were unruly and excited after the long gallop. We galloped about two and a half miles across the plain which was sandy and full of sage brush. When we got near the woods, which were on the right of the line, I heard some bullets whistling, but not the sound of the firing. In our front was an immense dense dust and we could see the shadows of Indians in that dust. Pretty soon Reno gave the command "Dismount and prepare to fight on foot." The battalion halted promptly and dismounted; and deployed very nicely. It surprised me because we had many recruits and green horses. The right of the line was at right angles to the woods. I heard no bugle calls during our advance, which took us 10 to 15 minutes after crossing the river.

The Indians appeared to be running around raising a dust. When we halted they seemed to be standing still waiting for us, five or six hundred yards away.

[INDIANS CIRCLE RENO'S FLANKS]

As soon as the line was deployed, Indians came out of the dust and went to our left, on the high bluffs. Came all around and soon were on our flanks. The line advanced seventy-five to a hundred yards and when the fire got on the left flank, it turned. Our fire was striking short, though their's reached us. They continued to come out and soon their fire was all around us to the front, left and rear; the only place we were not shot at was from the right, next the woods. The line remained there about ten minutes, during which time I saw Maj. Reno encouraging the men. He stood there and directed the fire.

Pretty soon Lt. Wallace directed my attention to Indians coming in on the other side of the woods. I started over with five or six men to see. The woods made a horseshoe loop and had a clearing inside. I crossed the clearing and saw some Indians through the woods, downstream. We stood there about ten minutes, when the trumpeter of my company came and said "Lieutenant, here is your horse." I said "I don't want my horse." I was then standing on the bank of the creek. He said "They are going out" and the men with me immediately mounted. I tried to check them but they would not listen: they appeared to be in a panic. I stopped at the creek trying to keep the men steady and as the last man passed I noticed the company guidon on the bank and told him to go and get it. He said it was too hot there for him and went on. I got the guidon myself; it was not more than forty feet away. I crawled up to the top and grabbed it. There were twenty or thirty Indians coming about forty or fifty yards away who scattered when they saw the head

["THE INDIANS FIRED A VOLLEY"]

of my horse over the bank. They fired a volley at me and I dropped down. By that time the command was leaving. I heard no trumpet calls while in the timber. I had seen Lt. Hodgson a few minutes before, leading his horse; he thought it was wounded, but I could see no wound and told him I thought it was a spent bullet. I saw two or three hundred Indians before the men left the timber, but I don't think any had gotten into the timber.

["I HEARD IMMENSE VOLLEYS"]

Soon after Maj. Reno left the timber firing commenced on the other side of the village. I heard immense volleys and more than half of the Indians left. Part went on the high bluffs and part down the river. Some picketed their ponies under the bluffs and laid flat, watching Reno on the hill.

One sergeant was killed on the skirmish line and two or three others wounded. Sergeant White was hit in the arm and afterwards went out with Maj. Reno. I judge it was from 20 minutes to half an hour from the time Maj. Reno deployed his men until the command left the timber. I looked at my watch every 10 minutes, it was between two and three o'clock when they left.

I remained in the woods till 9 P. M. The firing I heard started soon after Maj. Reno reached the hill. I could hear immense volleys on the other side of the village down the river. The fire lasted probably an hour and a half and then died off at a distance, with small shots, and soon died away. Before it stopped entirely the same Indians who left Maj. Reno came right back again, part of them going on the bluff and part across the plain to the south of his position on the bluff.

["THE FIRING I HEARD WAS CUSTER'S"]

I think the firing I heard must have come from Custer. Being in the valley I could hear better than from any other position.

I got back to Reno's command about 3 A. M., June 27th. I came out of the timber at Point "C" and tried to get to it the night of the 25th, but there were too many Indians between.

[THE INDIANS WITHDRAW]

I was down near our crossing ford "A" on the morning of the 26th between 10 and 11. I saw some Indians moving away and could hear the cries of the children and dogs; they passed five or six hundred yards away. It was several hours before all passed. I could hear the noise of the travois and of the dogs and children. While the women and children moved away, the warriors remained around Reno, keeping up a brisk fire until about 4:30, leaving in parties. My attention was first attracted to it while in the woods near Point "A". There was a solitary Indian fifty or sixty yards from us on a point. At about 4:30 he fired 4 shots into the air, and soon a Chief, whom I could not see, but could hear, commenced calling, and a lot of Indians left their places on the bluff and passed where I was. They went away singing, but still there were lots left on the bluff firing. About a half hour later, the same Indian fired four more shots into the air and the same Chief called out again; and another party of Indians left the bluffs. By the time all had left, it was six o'clock. I thought then that probably the command had left. I knew nothing of Custer's defeat and considered that we better stay there till dark, when there would be no fear of meeting Indians as we had the night before. As soon as it was dark I dropped into the river. The water was up to the armpits. We got across and on the bluffs. It was moonlight, but cloudy. When the moon was out of the clouds it was very bright and we were afraid there were still Indians there.

When we got nearly to the top I said we'd better not rise suddenly, because if there were still some Indians there, they would fire: so we laid flat and rolled over.

[BETWEEN 3000 AND 4000 WARRIORS]

On 29 June I visited the place where the Indian village had stood; it was three or four miles long and at some places a half mile wide. I estimate the number of lodges at twelve to fifteen hundred, and the effective fighting force between three and four thousand. At the time I thought there were more Indians than that.

I went over the Custer field on the 27th, volunteering to go with Capt. Benteen. Benteen, Lt. Bradley and Capt. Nolan [Nowlan] went up about five hundred yards from a natural ford we struck on the north side of the village, and there we found a dead body; that was the first, lying in the bottom of a little coulee. It was so disfigured as to be unrecognizable, but from marks on the pants we knew it was a trumpeter. Soon we found more bodies, scattered all over, wherever there was a chance to make a stand in the coulees. You could see that they had attempted to fortify themselves, but the country was such they could not protect the rear.

[THE BODIES OF CUSTER AND CALHOUN]

At last we got to the top of the knoll where Gen. Custer was, and several others, and the horses appeared to have been killed to form barricades. There were higher points all around, so they could not defend both front and rear, and they appeared to have been overcome by overwhelming numbers. I saw only a few cartridge shells. I am informed that the Indians pick them up.

I saw Calhoun's body and several others; part of the gray horse troop were in a ravine forty or fifty yards from the bank of the river—and in another one near Custer's body, toward the river and about 150 to 200 yards from it, there seemed to have been resistance. Their position was lower than the Indians and they had to defend both front and rear.

Whether the Indians who left Reno to go down stream got there soon enough to assist in the attack on Custer I don't know. They started when the heavy firing commenced, and that lasted an hour and a half.

[*"MOST OF THE INDIANS WENT DOWNSTREAM"*]

Not all the Indians left Reno to go downstream; numbers of them picketed their horses under the bluffs and went on the bluffs. I could see them from where I was, though they were not visible from Reno's position; but the great bulk of them went downstream as soon as they heard the heavy firing, and returned in much greater force than they went away.

Reno's timber position threatened the village; a short charge would have taken us into it; and while we were there it would hold all that part of the village to defend it. During the ten minutes I observed Maj. Reno on the skirmish line I admired his conduct. All officers and men did well.

[*TOM CUSTER'S CLOTHES?*]

On the morning of the 26th about daybreak, from the position I was in on the left bank, I heard a party of mounted men fording the river below. I could hear the clanking of the horseshoes and the splashing of the water. I had expected the command to return about daybreak to renew the attack on the village. Not knowing what had become of Gen. Custer, I thought he was with Maj. Reno all the time. I crawled up the bank of the river to see who they were, and to my surprise they were going out instead of coming in. They crossed 15 or 20 yards below me. I could not see them crossing, but after they crossed they came right opposite me. I recognized some of the horses of our regiment, and some of the men had on white hats and blouses. I noticed one whom I took to be Capt. Tom Custer; he had a buckskin jacket, a white hat and rode a sorrel horse; and I was certain it was he. I stepped to one side and called "Tom, send your horse across here." There was an Indian with him, whom I supposed was one of our Rees, as Tom always had some of the scouts with him.

They stopped and looked around, but could not see me. I said again "Here I am, don't you see me." Then some of the Indians saw where I was and gave a yell and sent a volley at me. Then I thought I was mistaken. These men had evidently been engaged in the attack on Custer and had taken their clothing and horses.

[BENTEEN'S APPROACH STOPPED INDIAN PURSUIT]

When Reno left the timber, the Indians followed; but when they got near the river, some of them yelled; and they all stopped running; and some pointed up the stream. When I saw and heard that, I expected Benteen was coming; and I looked up and saw his column approaching the ford where we had crossed; but before they reached it, they turned and disappeared to the right. The Indians watched that column probably ten minutes; and as soon as it disappeared the heavy firing commenced on the other side and they left.

CROSS EXAMINATION

There were about two hundred Indians on our right when we were in the timber; I don't know about the left. I was with the skirmish line all the time, and it withdrew into the woods the same time I did. I went to the top of the bank on the east side to get the guidon. The skirmish line was in the woods to my left at this time. The firing from the Custer field was at first very plain; the first volley; then it got further away and then died out. It started about the time Maj. Reno got to the top of the hill. It was steady for a long time and in volleys: after that it was scattering and lasted but a short time.

I think Maj. Reno had more Indians around him the evening of the 25th than were in the attack on Custer. I saw those around Reno, and make my estimate by comparison of the number in the village.

There were no evidences of any fight at the middle ford

"B". We found the tracks of two horses on the right bank, but they swung around and away. We followed these tracks to the body of the first soldier.

I think the men whose bodies were found in the ravine were in position to make a stand, but it looked like they had been separated from the main command and made a stand by themselves.

[NO EVIDENCE OF COWARDICE]

I saw no indications of cowardice on Reno's part; nor any want of skill in the handling and disposition of the men. When he halted and dismounted I said "Good for you," because I saw that if we had gone five hundred yards further we would have been butchered. Some of the shells I found were Winchester; which were used by the Indians. The Cavalry used the 45 calibre Springfield carbine.

RE-DIRECT EXAMINATION

The effect of sighting Benteen's column was to check the Indians' pursuit of Reno. The Indians watched it, as it appeared at first to be coming across, but it swung around and went off. I think it would have been better to have trumpet calls sounded in the timber, as many of the men were separated and could not hear voice commands.

I was with Girard and Jackson the night of the 25th. We went together from the first woods. I was holding onto the tail of Girard's horse. We were hunting the ford. The plain was full of Indians. We struck a band of them who evidently heard us coming, and were waiting for us. The first thing we heard was "How". Girard swung his horse to the left and struck for the woods full speed, and I let go; the other man did the same thing. The next time I saw them was when I joined Reno's command.

THE ELEVENTH WITNESS CALLED BY THE RECORDER WAS

SGT. EDWARD DAVERN,
Company F, 7th Cavalry

DIRECT EXAMINATION

I was Maj. Reno's orderly on the twenty-fifth and twenty-sixth of June, and was with Lt. Hare while the command was moving down the bottom after crossing the stream. The horses of the command were in tolerable good condition.

[A VARIATION OF CUSTER'S ATTACK ORDER]

Before we moved to the river, I heard Adjutant Cook give Maj. Reno an order; it was "Girard comes back and reports the Indian village three miles ahead and moving. The General directs you to take your three companies and drive everything before you. Capt. Benteen will be on your left and will have the same instructions." Those I believe were the exact words. This was near a tepee we passed, about a mile and a half or two miles from the river.

Just before we got to the ford I saw a few Indians (20 to 40) riding around in circles. I went with Lt. Hare to the left about two hundred yards away from the line, to get a shot at some Indians to our left. They were the nearest. They were not firing then. When the line halted I came back. The Indians were still circling around, getting thicker in front; and some were moving to the left; mostly singly. I saw Maj. Reno. He was near the woods; the skirmish line had swung to the edge of the woods and he was firing at the Indians with a carbine. They were seven or eight hundred yards away and were not firing much. Our line was firing very fast. I went on with Lt. Hare into an open glade and from there saw eight or ten tepees about a thousand yards away. Could just see their tops.

["THE INDIANS CAN'T BE DRIVING US!"]

I heard the fire grow pretty heavy and remarked to Lt. Hare "it can't be possible that the Indians are driving us."

I did not see the skirmish line on the plain break up. I saw it in the woods, where the men were mixed up and huddled together. The only way I knew the command was going to leave was seeing "G" Company men run for their horses: then I went for my own. They ran through the brush. The bullets were coming thick and fast, and but very few of "G" Company got out mounted. I found my horse and another tied to him, and led them both out. I met a "G" Sergeant and give him the "G" Company horse. When I got out I saw the command running as fast as it could. The horses were going on a run. I think the reason some of the men didn't get their horses was because they were so mixed up and demoralized. All the men that did get their horses got out.

THE RECORDER AT THIS POINT RECALLED TO THE STAND

LIEUTENANT DeRUDIO
for further
DIRECT EXAMINATION

I did not see Gen. Custer's column at all; but while I was in the woods Gen. Custer, Lt. Cook and another man I could not recognize came to the highest point of the bluff and waved their hats and made motions like they were cheering. But they soon disappeared. I judged by that that his column was behind the bluff. It was on the highest point on the right bank, just below where Dr. DeWolf was killed. It was not on Weir's point, but one nearer the river, where the river comes right under the bluff. The bluff is very narrow there—hardly wide enough for a horse to stand.

[CUSTER AND COOK AT POINT 7, WAVED HATS AND CHEERED]

He was about 1000 yards from me. *[The witness here designated by the figure 7 on the map the point where he saw Gen. Custer].* It was probably five or six hundred yards down the river from the hill afterwards occupied by Maj. Reno. I saw them only five or six minutes before Reno's retreat. I supposed Custer's command was coming down some of those coulees to join us but they did not; and as pretty soon after, firing began on the other side of the village, I argued that he went to attack the rear of the village. I believe his first encounter was near the middle ford "B"— that he was met there by the Indians and started for a position over the hill and the Indians followed him up.

[RENO COULD HAVE HELD TIMBER SEVERAL HOURS]

Maj. Reno could have held his position in the timber three or four hours by careful use of ammunition. But I cannot tell what effect Custer's attack would have had if he had stayed there for a quarter of an hour. I think the Indians were pretty well divided; half watching Reno and half watching Custer.

I went back for the guidon because I think it the duty of a soldier to preserve his colors at the risk of his life, though when I went, I did not think there was any danger.

CROSS EXAMINATION

The point where I saw Gen. Custer was about three to three and a half miles from the middle ford "B". I was then standing on the bank of the creek. This was six or seven minutes after the command went into the timber. It left five or six minutes later.

If Custer had traveled a mile and a half by the time Reno got on the hill, he would have been over the divide down in a coulee and would not have been in sight of Reno's command.

[CUSTER AND COOK WORE BLUE SHIRTS WITHOUT JACKETS]

I recognized Gen. Custer and Lt. Cook by their dress. They had on blue shirts and buckskin pants. They were the only ones who wore blue shirts and no jackets; and Lt. Cook besides had an immense beard. The third man I did not recognize and he may have been an orderly.

Gen. Custer had a birdseye view of the whole situation there; he could not see all of the village, but could see most of it; but after he left there was no further opportunity for him to see us. The middle ford "B" was the first opportunity to cross and support us by flank attack.

RE-DIRECT EXAMINATION

[THE MEN USED KNIVES TO EXTRACT SHELLS]

The men on our line fired rapidly. Those in the woods, slowly and deliberately. I noticed that when the men on the line fired fast they overheated their guns and had to use their knives to extract shells after firing eight or ten rounds.

I saw two Indians killed in front of us, and several wounded going back to the village. I saw some on the open line drop off their ponies. Lt. Hare got one.

THE INDIAN LOSSES
[W.A.G.]

In 1926, when summarizing the results of the battle, I closed Chapter VI of "The Story of the Little Big Horn" with the sentence: "The Indian loss was negligible." This statement was based upon all the information I was able to gather at that time, and little additional information has since been gained.

In Note 15½ of the series following the text of "The Story," I stated (p. 139), that two tepees were left standing in the Indian village, which contained the bodies of some 22 warriors, and that other bodies found on scaffolds and in trees along the trail the Indians took when on the evening of 26 June they left the Little Big Horn valley, brought the total of known Indian dead to about forty.

Early reports of the battle took for granted that the casualties of the Indians must have been at least as numerous as those of the troops, and stated this to be a fact, notwithstanding the Indian custom of carrying away their dead had made impossible any check upon their losses.

In 1886 Chief Gall was present at the tenth anniversary celebration of the battle, and among other things was asked: "How
many Indians were killed?" He answered: "Eleven down in that
creek, [i.e., Medicine Tail, then called Reno Creek], four over
there and two in that coulee." "How many were killed altogether?"
Gall replied: "Forty-three in all. A great many crossed the river
and died in the rushes. They died every day. Nearly as many
died each day as were killed in the fight. We buried them in trees
and on scaffolds going up Lodge Pole Creek toward the White
Rain mountains." ("The Custer Myth," p. 91).

Just what the above means is not clear. However, the story of
Mrs. Spotted Horn Bull, Sitting Bull's cousin, indicates that on
the day of the battle (25 June) the number of Sioux warriors
killed was twenty-two—the number found in the two tepees left
standing in the village. ("The Custer Myth," p. 87). As these
bodies were ceremonially dressed, and each tepee was surrounded
by the carcasses of ponies arranged in a circle, in number cor-
responding to the number of the dead warriors, it is obvious
that they were purposely left in pursuance of some tribal burial
custom, of which I have never seen an explanation.

In view of the fact that other bodies afterwards found in trees
and on scaffolds brought the number of known Indian dead to
"about forty," it may be that Gall meant, not that forty-three
were killed in the battle, but that this number included those who
died from wounds.

On the other hand, Gall's language is quite as susceptible of
the meaning that the Indian dead from wounds totalled many more
than forty-three. Unfortunately, there is no record from which
the measure of their loss may be determined: no one has ever
known how many died.

But if forty-three was indeed the Indian total, then the ratio
of killed was more than six to one, for the troops (including Indian
scouts and civilians slain), counted two hundred sixty-three who
lost their lives in combat.

In any event, the Little Big Horn was indeed "the greatest
victory ever won by the Indian warrior over the white soldier:
a greater triumph, even, than was Braddock's defeat." ("The
Story of the Little Big Horn," p. 4).

RE-CROSS EXAMINATION

I think it the duty of an officer to be the last in retreat and the first in a charge.

EXAMINATION BY THE COURT

[CUSTER'S NEAREST APPROACH TO THE RIVER]

From all indications, the nearest approach of Gen. Custer to the river was at the middle ford "B". The trail of two shod horses went there and then turned to the right. The nearest body was five or six hundred yards from Point "B", but there was no evidence of fighting nearer than that. There were several fords lower down the river, one of which the regiment used the day we left.

THE DIRECT EXAMINATION OF SGT. DAVERN WAS THEN
    RESUMED:

When I got out, some of the men were about ten yards away and some a long way off. There were Indians between —they kept along the flank at the head of the column. I heard no bugle calls while in the timber.

My horse fell while I was passing two dismounted "G" Company men. Some Indians on the left made a rush. I was thrown over the horse's head and when I got up saw that the "G" Company men were mixed with the Indians, and my horse was getting up. The Indians had run their ponies together and were dismounted. I got back on my horse and got away. I saw the bodies of the two "G" Company men lying down there afterwards. I crossed near Lt. Wallace. There were Indians on the right firing at him.

[THE CROSSING CLOGGED WITH MEN AND HORSES]

The men were trying to get out of the river. The opposite bank appeared to be clogged up with men and horses trying to get out. The men were in as good order as could be expected. About that time Lt. Hodgson jumped his horse into the river and it fell and got away from him. An "M" Company trumpeter was crossing near him and he caught his stirrups to help himself. He said something to the trumpeter but I could not hear what he said. He got out and that was the last I saw of him.

The Indians fired into the men while they were crossing. I did not see anyone return the fire. I crossed in the rear of the column a little below the others; the upper place was too crowded. The men did not stop after crossing, but ran on up the hill. I did not see Maj. Reno at all. I went part way up the hill and stopped. I saw two Indians higher up and to the left. The Indians in the bottom did not follow us at all.

[DR. DeWOLF KILLED]

I saw Lt. Wallace shoot at some Indians who were killing a man three or four ridges from us; the hill was divided into ridges or water cuts. I afterwards learned it was Dr. DeWolf that they were killing. When I got to the top I saw Maj. Reno. He asked me if I had any water. I said "No" and he gave me some. The firing had ceased except for some scattering shots from the Indians on the left.

[VOLLEY FIRING DOWNSTREAM]

Shortly after reaching the top I heard volley firing from down stream. It was not very distinct, but you could tell it was volley firing. No shots between the volleys. I could see Indians circling around in the bottom on the right away down and raising a big dust. I could not tell on which side of the creek; there are so many bends in it. I spoke to Capt. Weir about it. I said "That must be Gen. Custer fighting down in the bottom." He asked me where and I showed him. He said "Yes, I believe it is." That was maybe a half hour after getting on the hill, and I think after Capt. Benteen's column had arrived. Nothing was done at that time.

I don't remember hearing Maj. Reno give any orders, though he said something to some officer about going to look for Lt. Hodgson. I don't know who it was.

About an hour later Capt. Weir moved down the river, as I heard, to open communication with Gen. Custer. Shortly after, the whole command followed. The pack train had come up between one and two hours before. The command didn't go very far and it was probably fifteen minutes before it came back. Maj. Reno was at the head of the command and I was his orderly. The column halted and Maj. Reno sent for Capt. Weir who was ahead. Then we went back a short distance and threw out a skirmish line. The Indians were returning and Capt. Weir had just time to form when they arrived. We went back to a place a little to the right of our first hill.

The companies were then deployed; the pack animals removed into a depression. In the meantime the Indians were closing up—advancing on the command. The fight began and lasted till dark: it started about an hour before sundown, and lasted about two hours.

Maj. Reno sent me to the depression with his horse, so he would know where it was if he wanted it. I saw him several times going around the line, which was in a sort of circle. I reported to him after dark, and he ordered me to get his bedding and fix it for him in the depression. He told me to wait till midnight and then wake him, and then I could go to sleep. That was probably two hours after the firing ceased.

The next time I saw him was after he had the trumpet sounded in the morning; and I got permission to go on the line and was not with him that day [the 26th], tho' I saw him several times walking around the line.

CROSS EXAMINATION

I was a private then; I have been in service 16 years; an old soldier.

I knew McIlargy—I saw him re-cross the river coming

back from Maj. Reno's command; he said he was going to Gen. Custer. He was Maj. Reno's striker. I never saw him afterwards.

A short time after Adjutant Cook gave Maj. Reno the order *[here the witness repeated the order]* after the command started out, I saw him and Capt. Keogh both with Maj. Reno. I did not see anybody go with orders to Capt. Benteen, whose command was out of sight at that time.

When I got on the hill Capt. Weir was there. I don't remember seeing Capt. Benteen. The advance of the pack train was just coming in.

RE-DIRECT EXAMINATION

When I saw the dust and heard the firing, I remarked to Capt. Weir, "Gen. Custer must be fighting the Indians— they are circling around in the bottom." He said "Why do you think so." I said "I hear the firing, and see the dust, and see—the Indians have all left us."

RE-CROSS EXAMINATION

I saw no evidence of cowardice at any time on the part of Maj. Reno.

THE TWELFTH WITNESS CALLED BY THE RECORDER WAS

SGT. F. A. CULBERTSON,

Co. A, 7th Cavalry

DIRECT EXAMINATION

I was in Capt. Moylan's company. When we went down to the crossing I saw no Indians, but did see some dust. We left Gen. Custer at a tepee about three-quarters of a mile from the river and moved at a fast trot. After we crossed and formed, which took from 5 to 8 minutes, the command "Forward" was given, and we moved down the valley. After going half way, Indians came in on our left and front. Most of them would circle off to our left. A few shots were fired, some of which struck in the ground in front of "A" Company. We went on about a half mile further.

[250 INDIANS OPPOSED RENO WHEN HE HALTED]

There were, when we halted, about 250 Indians riding back and forth, and some crossed the bluffs on our left. They were about five hundred yards away and firing at us when we halted. I heard no firing from the command till we halted and deployed. I was at the extreme left of the line; the right rested near the woods. The skirmish line was about 250 yards long. We remained for some time on the skirmish line, some of the new men firing very fast, when the com-

[A CHANGE OF FRONT "BY THE RIGHT FLANK"]

mand was given to move by the right flank. Every man moved off by the right flank, toward the timber. I stopped when I arrived at the timber, with 3 other men. The balance went into the woods. One man had been wounded on the skirmish line and some others after they got in the woods. We were on the line about thirty-five minutes.

["THEY SAID THEY WERE GOING TO CHARGE"]

We fired three or four shots from the edge of the woods and then someone called to me to get our horses. Then a man of my company that was with us was wounded and we left him to get our horses. I went with Lt. Wallace. They said they were going to charge, and Sgt. McDermott and I rode with him. When we got on the hill we saw very few men in front of us, but a heavy body of Indians all around us. Lt. Wallace rode forward and we with him toward the river. The command was all ahead except a few straggling men. There were Indians to our right, left and front.

No heavy body of Indians had charged us while we were on the line, until just as the last man got off the line; then about 800, 8 or 10 deep, came round to our left.

[THE INDIANS FIRED FROM THEIR POMMELS]

As Lt. Wallace, McDermott and myself went toward the

river we could see the Indians riding along the flanks, firing into the command from their pommels. Some of them fired pistols as we came along.

I heard no order to charge and no bugle calls: I don't know where the order came from.

I only saw Maj. Reno a second while the skirmish line was being formed. He was riding toward the woods. I did not see him again till we got on the hill.

[INDIANS AT THE CROSSING]

As I came to the river there were numbers of Indians firing at all parties who were dismounted, killing horses and men as they could. My horse jumped into the river. I passed Lt. Hodgson who was in the water. I could not stop my horse to assist him. Lt. Wallace stopped on the other side to give what help he could. As soon as I got up out of the river I saw Capt. French and Sgt. Lloyd. He said to me that we ought to stop and protect the wounded. I told him to speak to Capt. French and he did. Capt. French said "I'll try—I'll try," and then rode on up the hill. But nothing was done, and the Indians fire was not returned at all.

I met Lt. Varnum about twenty-five yards above that with a wounded man. He asked me to dismount and help the man on his horse. I caught a loose horse of "G" Company and put the man on him and started up the hill again, slowly.

I don't know where Maj. Reno was at this time. I next saw him on top of the hill. The men were coming up, most of them dismounted. I went into the river at the same time as the others, but chose a place above to come out. Sgt. McDermott and I assisted our First Sergeant, who was wounded in the knee, to get up. Indians were firing on us from a high point.

["CUSTER IS COMING"—BUT IT WAS BENTEEN]

The first officer I saw on top of the hill was Capt. Moylan. He said he would not sell his horse for something, I don't know what. Maj. Reno was then riding down to where he took position. In about 5 or 10 minutes I heard them say that Gen. Custer was coming; but it turned out to be Capt. Benteen.

I heard Maj. Reno order Lt. Varnum to do something, but I don't know what. The lieutenant said his horse was worn out, but if he could get another horse he would go. I went to where most of my company were and as the wounded men came up we took care of them.

[RENO AND VARNUM ASK ABOUT HODGSON]

Capt. Moylan asked me what men were wounded or missing and I told him; then Lt. Varnum asked me if I had seen Lt. Hodgson and I told him. Maj. Reno came up and I told him also. He asked if I could find him. I said I thought so and he said he was going for some water, and that I should go with him and ten or twelve men. We went down to the river and found a body at the edge of the river. It was one of my own company. We filled our canteens with water, and then a little further up the hill, we found Lt. Hodgson's body. His watch and chain had been taken, but Maj. Reno took off his class ring: as we went on up the hill we found a "G" Company man who had lost his horse and had hidden in the brush. We took him out and went on up the hill. Several men had been hit there and we all stood a chance of being killed by Indians who were on a hill to our right.

[WEIR MOVES; COMMAND FOLLOWS—RETREATS]

About fifteen or twenty minutes after we got back, Capt. Weir's company moved out and the pack train was just coming up. My company had four wounded and we carried them in blankets. It took six men to each wounded man and the rest to take care of and lead the horses. We moved half or three quarters of a mile and then were ordered to return. Capt. Weir was then being driven back and was about 600 yards ahead of us at the time.

After the return of the command Lt. Mathey ordered me to bring four men from the line and take off the packs and make breastworks for the wounded. While we were doing this one man was instantly killed. We took off the packs by Maj. Reno's order and built breastworks for the wounded.

[HEAVY VOLLEYS HEARD DOWNSTREAM]

Before I went down to the river with Maj. Reno to find Lt. Hodgson's body, I was sitting near Lt. Varnum talking with Lt. Edgerly. We heard firing from down below. At first it was a couple of volleys, very heavy. Afterwards it was lighter and appeared more distant. Lt. Varnum remarked that Gen. Custer was hotly engaged or was giving it to the Indians hot, or words to that effect; and in a few minutes Maj. Reno came up and we went down to the river and I did not hear it any more. If there was any after that the hills broke the sound.

Maj. Reno came up to us while the firing was going on, a few minutes after Lt. Varnum had remarked the firing, which after the volleys, sounded more like skirmish firing. The command moved down stream a few minutes less than an hour afterwards.

MAJOR RENO AT THIS POINT RECALLED

LT. DeRUDIO,
for further
CROSS EXAMINATION

While in the timber Girard said it served him right to get in such a position, not having stayed with the pack train; that he was not employed to fight.

RE-DIRECT EXAMINATION

So far as I know, it is not the duty of an interpreter as such, to fight.

THE CROSS-EXAMINATION OF

SERGEANT CULBERTSON
then began

On the way to the timber I heard Maj. Reno say to "G" Company not to get excited; that they would have hot enough work soon.

There was a very large cloud of dust in front of the Indians as we moved down the valley; but there were from 100 to 150 Indians, and at times more, riding back and forth outside it. Maj. Reno's Adjutant deployed the left of the skirmish line, and he, the right.

[THREE MINUTES FROM DESTRUCTION]

If the line had not been retired within three minutes from the time it was, I don't think anyone would have gotten off the line. I don't think Maj. Reno could have held the timber

[1000 TO 1200 WARRIORS]

but a very few minutes. My estimate of the number of Indians about his position on the skirmish line and in the timber is about a thousand to twelve hundred. I always knelt before I fired, but most of the men were new and never under fire before, and they fired at random. I fired twenty-one shots, but one of the men told me he fired sixty. The firing I heard downstream while on the hill was no heavier than we had on our skirmish line, and I don't think anybody had any impression that Gen. Custer was having any more trouble than we were. Maj. Reno exercised caution over his command on the 25th and I saw him in very dangerous and exposed positions during the afternoon and evening and also on the 26th.

[NO IDEA CUSTER DESTROYED]

During the night Lt. Varnum asked Sgt. McDermott if he would volunteer to go with him to take a dispatch to Gen. Custer. Sgt. McDermott said he would not volunteer, but would go if detailed. Lt. Varnum said it was very likely that he would have to go and wanted McDermott to go along. It was the general impression among the men that Gen. Custer had wounded and could not come to us, just as we could not go to him. There was no idea that he and his command could possibly be destroyed.

I heard Capt. Weir ask Capt. Moylan if, when he was Adjutant, Gen. Custer gave him any particular orders about doing anything. Capt. Moylan said "No", that when he was Adjutant, Gen. Custer never told him what he was going to do; he would order him to tell the company commanders to go to such and such places and that was all.

As we were crossing the tributary to the Little Big Horn while on the way to the crossing ford, I heard Adjutant Cook tell the men to close up; there was hot work ahead for them. The horses were not unmanageable, but some of the men were very poor riders. Point "B" was as good a ford as Point "A".

Girard told me, the night of the 26th, that he lost his watch and that he threw his rifle into the river, trying to get away.

[RENO NO COWARD]

I saw no evidence of cowardice on the part of Maj. Reno at any time.

RE-DIRECT EXAMINATION

Altogether, during the two days I saw Maj. Reno 4 or 5 hours. I base my opinion on that.

[TOO MANY RECRUITS?]

Most of "G" Company were recruits, about half, and about a third of "A"—I don't know about "M"; and they detailed the oldest men for horse holders. About one in ten of the new men had seen prior service; they had had very little training; were very poor horsemen and would fire at random.

RE-CROSS EXAMINATION

About all the instruction they had had in the duties of a soldier were what Maj. Reno had given them that spring. Most of the time they were on some other duty that gave no chance to learn how to fight.

RE-DIRECT EXAMINATION

The recruits were brave enough but had not had the time nor opportunity to make soldiers—some of them were not fit to take into action.

THE RECORDER THEN CALLED HIS THIRTEENTH WITNESS

JOHN MARTIN, TRUMPETER
Co. H, 7th Cavalry

DIRECT EXAMINATION

I was orderly trumpeter to Gen. Custer on June 25th. At the tepee on the right side of the river Maj. Reno's column took off to the left and we took off to the right. It was at a ravine; we could see hills on both sides. We remained on the right side of the river and went on the jump

[CUSTER STOPPED ONCE—TO WATER HORSES]

all the way: Gen. Custer did not go near the river at all: he halted only once, at a little creek to water the horses for about five minutes. We were there about 10 minutes altogether, and the General directed the commanders not to let the horses drink too much.

He left that watering place and went about three hundred yards in a straight line; then turned to the right a little and traveled four or five hundred yards and then there was a big bend on the hill; he turned these hills and went on top

[THE SLEEPING VILLAGE]

of the ridge. All at once we looked on the bottom and saw the Indian village; at the same time we could only see children and dogs and ponies—no Indians at all. Gen. Custer appeared to be glad to see the village in that shape and supposed the Indians were asleep in their tepees.

We could see the bottom from the ridge but could not see the timber because it was under the hill—nor anything of Maj. Reno's column.

I rode to the left and rear of Gen. Custer, and about two yards from him. That was my position as orderly.

The gray horse company was in the center of the column. We could see the river while on top of the ridge, but after we went down a ravine we could not see the river or timber or anything else. We heard no firing as we went down.

[CUSTER MOVED AT THE GALLOP]

Gen. Custer's column moved always at a gallop. It was about a mile and a half from the watering place to the point on the ridge where we could see the village.

After he saw the village, he pulled off his hat and gave a cheer and said "Courage, boys, we will get them, and as soon as we get through, we will go back to our station."

[CUSTER TO BENTEEN—THE LAST MESSAGE]

We went more to the right from the ridge and down to a ravine that led to the river. At the time Gen. Custer passed the high place on the ridge or a little below it he told his Adjutant to send an order back to Capt. Benteen. I don't know what it was. Then the Adjutant called me. I was right at the rear of the General. He said "Orderly, I want you to take this despatch to Capt. Benteen and go as fast as you can." He told me if I had time and there was no danger to come back, but otherwise to remain with my company which was with Capt. Benteen.

My horse was tired and I went through as fast as he could go. The Adjutant told me to follow the same trail we came down.

[RENO ENGAGED; MESSAGE DELIVERED]

After I started back I traveled five or six hundred yards, perhaps three quarters of a mile, and got on the same ridge where Gen. Custer saw the village. I looked down and saw that Maj. Reno's battalion was engaged. I went on to about three or four hundred yards above the watering place and met Capt. Benteen. I delivered my despatch to him and told him what Lt. Cook had told me. Capt. Benteen read the despatch and put it in his pocket and gave me an order to Capt. McDougall to bring up the pack train and keep it well up.

Capt. Benteen asked me where Gen. Custer was. I said I supposed that by that time he had made a charge through the village. I said nothing about Maj. Reno's battalion. He did not ask about it.

[CUSTER WAS GOING AHEAD]

When I left Gen. Custer he was going ahead: the Adjutant stopped to write the despatch. It took me three quarters to an hour to get back to Capt. Benteen: it was fifteen or twenty minutes after I looked down from the ridge and saw Reno in action before I met Benteen.

I went at once to Capt. McDougall about 150 yards. He was in front of his troop, and the packs were pretty well together. I delivered my message and joined my company.

After delivery of Custer's despatch to Benteen, he moved a little faster. The packs were coming on—some walking, some running, some trotting.

[BENTEEN STOPS TO HELP RENO]

We followed Gen. Custer's trail till we got on the same ridge where I saw Reno engaged. About the time we got there we saw Reno's battalion retreating to the same side of the river we were on. We joined Reno and the packs came up in about fifteen minutes. After the packs were all up, we moved down the river in about one and a half hours. I was right in front of the column and could see Indians after we got to the head of the first ravine. We halted then and Capt. Weir wanted to take his company down the stream to see Gen. Custer. He went a little to the right and

[WEIR ADVANCES, RETREATS: INDIANS FOLLOW]

came back again. The Indians were leaving Gen. Custer and coming back to us, firing; the bulk of them came to where we were. The column then turned back as it was in a bad position: the Indians were on both flanks and the ravine was very deep and we could not go through. We took position a little further down the stream from where we first saw Maj. Reno.

I saw Maj. Reno when we took position and again that night at 12 P. M., when he sent an order to sound reveille at 2 A. M. No calls were sounded that night. The Indians commenced firing after reveille and kept it up. Maj. Reno was in the center of the corral at reveille and afterwards was around the skirmish line examining the position.

I was the only one who sounded calls. The second day, after the Indians left, I sounded retreat, recall and march, so that if there were any of our friends in the ravines they would hear and come up.

CROSS EXAMINATION

I judge it was about noon when Gen. Custer and I were on the ridge and saw the village. I did not see Gen. Custer after that. His command was galloping when I left. When I saw the Indian village there was no dust at all; just dogs and children playing around the tepees. Gen. Custer said

["THE INDIANS ARE ASLEEP IN THEIR TEPEES"]

"Courage boys, we have got them; the Indians are asleep in their tepees." I was sent back from about the head of the ravine that Custer went down toward the river. *[Here the witness designated the point by marking the figure 8 on the map].*

After I saw Maj. Reno engaged, I traveled about two miles to Capt. Benteen. It took about three quarters of an hour to come back with Benteen's command.

I was about an hour and a half going from Custer to Benteen and about three quarters of an hour back to the ridge. I can't say how long it took; two or three hours. I judge I went about five miles, but I cannot judge the times and distances. I do not know.

RE-DIRECT EXAMINATION

The ridge from which Gen. Custer and I saw the village is the highest point around there. I met Capt. Benteen before I got as far as the tepee; was not in sight of it. I don't think I crossed Maj. Reno's trail at all. I can only guess at the time. I had no watch.

RE-CROSS EXAMINATION

Only the Indian scouts went to the top of the high hill. Gen. Custer did not go himself. His brothers and his nephew were with him there on the hill, and he sent messages to the companies.

THE RECORDER HERE RECALLED

SERGEANT DAVERN

DIRECT EXAMINATION

Maj. Reno generally carried a carbine and pistol. I always handed him his carbine when he mounted. The night before the fight he kept his own pistol. He had a carbine and pistol the 25th, but not after we got on the hill. I told him I'd lost my carbine when my horse fell and he said he had lost his carbine and pistol also. He did not say how or when.

CROSS EXAMINATION

Maj. Reno had a carbine on the hill but I don't know whose: my conversation with him was just as we got to the hill; he was mounted, and it was before the line was formed. He spoke about water and gave me a drink.

RE-DIRECT EXAMINATION

It was an easy matter to borrow a carbine or pistol on the hill; you could find one most any place.

THE FOURTEENTH WITNESS CALLED BY THE RECORDER WAS

CAPT. F. W. BENTEEN,

7th Cavalry

DIRECT EXAMINATION

On June 24th we marched till about three o'clock [P.M.], and bivouacked without order to unpack mules or unsaddle horses, and on the next morning when we moved I got no orders. The command moved and I followed the rest.

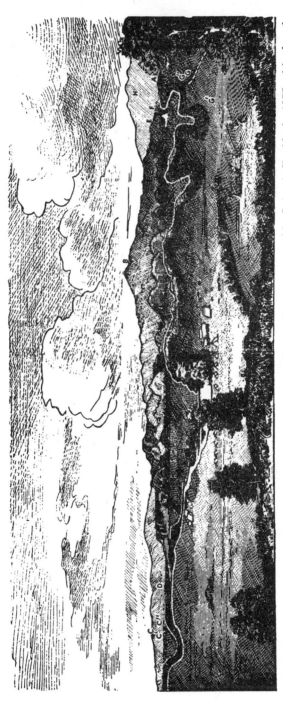

The Little Big Horn battle field one year after the battle. Drawn by an artist with Colonel Sheridan's 1877 visit for the N. Y. Graphic. The tents and wagons pertain to Colonel Sheridan's command.

A. Where Reno first crossed the river.
B. Custer's position at time of Reno's first crossing.
C. The scene of the "last stand."
C′. Bodies of men and horses of Custer's command here.
C″. "Dead men by companies" in this ravine.
D. Ford which Custer approached.
E. Ravine down which Benteen led charge to obtain water.

F. Southern line of rifle pits, where Hodgson was buried.
G. Reno's skirmish line formed here. (Dotted in by Benteen)
G′. Farthest advance of Reno's skirmish line.
G″. Reno dismounted here. (Inked in by Benteen)
H. The Rosebud mountains.
D-B-E-F. "Bad Lands" Buttes.

[CUSTER DISCREDITS HIS SCOUTS]

The battalion organization was made after we had marched about four hours. I think at the first halt an orderly came to me with instructions for the officers to assemble. No bugle call was sounded. Gen. Custer told us that he had just come down from the mountain; that he had been told by the scouts that they could see a village; ponies, and tepees and smoke. He gave it to us as his belief that they were mistaken; that there were no Indians there; that he had looked through his glasses and could not see any and did not think there were any there. Other instructions were given; these were that the officer who first reported that his company had carried out his order that a non-com and six men should be with the packs, and that the men should have 100 rounds of ammunition in their belts and in the saddle bags, should have the advance. I reported first and was given the advance.

[CUSTER'S ORDERS TO BENTEEN]

We moved then probably 8 miles and halted in a kind of valley surrounded by high hills, and there the division into battalions was made. I received three companies and was sent to the left to a line of bluffs. I don't know how many battalions, or who was put in command. It was not told to me at all. My orders were to proceed out into a line of bluffs about four or five miles away; to pitch into anything I came across and to send back word to Gen. Custer at once if I came across anything. I had gone about a mile when I received instructions through the Chief Trumpeter that if I found nothing before reaching the first line of bluffs to go on to the second line of bluffs with the same instructions. I had gone I suppose a mile further when I received orders through the Sergeant Major that if I saw nothing from the second line of bluffs then to go into the valley, and if there was nothing in that valley to go on to the next valley. The angle of my march to the route of the regiment was about 45°, a left oblique. The pack train, at the first halt, was close up. I don't know where it was at the second halt, but I suppose, close to the rear.

Gen. Custer also instructed me to send an officer and six men in advance of my battalion and ride rapidly. I selected my first lieutenant and six men from my own company and sent them ahead; but the greater part of the time I was ahead of them with my orderly, the battalion coming on as fast as it could.

[BENTEEN'S MARCH]

I went to the second line of bluffs and saw no valley and I knew the Indians had too much sense to go to any place over such a rugged country—that if they had to go in that direction they had a much better way to go. The last I saw of the column was the gray horse troop at a dead gallop. I had an idea that Gen. Custer was mistaken as to there being no Indians in that vicinity; and as there were no Indians there and no valleys I thought my duty was to go back to the trail and join the command.

The route back was the same as going over, bearing to the right at the same angle. I struck the trail about a mile ahead of the pack train. I saw it coming on the trail. I then followed the trail to a kind of morass. My horses had not been watered since 6 or 8 o'clock the evening before and I formed them around this morass and watered them. As I moved out from there, two mules from the pack train rushed into the morass and were stuck in the mud. I then went on, I suppose, about seven miles when I came to a burning

[CUSTER'S MESSENGERS]

tepee which contained a dead warrior. A mile or so from that I met a sergeant coming back with instructions to the Commanding Officer of the pack train, to "hurry up the packs." I told him the pack train was about seven miles back and he could take the order back as I had nothing to do with that; that Capt. McDougall was in charge of the pack train. About a mile or so further on I met Trumpeter

Martin who brought a written order which I have. It has no date. It says: *"Benteen, come on—big village—be quick—bring packs. P. S. Bring packs. W. W. Cook."* It was about two miles from where Maj. Reno first crossed the Little Big Horn that Martin met me and about two and a half miles from the burning tepee. I did not know whose trail I was following. I asked Martin, after reading the note, about the village. He said the Indians were all "skedaddling"; therefore there was less necessity for me to go back for the packs. I could hear no firing at that time. I was then riding four to five hundred yards in advance of the battalion with my orderly. Capt. Weir was about two hundred yards in my rear. I waited till he came up and handed him the note. I asked him no questions and he did not volunteer advice.

[BENTEEN REACHES THE RIVER AND JOINS RENO]

When the command came up I ordered a trot and went on ahead to the crossing of the Little Big Horn at the ford "A." That was my first sight of it. There I saw an engagement going on and supposed it was the whole regiment. There were twelve or thirteen men in skirmish line that appeared to have been beaten back. The line was then parallel with the river and the Indians were charging through those men. I thought the whole command was thrashed and that was not a good place to cross. To my right I noticed three or four Indians four or five hundred yards away from me. I thought they were hostile, but on riding toward them found they were Crows. They said there was a big "pooh poohing" going on. Then I saw the men who were up on the bluff and I immediately went there and was met by Maj. Reno. I did not consider it necessary for me to go back for the pack train as it was coming, and the Indians could not get to it except by me.

["I HEARD LITTLE FIRING"]

I heard very little firing at all. After the time I got on the Reno hill not more than 15 or 20 shots. While at the river

I could both hear it and see it about two miles away. My effective force was about 125 men. As to the time I reached Maj. Reno on the hill, I know only from Lt. Wallace that it was 12:10 when I started off to the left, and it must have taken 3 hours to go where I did and back. I reached Reno, I think about 3 P.M. The pack train was not yet in sight. I should think it was an hour and a quarter to an hour and a half before it arrived.

When Custer ordered me to move off to the left Reno was not present.

Reno's men appeared to be in good order, but pretty well shaken up. Men climbing a big bluff on foot would be pretty well blown, and so would the horses. They were not in line of battle but scattered around, I suppose to the best advantage. They all thought there was a happier place than that, I guess.

[THE INDIANS CHECK PURSUIT]

The Indians saw me about the same time I saw them and checked their pursuit. Four or five hundred came to the highest point of land there; they were nearly a mile away. There were about nine hundred circling around in the bottom.

I showed Reno the order I had from Cook and asked him if he knew where Gen. Custer was. He said he did not; that he had been sent in to charge those Indians on the plain and that Gen. Custer's instructions to him through Lt. Cook were that he would support him with the whole outfit; and that was the last he had seen or heard of him and he did not know where he was.

[NO KNOWLEDGE OF CUSTER'S WHEREABOUTS]

I had no knowledge or impression where Custer was or on which side of the river. My impressions from Martin were that the Indians were "skedaddling" but my first sight of the fight showed that there was no "skedaddling" being done by the Indians, and I, of course, thought that was the whole command and if so, it was whipped. When I found

it was not, I supposed Custer was down the river. I did not
say so to Maj. Reno, as he should have known more about
Gen. Custer than I could. Reno did not explain to me why
he had retreated from the bottom to the hill; nor did he
express any solicitude or uneasiness about Custer. Nor did
I; I supposed Gen. Custer was able to take care of himself.
Reno was just as cool as he is now; he had lost his hat in
the run down below.

[“I HEARD NO VOLLEYS”]

The only firing I heard that I did not see, and which came
from the direction Custer had gone was the 15 or 20 shots
that seemed to come from about the central part of the village, about at the ford “B.” The village was in 2 divisions.
I have heard officers disputing about hearing volleys. I heard
no volleys.

[THE DOWNSTREAM MOVEMENT DRIVEN BACK]

About half an hour after our arrival on the hill Capt.
Weir sallied out in that direction in a fit of bravado, I think,
without orders. I think it was before the packs came up.
There was no movement downstream ordered, that I know
of; but I afterwards went down in the same direction with
my battalion to the highest point and had the troops defiled
on the bluffs to show Custer our position if he was down
there. The bulk of the troops followed. Reno was not there—
probably then at Hodgson’s body and picking up wounded.
We went down about a mile. I suppose this figure 7 on the
map is intended for that point.

A movement could have been made down the river in the
direction Custer had gone immediately upon my arrival on
the hill, but we would all have been there yet. The whole
command could have gone as far as I went, but no further.
We were driven back.

[THE RETREAT AND FORMATION FOR DEFENSE]

From that point I had my first sight of the village. It was
the only point from which it could be seen. I saw about

eighteen hundred tepees, no sign of troops or fighting. We had not been there but two or three minutes before the gorge was filled with Indians rushing toward us, and then we fell back to where we were corralled. I was for halting before we got there, so as to check the Indians and to select a better place while we had time and not be rushed over by them, but Maj. Reno thought it best to go back to where he first got on the hill. The line was formed in an irregular ellipse, with the up-river side of it knocked off: there was a flat where our pack animals and horses were corralled and the line formed around it in the shape of a horseshoe, one prong of the horseshoe extending further than the other. The Indians surrounded us there and kept it up pretty lively as long as they could see. I was on the long prong of the horseshoe:—the short point was turned in at right angles—Capt. Moylan had this.

I had left one company back on the ridge with orders to hold it at all hazards, but that company got back as quick as the others. Then I sent Capt. Godfrey's company to another hill to check the Indians till we could form. I saw Reno there; he came back with me and talked with me. I don't know that he gave any order to retire from the advanced position. Orders were not necessary about that time. The first I know as to the formation of a line was when I told Lt. Wallace to place his company at a spot I pointed out. He said he had no company, only three men. I told him to go there with his three men and I would see he was supported; and from that the line was formed. Maj. Reno might have been at the other end or in the center after the

[2500 OR 9000?]

line was formed: I saw him in the center. I thought then that there were about 2500 Indians surrounding us, but I think now there were eight or nine thousand.

[THE FIGHT ON THE HILL]

The location of the troops around the horseshoe shaped

line was first, at the angle, Company A; then followed Companies G, D, B, M and K. I was not assigned to any particular part. My company was on the extreme left. After our line was formed it was about as lively a fire as you would like to stand up under. You had only to show a hat or a head or anything to get a volley toward it. It was about 5:30 when we got our line finished, or maybe later. We were under fire two and a half to three hours. The Indians had parties as large as a regiment standing around in the bottom looking on; there was no place to put them; fully 2000 were around us waiting for a place to shoot from. The Indians close to us did not expose themselves; the only thing you could see would be the flash of a gun. They came so close that they threw arrows and dirt over at us with their hands and touched one of the dead men with a coup stick. That was the next morning. That afternoon was like the second day; we could see nothing to shoot at. We got volleys, but could not return them.

["NEXT MORNING THE FIRE WAS HEAVIER"]

The night of the 25th Maj. Reno was up on the hill where my company was and ordered me to build breastworks. I sent for spades but there were none. I thought it unnecessary, but the next morning the fire was much heavier and I had a great deal of trouble keeping my men on the line. I had to run them out of the pack train, and I brought up sacks of bacon and boxes of hard bread and pack saddles, and made a redoubt. I took 12 or 15 skulking soldiers and packers to that place and turned the redoubt over to my First Lieutenant and told him I intended to drive the Indians who were close to us from the ravine. I did so and we then got water. Maj. Reno was at the time on the other end of the line, where he thought the main attack would come. After getting to the water I sent word to Reno to get all the kettles, canteens, pots and other receptacles together and fill them, as I had secured the water. I then told Reno

I was being annoyed by a cross fire from every quarter and
was unprotected, save by the breastworks and asked him
if I might drive those Indians out. He said "Yes" and we
did it. I gave the order—told the men to go, and went with
them. I do not think Maj. Reno did.

[RENO'S CONDUCT ALL RIGHT]

I think that his conduct was all right; I saw him every
15 or 30 minutes those two days and during the night of
the 25th was with him nearly the whole time. I could have
tried to join him in the timber, but would not have attempted
it without first getting the pack train; but my losses would
have been much greater. The pack train was in no danger;
if the Indians had attempted to attack it, I could get there
quicker than they could. What we did was the best that
could be done; if I had to do it again I would go over the
same trail. I could not improve it.

[RENO'S POSITION IN THE TIMBER]

The position in the timber first taken by Reno was an A-1
defensive position, and could have been held five or six hours,
depending on the size of the attacking force. Against 900
it was defensible; but the 900 would have been reinforced
by another 900, and the next morning they would all have
been killed. It could, however, have been made more defensible than the position on the hill, with axes and spades.
But there were few axes, and only five spades. The position
did not threaten the village much, though only six or seven
hundred yards away, because they could pull down their
tepees and take them away. It would hold a large force of
Indians between there and the village to prevent a charge,
but they had enough to do it; eight or nine hundred was only

[JUNCTION IN THE TIMBER USELESS]

a small part of what they had. If I had joined Reno in the
timber with the pack train, it could not have made a particle
of difference so far as Custer was concerned. The seven com-

panies would have been as completely corralled there as on the hill. Gen. Custer would have had to look out for himself the same as he did; and how he did, you know. Doubtless the abandonment of the timber by Reno released numbers of Indians for attacking Custer, but I don't think they had any use for them down there. There was not a foot of unoccupied ground in that country; there were Indians everywhere, from 12 feet to 1200 yards away.

[CUSTER'S ROUTE]

I examined what I thought was Custer's route, but I think now I was mistaken. I supposed he had gone to the ford ["B"], down through a canyon-like ravine, but I now think Custer went to the right of the second divide and not to the river at all. On the morning of Gen. Terry's arrival I asked permission to take my company and go over the battlefield of Gen. Custer. I did so and followed down the gorge, but I am now satisfied he did not go that way.

CUSTER'S ROUTE TO THE BATTLE RIDGE
[W.A.G.]

For some months after the battle of the Little Big Horn, belief was general that Custer had ridden down a branch of the ravine now known as Medicine Tail Coulee, in an attempt to force passage of the ford which lies at the coulee's mouth, and thus assail the flank of the Indian village. And it was upon this accepted theory that Lt. Maguire drafted his map, upon which in boldly dotted lines, the route then conceived to be the one that Custer followed, is clearly indicated. It shows his supposed approach behind the crest of the bluffs that line the easterly bank of the river until the way lay open for a quick turn to the left and a dash for the ford, designated on the map by the letter "B." There it was supposed, he met such strong resistance that he was forced back and to the north, in two separate columns, the first of which retreated to the ravine (designated "H" on the map) where it made a stand, many bodies of "E" Company men being found there. Thence the survivors of this column fled northeast, to the hill marked "E" where, mingling with the remnants of the second column, "Custer Last Stand" was made. The second column rode further to the east before it headed north to the elevation since known as Calhoun Hill (designated "D" on the map), where it too made a stand, flanked on its right by Keogh's Company "I" along the battle ridge. The survivors of this column, it was supposed, fell back to the hill "E," joining Custer and his faithful few who still fought on till all were killed. This was the accepted picture of the fight for many months, and until it dawned upon the numerous observers who visited the battlefield during 1877, and even before the winter of 1876 set in, that no bodies, either of men or horses had been found anywhere near the ford "B," the body nearest the ford being at least a half mile distant. Capt. Benteen, who with his company rode over the Custer field on the 27th, said during the Inquiry that though he had formerly believed that the Maguire map correctly indicated Custer's route, he "never could account for the fact that there were no dead bodies at that ford: for if he had gone down to the river and was attacked, there would have been horses and men killed there; but there were none. I don't think he got within three furlongs from the ford."

The Indians too, were in general agreement that Custer did not closely approach the middle ford ("B"), though it is true that some of them insisted that he not only did approach it, but that the advance of his column actually crossed the river, thus accounting for the several dead soldiers found within the limits of the village site. The preponderance of the evidence, however, and particularly that of the circumstantial evidence—the total absence of any sign of conflict at or near the ford, leads inevitably to the conclusion that Maguire's theory was based upon false premises, and that the route he mapped for Custer and his force was due to misconception of the facts. However that may be, Maguire should not be saddled with the onus of the error. The mistake was not his, but that of his informants, the officers of the Seventh, who at the time were convinced of the correctness of his theories, because those theories were but an adoption of their own.

It remains then to inquire, since the Maguire route appears to be discredited, by what route did Custer come to the battle ridge. This question has never yet been answered satisfactorily, and in my opinion, never will be. There is, unfortunately, little to go on except the stories of the Indians, and they are in hopeless disagreement. It is true, no doubt, that many of the discrepancies and contradictions found in Indian accounts as they have come down to us, are the result of bad interpreting; indeed, I feel sure that this is so. But it is a condition which cannot now be remedied; we cannot edit tales, most of which were recounted seventy-five years ago, by saying, as some have seemed to do: "This stor: is not correct; he *ought* to have said *this,* but the story makes him say *that.* I think he said what he ought to have said, and therefore, he did say it." This is a comfortable way to write history if one can get away with it, whatever may be thought of its ethics.

But does it really matter how Custer came to the battle ridge? We know he did arrive there, because he and most of his men were found there. But as to his approach, General Godfrey had his own idea; so also did Mr. Curtis, who wrote "The North American Indian"; and they were as far apart as the poles. Both routes are plotted on the U. S. Geological Survey Contour map at page 146. On the other hand, Fred Dustin, in "The Custer Tragedy," appears to have accepted the Maguire theory intact, while Dr. Kuhlman in his "Legend into History" comes up with a brand new one that differs materially from all the others. All these gentlemen wrote history and wrote it well; each expressed his honest convictions, and each offers a feasible and possible route. When so many who speak with authority differ with each other so completely, and the Custer story is not affected in the least, I think it proves the point of such small importance that I shall spare the reader any guesswork of my own.

The nearest body to the middle ford "B" was six to eight hundred yards from it.

["A PANIC 'TILL THE LAST MAN WAS KILLED"]

I went over the battlefield carefully with a view to determine in my own mind how the fight was fought. I arrived at the conclusion then as I have now that it was a rout, a panic, till the last man was killed; that there was no line formed. There was no line on the battlefield; you can take a handful of corn and scatter it over the floor and make just such lines. There were none; the only approach to a line was where five or six horses were found at equal distances like skirmishers. Ahead of them were five or six men at about the same distances, showing that the horses were killed and the riders jumped off and were all heading to get where Gen. Custer was. That was the only approach to a line on the field. There were more than 20 killed there. To the right there were four or five at one place all within a space of twenty or thirty yards. That was the condition all over the field and in the gorge.

[EVIDENCE OF A STAND]

Only where Gen. Custer was found were there any evidences of a stand. The five or six men I spoke of were where Capt. Calhoun's body was; they were of his company. If I am not mistaken, there were twenty-two bodies found in a ravine, fifty to seventy-five yards from the river; they had, I think, been killed with stones and clubs. They were unarmed—I think wounded men. They had gone into the ravine, the Indians say, possibly to hide. There was a trail leading to a crossing about a hundred yards above that ravine: but I could cross that river almost anywhere.

[CUSTER DID NOT GET NEAR FORD "B"]

In my opinion the route taken by Gen. Custer is not properly indicated on the map, though until recently I had believed it was; but I never could account for the fact that there were no dead bodies at that ford ["B"], for if he had gone down to the river and was attacked there, there would have been horses and men killed there, but there were none. I don't think he got within three furlongs of the ford.

I counted seventy dead horses and two Indian ponies on the field. I think in all probability the men turned their horses loose without any orders to do so. Many orders might have been given, but few obeyed. I think they were panic-stricken; it was a rout as I said before.

The village, as I saw it from the one high point, I esti-

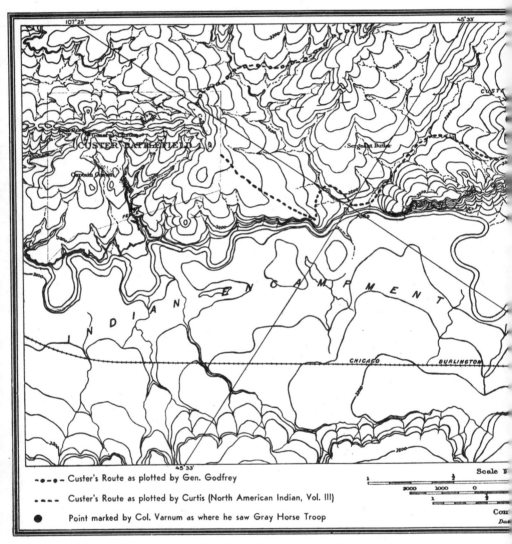

- •- •- Custer's Route as plotted by Gen. Godfrey

- - - - Custer's Route as plotted by Curtis (North American Indian, Vol. III)

●   Point marked by Col. Varnum as where he saw Gray Horse Troop

Contour map of the battlefield. (U. S. Geologica

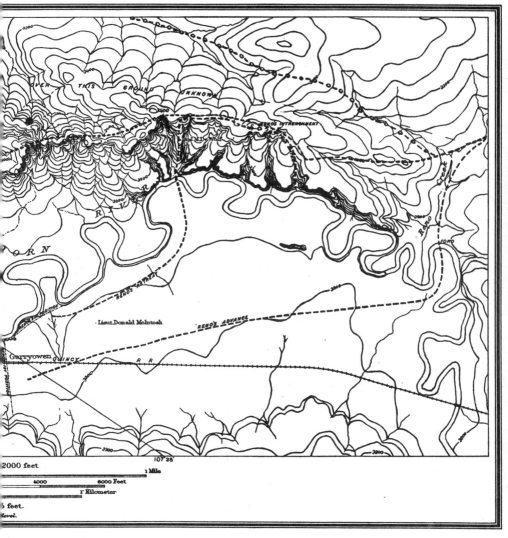

Custer's route as supposed by Curtis and Godfrey.

[THE INDIAN VILLAGE—ITS SIZE]

mated at 3 to 4 miles long. There were about 1800 tepees, probably averaging 4 to 7 warriors to the tepee. I saw it when it moved—it started about sunset and was in sight until darkness came. It was in a straight line about three miles long and I think a half mile wide, as densely packed as animals could be. They had an advance guard and platoons formed and were in as regular a military order as a corps or division.

CROSS EXAMINATION

I saw no evidence of cowardice on Reno's part. I found it necessary at one time to caution him about exposing himself. I told him to be careful how he stood around in front of the point, where we were making rifle pits, as volleys were coming constantly. At that particular time the fire was irregular and not very heavy.

["THERE WAS NO PLAN AT ALL"]

When I received my orders from Custer to separate myself from the command, I had no instructions to unite at any time with Reno or anyone else. There was no plan at all. My orders were "valley hunting ad infinitum." The reason I returned was because I thought I would be needed at the ridge: I acted entirely upon my own judgment. I was separated from Reno possibly fifteen miles when at the greatest distance.

Trumpeter Martin came at a jog trot, and told me the Indians were "skedaddling." I moved at a trot from then till I joined Reno. I moved at a trot all the time from when I left Custer till I met Reno except when watering the horses.

Reno could not have expected me to join him; there were no orders for me to do so. It was about eleven miles from the tepee with the dead warrior that Custer gave me the order to diverge. I passed from the sight of the column in about three quarters of an hour. I could not tell how far

Custer was from the lone tepee when I lost sight of the column. It might have been 5 or 6 miles, or more.

[NEVER ORDERED TO JOIN RENO]

No order was ever sent me to join Reno's command; the one brought by Trumpeter Martin was the only one I got. When I left I did not know that Reno had any command; the division had not been made yet; and I don't think Reno knew anything about it at the time I left. When I passed he asked me where I was going and I told him I was going to the left with instructions to pitch into anything I came across. The next time I saw Reno was on the hill. I think that he replenished his ammunition from the pack train. I heard so, but did not see it.

[NO ONE IMAGINED CUSTER DESTROYED]

The farthest down stream any company of Reno's got was about a half mile below that highest point. I planted a guidon there as a guide to our position for Custer. His battlefield is not visible from there—I know that positively, though some officers think it was. Not a soul in the command imagined that Custer was destroyed till Gen. Terry came up; that was our first intimation; up to that time we were wholly ignorant of his fate. Except for the battle of the Washita there was no historical example, so far as I know, of the destruction of a command equipped as his was. From all the circumstances it is my judgment that his fight lasted from fifteen minutes to half an hour or an hour; not more than the latter. I do not think it would have been possible to have communicated with him even if we had known where he was.

It was after we had marched eight or ten miles on the morning of the 25th when Gen. Custer said he did not believe there were any Indians in that country. It was about ten o'clock that morning. I started off to the left shortly after 12 o'clock by Lt. Wallace's watch. I did not look at my own watch that day or the next, though I kept it wound.

[WE BELIEVED OURSELVES ABANDONED]

It was the belief of the officers on the hill during the night of the 25th that Gen. Custer had gone to Gen. Terry and that we were abandoned to our fate.

RE-DIRECT EXAMINATION

Maj. Reno knew I went to the left, but not what orders I had. If different parts of a command were expected to cooperate I should think it very necessary to communicate orders to other officers. When I left, Reno had no command that I knew of—he had no reason to believe I was to his left and rear or that I was following the same trail. I scarcely knew myself what I had to do. As I said, "I was 'valley hunting.' " He had no right to expect any assistance whatever from me.

[CUSTER BELIEVED NO INDIANS WERE THERE]

If there had been any plan of battle, enough of that plan would have been communicated to me so that I would have known what to do under certain circumstances. Not having done that, I do not believe there was any plan. In Gen. Custer's mind there was a belief that there were no Indians nor any village. Not knowing where they were, I do not know whether there was need of a battle plan. I was sent off to hunt up some Indians. I was to pitch into them and let him know; and then I expected him to come back to me. And if I had found them, the distance would have been so great that we would have been wiped out before he could get to us. The country did not force me to bear to the right: I could have gone on in as straight a line as the country would admit, all the way to Fort Benton.

It would have delayed me an hour and a quarter to wait for the packs to come up after I got the Martin order—I could not have expedited it by going back for them, as a sergeant had already done that. From that tepee to ford "A" was about four miles; and from ford "A" to Reno's position, about two miles. If I had waited for them I would have halted about half way between. I heard no firing till I arrived at the ford, when I both heard and saw it—about 900 Indians engaged in demolishing about thirteen men on a skirmish line. They were charging and re-charging through them. I suppose Reno had retreated and these men were left behind.

["MY GOING BACK WAS PROVIDENTIAL"]

The three orders I got from Custer did not indicate that he expected me to cooperate in any attack on the village. The first two were things he forgot to tell me as he started off, while the column was in plain sight. The order to send him word if I found anything showed that he did not believe there was any village there. Of course, it would be expected that the whole command would cooperate with whatever detachment found the hostiles, and to notify the others—but I am convinced that when the order brought by Martin reached me Gen. Custer and his whole command were dead. It was then about three o'clock. It was not evident to me that he expected me to be on the trail; he could have expected no such thing; from the orders I started out with, he could not possibly have known where to find me within 10 or 15 miles. My going back was providential or accidental or whatever you may be pleased to term it. I suppose that Custer had found what he sent me out to find, and he wanted me quickly as possible; and I got there as soon as I could. I could not possibly tell what he may have thought. He would have known that I would come up with the column if I found no Indians.

[CUSTER'S ORDER SENSELESS]

From my orders I might have gone on 20 miles without finding a valley; still I was to go on to the first valley and if I did not find any Indians, I was to go to the next valley. Those were the exact words of the order. No interpretation at all. I at least had to go to the second valley. I understood it as a rather senseless order. We were on the main trail of the Indians; there was plenty of them on that trail. We had passed through immense villages the preceding days and it was scarcely worth while hunting up any more. We knew there were eight or ten thousand Indians on the trail we were following. Gen. Crook had fought these same Indians seven days before we did and he saw enough of them to let them alone. He had a larger force than we had, yet he remained from the 17th of June to the 15th of August waiting reinforcements, and did not think it prudent to go after those Indians. I know there was a large force of Indians and knew it at the time. Why I was sent to the left I don't know. It was not my business to reason why; I went. The facts about Gen. Crook's fight were not known at the time; but we could see the trail. *[Here the witness repeated in detail Gen. Custer's orders to diverge to the left].* I did not get to any valley, and did not see the valley of the Little Big Horn till I came to ford "A," where I first saw the river. I consider that I violated my orders when I struck to the right. If I had carried them out I would have been at least twenty five miles away. I don't know where I would have been. As it was, I was certainly too far to cooperate with Custer when he wanted me. He could have found out what was behind that line of bluffs by following the trail he was on.

BENTEEN'S MARCH
[W.A.G.]

It is next to impossible to trace precisely the route travelled by Benteen and his battalion from the time they left the column at 12:10 p.m. until they again hit the trail of the regiment near the morass where the horses were watered.

They reached this morass in advance of the pack train, which had followed the trail of the regiment, and were apparently about to continue their march when the first pack mules arrived, and mad with thirst, rushed into the morass and bogged down. Benteen assisted in extricating some of them, and then proceeded.

The train had perforce moved very slowly. Pack mules were something new for the Seventh Cavalry, and much halting and repacking became necessary along the route, because packs slipped, became unfastened, or lost their contents. There were not enough packers—all civilians—to keep the train moving steadily.

Benteen hit the trail of the regiment sometime between 2 and 3 o'clock, and was on his way after halting to water his horses, in time to reach the river just as the last of Reno's men—those who had lost their mounts—were being slaughtered in the valley. He reached Reno on the hill about 4:20, the time noted by Godfrey in his diary.

His orders from Custer had required Benteen to go to a line of bluffs several miles off to the left, in a search for Indians. If he found none at the first line of bluffs, he was to go on to the second line and into the valley beyond; and if he then had found no Indians, on to the second valley. He went to the second line of bluffs, and having found no Indians, was forced by the nature of the terrain, and the necessity of preserving his horses, to turn to the right and skirt the base of the bluffs, sending his Lieutenant to the top numerous times to scan the terrain for Indian signs. None were found; and Benteen, satisfied that no Indians were there, returned to the trail of the regiment. He had carried out the spirit of his orders, while disregarding the letter.

The distance he travelled, and the extent to which he diverged from the regiment's trail can never be definitely determined except by the time the march consumed. Edgerly thought that the battalion went about 2½ miles off the trail before turning to the right; Godfrey says it was five miles. Benteen himself said that the first line of bluffs was "four or five miles away."

If we knew definitely where the regiment was when Benteen departed, the distance to the second line of bluffs might be ascertained. But we cannot be too categorical about it, for dispute still goes on as to which branch of Reno Creek the regiment followed. So also with the morass where the horses were watered and the packmules bogged down. Neither can its location be definitely spotted, though my good friend Dr. Kuhlman thinks otherwise.

It is generally accepted, however, that the lone tepee was located at the forks of the middle and nothern branches of Reno Creek, approximately three miles from the point where Reno crossed the river in attack. Benteen reached the terrain overlooking the river about 4:15, at which time he was seen by the Indians in the valley, who thereupon ceased their pursuit of Reno.

The battalion had travelled at a trot much of the time since it left the column at 12:10. At the trot cavalry would cover from 6 to 8 miles an hour, depending on terrain. The halt at the morass probably consumed half an hour out of about four and a quarter hours, leaving three and three quarters hours of marching time. Averaging the march at seven miles per hour, and allowing for halts, it is fair to assume that Benteen had covered altogether some twenty-two miles by the time he joined Reno on the hill.

Benteen estimated the distance from the morass to the lone tepee as about seven miles, an over-estimate. Edgerly says three miles, which is believed more nearly correct. A mile further on, he was met by Sgt. Kanipe of "C" Company who carried a message to the Commander of the pack train; another mile, and he was met by Trumpeter Martin with Custer's message to "Come on—be quick—bring packs." He was then, he says, about two miles from Reno's crossing, toward which he rode until turned to the right by the Indian scouts who pointed out Reno's hill position about a mile away. These distance estimates add up to 8 miles, more or less, from the morass to Reno. Eight from 22 leaves 14, which I submit is reasonably close to the 15 mile estimate Benteen made of his Indian hunting excursion to the left; and assuming his and Godfrey's figures as reasonably accurate, ten of the fourteen may be accounted for by his left oblique to the bluffs and his right oblique back to the trail, which leaves four miles as the probable distance he rode along the base of the bluffs. If Benteen's distance estimates were even reasonably accurate, supported as they are by the over-all estimates of both Edgerly and Godfrey, the first of whom said they "made a circuit of about fourteen miles" and the latter, "we travelled 12 to 15 miles before we again struck the trail," they indicate, as it seems to me, that those who maintain that Benteen was at no time beyond supporting distance from the rest of the regiment, should sit down with a piece of graph paper and a pencil and draw themselves a picture. If they will take the trouble to do this, they will discover that Benteen was beyond supporting distance considerably more than half the time from 12:10 to 4:20. After 4:20 there was a possible period of some 25 minutes when, had he known of Custer's whereabouts, he might, by galloping all the way, have reached the battlefield four and a half miles distant by 4:50. Had he done so, he would have arrived too late to help Custer, who with his men were now beyond all human aid.

Martin did not tell me until we were on the high point, which side of the river Custer was on; then he pointed out the place where he was sent back. I did not send him to the pack train; if he went there he did so on his own.

[CUSTER'S OWN STATEMENT]

The only evidence I have that Gen. Custer did not believe, before I left, that there were Indians in the valley is his own statement—nothing else.

I think after Custer sent Reno across to charge the Indians his intentions were to get in the rear of the village and attack them from the left. His plan of attack was therefore known only to himself and not to Maj. Reno, for he must naturally have expected his assistance to come from the rear and not from the front. When I joined Reno on the hill, neither of us had any knowledge of where Gen. Custer was.

["WE WANTED TO KNOW WHERE CUSTER WAS"]

The reason we moved downstream after I joined Reno was the presence of about nine hundred Indians on the other side who seemed pretty vigorous and well armed: and we wanted to know where Custer was.

The advance of the pack train was not in sight when I met Maj. Reno. It was over an hour before the ammunition packs came up. I saw them coming. I did not want any ammunition and was not particularly interested in them.

["AS FRIENDLY TO CUSTER AS I EVER WAS"]

I have never expressed an opinion adverse to Maj. Reno's conduct to any officer. I was on as amicable terms with Gen. Custer on the 25th of June as I ever was with him.

[The Recorder asked whether the witness entertained a good or bad opinion of Gen. Custer as a Commander, to which question Maj. Reno objected as beyond the scope of the Inquiry. The Court sustained his objection].

RE-CROSS EXAMINATION

My idea in striking to the right was that there was more for me to do on the trail; that there was or would be fighting on the trail and that I had better go back and help. I thought I had gone as far as I should and would be needed on the trail.

There were no limitations with regard to the distance I was to go in the direction Custer sent me, except as to finding the first and second valleys I did not find; and it became my duty to bring up the packs when I received the order through Trumpeter Martin. I waited for them on the hill where Maj. Reno made his stand.

[THE INDIANS REMAINED HALF AN HOUR]

The 900 Indians I saw in the valley remained there perhaps half an hour after we were together, and then most of them went down the river toward the ford "B." Not all left at any time. I think they expected Maj. Reno to come across the plain again and had arranged an ambush for him if he tried it.

["NO ROYAL ROAD TO DEATH"]

The position of the bodies on the Custer battlefield indicated that the officers did not die with their companies, for only three officers were found with their companies. That ʾws that they did not fight by companies. All the officers, ᵪcept Col. Keogh, Capt. Calhoun and Lt. Crittenden were on the line with Custer. That would not be the fact if the command was overwhelmed while making a stand.

If there had been a charge it was the business of the officers to lead it. They would have been with the men: there is no royal road to death in a charge. The officers' bodies, including Gen. Custer's, were in a position which indicated that they had not died in a charge; there was an arc of a circle of dead horses around them.

Re-direct Examination

The bodies of Dr. Lord, Lt. Porter, Lt. Harrington and Lt. Sturgis were never found. If they had had lines, the officers would have died with their men. Lines could have been formed, but lines were not formed; they probably had no time to form lines. I think possibly that is the just conclusion. Gen. Custer might have fled the field and saved a part of his command, and I think discretion would have been the better part of valor had he done that.

FIRST LIEUT. W. S. EDGERLY,
7th Cavalry

DIRECT EXAMINATION

I was 2nd Lt. in Capt. Weir's Company "D," and under Capt. Benteen from the time he separated from Gen. Custer's column, until we joined Maj. Reno on the afternoon of June 25th.

[THE DIVISION INTO BATTALIONS]

After moving over the divide between the Little Big Horn and the Rosebud, Gen. Custer gave the command "Halt." I was close to him, riding with Captains Benteen and Weir. I saw Gen. Custer and Adjutant Cook dismount and make the division into battalions as I suppose, with pencil and paper; and then they were announced: that Maj. Reno would have "A," "G" and "M," Capt. Benteen "K," "D" and "H,' and one battalion was given to Capt. Keogh and one to Capt. Yates; and Capt. McDougall with one company was to be the rear guard.

Capt. Benteen was ordered to move to the left at about an angle of forty-five degrees and to pitch into anything he came to. Maj. Reno's orders were to move down the valley and attack anything he came to—those were all the orders I heard. Maj. Reno was not present when Benteen got his orders: he had about a hundred and twenty-five men and Reno about the same.

[BENTEEN'S MARCH]

Benteen moved in the direction ordered. I judge in about a mile we came to very high bluffs. Capt. Benteen sent Lt. Gibson to the top of them to report what he saw. He came back and reported he saw more bluffs and no Indians. We skirted along under those bluffs, and I think Lt. Gibson went to the top of the bluffs four times in six miles. One time when he came back, a messenger came with an order to Capt. Benteen from Gen. Custer. I don't know what it was; about two miles further on another messenger came to Capt. Benteen. Then we kept on and from that time made no further effort to go to the left, as all the reports from Lt. Gibson were that the country was very broken; and no Indians to be seen. We kept along skirting the hills and finally came into the valley; there were some foothills between us and the valley and the pack train was just going down. We went on to the watering place, which was seven or eight miles from where we started and about half way to where we found Maj. Reno. We watered our horses hurriedly and went on. When we had gone about a mile Trumpeter Martin came with the written message to Capt. Benteen, signed by Lt. Cook as Adjutant. That order was shown to Capt. Weir and myself. It was to the effect 'We have struck a big village: hurry up and bring up the packs." There was a P.S.—"Bring up the packs." The remark was made by someone—Capt. Weir or myself, that Gen. Custer could not possibly want us to go for the packs as Capt. McDougall was there and would bring them up. We went on without halt or delay, Capt. Benteen putting the order in his pocket. About a mile or two from there we came to a lone burning tepee. Capt. Benteen and I looked in and saw a dead Indian. We then went to the head of the column and saw Indians to our right whom we afterwards found were our own scouts watching the battle. When we came to about a mile from where Reno crossed the river, we saw mounted men in the bottom, but could not see whether they were Indians or white men. About a half mile from the crossing we saw a body of men going over the bluffs. Someone said they were Indians. Someone else said "I don't know," in a doubtful way. Near the crossing we saw the scout Half Yellow Face, and he beckoned us to come to the right. We did so and the Indians fired at us from the bottom but did us no harm. A few bullets struck at our horses' feet. We went up about a half mile and found Maj. Reno on the top of the hill with his command.

Benteen changed direction to the right about six miles after we started down the valley after going to the hills. We could not see Custer's column 10 minutes after we went to the left.

During the march, a sergeant of "C" Company came from Custer with a message to bring up the packs. Capt. Benteen said he thought Custer had made a mistake—that Capt. McDougall was in charge of the packs, and he showed him the place and he went on. It was before we got to the watering place, some time before Martin came up.

[A 14 MILE CIRCUIT]

We traveled about nine miles after leaving Custer before we struck the trail again; made a circuit of about fourteen miles. I don't think we were more than two and a half miles from the general direction of the trail at any time.

I heard Trumpeter Martin speak to the orderly behind Capt. Benteen. He was laughing and seemed much elated. He said it was the biggest village he ever saw and that they had found the Indians all asleep in their tepees; that Maj. Reno was charging it and killing everything, men, women, and children.

[WE FOLLOWED RENO'S TRAIL]

We struck the trail about a half mile from the watering place. It was about three miles on to the burning tepee and three and a half from the tepee to the river.

The advance of the pack train got to the watering place while we were there; the animals were tired and were being whipped along. They stretched back for two miles.

We traveled at a fast walk from the watering place, and the same after Martin came. We were at the watering place 8 or 10 minutes. We followed Reno's trail to near the crossing, and intended to cross the river at the time we were diverted to the right.

We heard no firing till we got to the crossing; perhaps some faintly, a mile before. It pertained to Maj. Reno's command. I heard no heavy firing; it was faint and irregular. I saw a great many Indians in the bottom, about 800 to 1000, before we saw the command on the hill.

[RENO AND VARNUM EXCITED]

When we arrived on the hill, one of the first officers I saw was Maj. Reno. He was mounted: had lost his hat, and had a white handkerchief around his head. He was in an excited condition, and as we came up he turned and discharged his pistol towards the Indians, 1000 yards away. About the same time, I saw Lt. Varnum; he also had lost his hat and had a white handkerchief around his head. He was excited and crying, and while telling us about what had occurred, he got mad and commenced swearing and called for a gun and commenced firing at the Indians. About that time Capt. Moylan came up and said "For God's sake, give me some water;" he said he had twenty-five wounded men dying of thirst.

There were a few Indians on a point firing. Company "D" at once formed a skirmish line; so I did not observe the command closely. I was surprised, after the ride they had that they were so little excited. I remember one man who was perfectly cool, and came up the hill holding a scalp he had just taken.

[THE INDIANS REMAINED AWHILE]

The Indians in the bottom remained there a while. I occasionally looked and saw great numbers of them. Some stayed all the time; till Company "D" moved out, nearly all stayed there. After that, when I came back from going with Capt. Weir to the hill, the bottom was nearly deserted. I judge they had gone downstream.

[HEAVY FIRING BY VOLLEYS]

Shortly after I got on the hill, almost immediately, I heard firing and remarked it—heavy firing, by volleys, down the creek. Capt. Weir came to me and said Gen. Custer was engaged and we ought to go down. I said I thought so too.

He went away, walking up and down anxiously. I heard the fire plainly. The First Sergeant came up then and I saw a large cloud of dust and thought there must be a charge and said, "There must be Gen. Custer; I guess he is getting away with them." He said "Yes sir, and I think we ought to go there." I did not answer him. Shortly after, Capt. Weir came up again. I think he had been gone about ten minutes. By that time the firing had almost ceased. Capt. Weir asked me what I said to going with "D" Company if they would not go with the whole command. I said I would go. He said he would go and ask permission from Maj. Reno or Capt. Benteen. Soon after, he came back and called his orderly, mounted and went off. I mounted the men and started out without orders supposing he had got permission to go. We went down about one and a half miles; he keeping on the

[INDIANS FIRING AT OBJECTS ON THE GROUND]

ridge and I in a sort of valley. When we got on the ridge we saw a great many Indians riding around and firing at objects on the ground. They saw us at the same time we saw them. Pretty soon Capt. Weir saw them start for me, and he signalled to swing to the right. I obeyed and came around up on the hill and saw Capts. Benteen, French and Godfrey with their companies; and also saw Lt. Hare speak to Capt. Weir.

The firing down the valley was perfectly distinct and was heard by everybody about me. It lasted about three quarters of an hour; the scattering shots and all. Maj. Reno was on the line when I saw him, about 75 yards nearer the stream, and about on a level with me.

[THE MOVEMENT DOWNSTREAM]

It was about three quarters of an hour after we joined Reno that the movement downstream was made by Capt. Benteen and his command. Capt. Weir's company had started out about fifteen minutes before.

I think the cloud of dust I saw was on the left bank of

the stream, and was made by Indians coming from the fight towards the village and discharging their pieces as they came on.

When Company "D" joined Benteen, French and Godfrey on the height, we moved with them. Benteen took the most advanced position; "D" Company took a spur at right angles to his position; French formed in the rear of that, and Godfrey in rear of French; the latter being on a spur facing the Indians. The Indians opened fire on us as we took posi-

[RETREAT TO RENO HILL]

tion. After a little while Benteen moved back toward the corral. I don't remember seeing Maj. Reno till we got back. In a short time Capt. Weir moved back by himself towards where Maj. Reno had selected a position. The next thing, Capt. French spoke to me, and said the order was to move back. I said I thought not. I had heard no such order. He waited about five minutes and then said the order had been given to move back and he was going. He mounted his men and moved off at a gallop. I then gave the command "mount" and moved off at a trot. As we got within about 60 yards from that point I saw "K" Company with Capt. Godfrey and Lt. Hare, their men dismounted, and the horses being led back. They had seen us coming and Capt. Godfrey had turned back and covered our retreat in the most brave and fearless manner.

[WEIR ABANDONS WOUNDED SOLDIER]

On going back I passed a man of "D" Company, wounded. He looked at me and I told him to get into a hole and I would form a line, come back and save him. When I passed "K" Company, I saw Capt. Weir and told him about the wounded soldier and that I had promised to save him, and asked him to throw out a skirmish line for that purpose. He said he was sorry, but the orders were to go back on the hill. I said I had promised to save the man. He said he could not help it; the orders were positive and we must go back. We went back and took position on the opposite side of the line from Capt. Benteen's company.

We had hardly got back on the hill when the heavy firing commenced, and we returned it, firing volleys and lying flat. Most of the firing had been individual while in the advanced position, though the engagement was general. "H," "D" and "M" were engaged, but the fire was not heavy there.

[THE COMMAND ORDERED BACK—NOT DRIVEN]

The command was not driven back from the advanced position; we were ordered back. Our only casualty was the man I spoke of.

We moved out along the ridge to that Point 7 and then down the valley toward Point 8. We went about one and a half miles and then swung around. After meeting the other companies we moved to Point 9. [*The witness here placed the figure 9 on the map*]. It was about three quarters of a mile from Point "B." I don't recollect seeing Reno there. I saw him when we got back, walking in the rear of "K" Company which was on the left of "D" Company. I did not hear him give any orders: I think Capt. Weir must have

[THE FIGHT ON THE HILL]

placed "D" Company. We were not in position more than a minute when the fight commenced and kept up till long after dark; lasted one and a half to two hours. The Indians came to close range; over a thousand of them, judging by those on the left where I was.

[RENO]

The next time I saw Maj. Reno was about nine o'clock. He seemed to have come from the other end of the line. I saw there was a gap between "M" and "B" Companies and also between "G" and "A" Companies. I asked him if I should close them. He said "Yes" and I then went and gave his orders to close them. I was afraid the Indians might charge through these gaps in the morning. I did not see Reno during the engagement; only Capts. Weir and Godfrey. They were walking up and down under fire, and encouraging the men. After the firing ceased I slept till about 1:30 A.M., when Capt. Weir woke me and told me to improvise a picket line for the horses, so that all the men could be on the line. I did so.

I saw Maj. Reno over there, lying on some blankets. He asked me what I had been doing. I told him I had been asleep. He said "Great God, I don't see how you can sleep." I saw him several times behind Capt. Benteen's line near the horses. We dug shallow rifle pits during the night; there were only a few spades and 2 axes. We built little trenches around the crest of the hill by Maj. Reno's orders, and he walked around superintending it. There was no firing at that time. It began again at 2:30 a.m., before daylight, very heavy, and continued till about ten o'clock, and then fell off. Some of the Indians withdrew and only sharpshooters remained after that. I saw Maj. Reno many times the 26th. He laid in a pit with Capt. Weir and also walked over to Benteen's line. Asked me if I had a place.

["CHARGE AND GIVE THEM HELL!"]

At one time there was a break in Benteen's company and the men were, I thought, rushing back to where I was. Soon after Capt. Benteen came over and stood near me. The bullets were flying very fast and I did not see why he was not riddled. He was perfectly calm, a smile on his face. He said to Maj. Reno: "We have charged the Indians from our side and driven them out. They are coming to our left and you ought to drive them out." Maj. Reno said "Can you see the Indians from there?" He said "Yes." Reno replied "If you can see them, give the command to charge." Benteen said "Alright, ready boys; now charge and give them hell!" The whole line was then in the pits. Reno was up on his elbow, at the left of the line. The men charged forty or fifty yards and then Reno ordered them to get into their holes again. We could not see many Indians. They were behind the points; but there were a great many of them there and we could just see heads popping out.

[A COMPANY COMMANDER'S FIGHT]

When I first arrived Maj. Reno was excited, but not enough to impair his efficiency, or have a bad effect on the troops. He did everything that was necessary, which was little, because all the officers could see what ought to be done. There was no occasion for any particular control by the Commanding Officer. So far as I could see the company commanders fought their own companies to a great degree. I saw Reno walk across the line as I saw other officers, and he seeemed very cool; and I think the position we had was the best possible within a radius of many miles.

The men, too, were very cool. I don't think any particular man inspired them with courage or coolness. I have no doubt that when Capt. Benteen was on the ridge every man admired him; but I don't think it was necessary to inspire the men.

[RENO WAS COMMANDING OFFICER]

Maj. Reno exercised the functions of a Commanding Officer so far as I know; but as I say, few commands were given. He would have seen the gaps in the line himself; he was coming to that part of the line from Benteen's position when I reported them to him.

[THE INDIAN VILLAGE MOVES]

I saw the village moving about 4 o'clock the 26th. It was two and a half to three miles long and from a half mile to a mile wide. I thought before the ponies commenced to move that it was like a lot of brown underbrush; it was the largest number of quadrupeds I ever saw in my life and very close together. It looked as though a heavy carpet was being moved over the ground. I judge that there were twenty thousand ponies: the Sioux average 6 or 8 ponies to a man. The population of the village I estimate about six or seven thou-

sand. A great many had no families there. I think the warriors numbered about 4000 at least. This opinion is based
on what I saw and what I have since learned from the Indians.
There were many war parties there and they do not carry
their families. The statements of individual Indians are not
of much value—they will usually rather lie than tell the
truth; and they usually try to make their statements and opinions coincide with those of the person they are talking with.

[THE SIZE OF THE VILLAGE]

I rode over the ground occupied by the village. It was
over 3 miles long and a half to three quarters wide along
the stream. I could not estimate now the number of lodges
that had been there. The Indians move their lodges frequently,
and ground that had been occupied by lodges would not correctly indicate the number, without some other signs.

[CUSTER AND HIS DEAD]

All I saw of Custer's trail was on the 28th when we went
to bury the dead. We formed skirmish lines so as find them
all. We found a few three and a half miles from our hill
position. As we came to the first hill where they were at
all thick, Maj. Reno called Capt. Moylan to identify them.
I went with him and we found Lieut. Calhoun in the rear
of his first platoon, and about twenty or thirty feet away,
Lt. Crittenden, in the rear of the second platoon.

I got permission to go on and went to Capt. Keogh's company. They were in an irregular line. My impression was that
they had formed line on the left of Calhoun and had fallen
back, some faster than others. Capt. Keogh had evidently
been wounded as we found that his leg was broken and the
sergeants of his company had got around him and were killed
with him. There were no regular lines, but still evidences
that there had been. After recognizing Keogh's body I went
on toward a high point one or two hundred yards off and
came to Gen. Custer's body. About 15 feet from him was
his brother's body. A short distance away was Lt. Reily and

then Lt. Cook; and there were bodies lying round as far as we could see in irregular positions. There were a good many soldiers killed around Gen. Custer. There were no evidences of company organizations there—it seemed to have been a rallying point for all of them. I think that was where Gen. Custer planted the guidon. It was the last point—not the highest—but the highest in the immediate vicinity. There were bodies between Gen. Custer and the river, but I did not go down there. There were evidences of fighting to about a half mile from the river.

Knowing the men as I did, I have no doubt that they fought desperately for a few minutes. I did not go over the entire field. Around Custer were evidences of a rallying point and around Keogh and Calhoun evidences of fighting, but not of rallying points. There were no evidences of officers abandoning their men in a disgraceful or cowardly manner. I believe Gen. Custer fought very desperately.

In a desperate struggle like that it would be impossible to find the men lying in regular and perfect lines—they would appear in scattered position.

[RENO'S HILL POSITION]

Maj. Reno's position on the hill was two and a half or three miles from the bulk of the village; which was close to the bank of the stream beyond the timber, near where we first saw Maj. Reno. The nearest dead of Custer's were about a half mile from the middle crossing "B."

CROSS EXAMINATION
["EXCITEMENT IS NOT FEAR"]

I do not pretend to give the history of all Maj. Reno did—only my own personal knowledge. I never expected him to be ubiquitous. The nature of the fight was such that no special directions from him were necessary. I saw no evidence of cowardice on his part. I distinguish excitement from fear, most emphatically. In the charge suggested by Capt. Benteen, Maj. Reno accompanied the troops. Capt. Benteen did not.

The weather was extremely hot—there were some sprinkles of rain, but it was intensely hot.

[BENTEEN'S MARCH]

Capt. Benteen moved to the left about twelve and a half miles from the ford "A" crossing; he moved immediately after getting his orders and Reno halted to let us pass. Reno then moved on toward the village. Gen. Custer in person gave the orders, I think. What orders he may have given Maj. Reno afterward I do not know. I did not see him after that.

As I have said before, we [Benteen] went to the bluffs at the end of the valley and Lt. Gibson would go on top while we skirted the edge. The idea I had was that if the Indians ran out of the village we would strike them to the left; and if to the right, some other part of the command would.

I do not mean that Benteen was at no time more than 2½ miles from Custer's troops. General Custer moved much faster than we did and I think went nearly on a straight line to where Reno crossed.

After Benteen received the Martin order, we kept on at a fast walk, as fast as I thought we ought to go, though I was anxious to go faster. He went at a proper rate of speed to keep the horses in condition.

I think Reno halted on the hill, not to bring up the packs, but because he had found a good position; and Benteen halted because he had found Reno, attacked by Indians.

[AMMUNITION REPLENISHED]

After the ammunition of the men who had been engaged in the timber was replenished and the wounded cared for, the advance downstream was made. All I know about any orders Maj. Reno gave to Capt. Weir is what Capt. Weir told me. I don't think Maj. Reno knew that Capt. Weir had left a wounded man.

[CUSTER'S MESSENGERS]

Capt. Benteen received four orders from Gen. Custer after

we started off to the left. I saw a person approach and speak to him and ride away: then the Sergeant Major came and spoke with him and rode away. After that a Sergeant of "C" Company—either Sgt. Knipe or Sgt. Hanley—I think the latter*—came to him with reference to the pack train and

was sent back towards Capt. McDougall. Trumpeter Martin was the last. When we came near where Maj. Reno was, Half Yellow Face beckoned us. The place where the "C" Company Sergeant came to us was about half way from where we started over the divide to where we met Maj. Reno.

[WHO FIRED THE VOLLEYS]

I did not at the time think that the firing I heard and the dust I saw in the field below came from the Indians returning to the village from Custer's battlefield, but I now think that much of it did. It is the custom of Indians to do a great deal of firing to celebrate a successful fight.

At the time I heard the firing, Reno was about 4 miles from the Custer field. The packs were not then up. We did not advance till after the heavy firing had ceased.

[CUSTER'S FIGHT WAS SHORT]

I believe Custer's command were all killed in 20 minutes to a half hour from the time the Indians first attacked them; within 30 or 35 minutes after the first firing I heard which was almost immediately after I got on the hill. Reno had been there a very short time; some of his men came up after we got there. Nobody had any idea that Custer was destroyed; the belief was general that he had gone to join Terry.

RE-DIRECT EXAMINATION

Whether a Commander in an engagement of that kind would show coolness or excitement would depend largely upon the temperament of the man and the way he regarded the fight.

---

* It was Sgt. Knipe (also spelled Kanipe.) Ed.

The firing I heard did not recede. Reno made no effort to find out what had become of Custer during the night of the 25th. There were scouts there that night. The gaps in the line existed for about two and a half hours before they were filled.

MAJ. RENO NOW RECALLED

CAPT. F. W. BENTEEN
for further

CROSS EXAMINATION

The "C" Company sergeant who came to me had verbal orders to the Commanding Officer of the Pack Train, and I did not consider that an order to me. The pack train was not a part of my column or command. Trumpeter Martin reached me about half way between the burning tepee and the ford "A." It is about three miles from the tepee to the ford.

I did not see Reno fire a pistol as I came up.

LT. EDGERLY
(recalled)

Any impression I might have had as to the part Maj. Reno was to take is my own, except the order to charge toward the village. That was the only one I heard given him.

THE RECORDER'S SIXTEENTH WITNESS WAS

B. F. CHURCHILL,
a civilian packer

DIRECT EXAMINATION

I started from the mouth of Powder River with the Custer expedition, as a packer, five days before the fight. The first we heard of it was about two and a half miles from the Little Big Horn near a tepee. I judge it was about ten or eleven o'clock. I had no watch so it is a mere guess as to time.

[AMMUNITION HURRIED FORWARD]

We had orders that morning to move out, and after that received none till we got to that tepee. We then had orders to take the ammunition mules out and go ahead with them. We had 175 mules in the train altogether.

Myself and a man named Mann took one mule, and who took the other I don't know. He led it and I licked it along as fast as I could. We traveled about two miles to reach the column; it took us about 8 to 10 minutes.

At the watering place one mule was mired; several were pulled out; some were left and some went on. I did not notice any troops there. It is customary to string a pack train out.

When we reached Reno I didn't notice whether there were any soldiers in the bottom. I saw some coming up the hill; some mounted and some on foot. I saw eight or ten Indians about 5 minutes after we got there. They started out of the timber to go up the river; those were the only Indians I saw in the bottom. Several men commenced firing from the bluff —Capt. French among them, at these Indians going up the river, on the other side.

[AMMUNITION UNPACKED]

We unpacked the ammunition mules and then had to pack them up again. I heard no firing for about one and a half hours; then heard it down the river. I took it to be volleys and spoke of it to some of the men. I heard four or five volleys. It seemed to be two and a half or three miles away; it was not a very plain report of guns. It was in the right direction to have come from the Custer battlefield. It lasted one and a half to two hours—before the Indians came back on us.

[FIRING FROM DOWNSTREAM]

From the hill position I could see a few tepees in the village. There were not many Indians attacking us at the time, but when they came back they came in force. The firing I heard appeared to come from the lower end of the village. Others heard it, and spoke of it. After we had packed the ammunition again we moved downstream—we were about an hour going down and back. The boxes of ammunition on my mule were not opened till after we came back from downstream. We had unpacked it when we first arrived supposing they wanted it at once. Why it wasn't used I don't know. The rest of the train came stringing in in a short time. I think Capt. Benteen's command got there a few minutes before we arrived with the mules. I saw them coming.

[THE PACKS MOVED SLOWLY]

The train moved on the advance very slowly and came back on the same trail. We then corralled it and threw out a picket line and tied the mules to it and unpacked. This was by Capt. Mathey's order. The fight commenced about a half hour after we got back. The officers who seemed to be directing it were Capts. Benteen and Weir.

[WAS RENO DRUNK?]

I did not see Maj. Reno that afternoon; but did after dark, about 9 or 10 o'clock. A Mr. Fritz [sic.] was with me. We had started out on the line to get our blankets and something to eat, and saw Maj. Reno standing there, though we did not notice him till he spoke to Fritz. He asked Fritz what he wanted. Fritz said he was after something to eat. Maj. Reno then asked him if the mules were "tight." It sounded like "tight" but Fritz thought he meant "tied," and said "yes." Maj. Reno again asked if the mules were "tight" and Fritz asked him what he meant by "tight" and then some words passed between them and Maj. Reno made a pass to strike Fritz; and some whiskey flew over me and Fritz. At that Maj. Reno stepped back and picked up a carbine— whether he intended to strike Fritz with it I don't know. I took Fritz by the shoulders and pulled him away. That was the last I saw of Reno that night. He was, I thought, under the influence of liquor. [*Here Maj. Reno protested but did*

*not formally object to the admission of this testimony as
irrelevant to the charges he had come to meet*].

I saw him the next day about nine o'clock; he was lying
behind the pack saddles and hardtack boxes that we had
piled up as breastworks. This was at a time when the rest
of the command was doing some pretty heavy firing—most
of them. I saw him when I went down to the horses to get
ammunition out of my saddlebags. He was not firing, but
he had a carbine lying on the ground under his head. The
firing that day began at daybreak and lasted till ten or ten
thirty o'clock.

CROSS EXAMINATION

I heard the firing from the direction of Custer's field while
we were packing up. I suppose the command moved out when
they heard the firing. I don't know what else sent them. The
only firing I heard was the 5 or 6 volleys. I judge by the time
the Indians came back on us that it lasted an hour and a
half. I heard none after we had moved out and come back.
We had enough to attend to without listening for outside
firing at that time. Whether Reno staggered or stepped forward when he struck at Fritz, I don't know. I did not notice
any stammering, nor did I notice his condition the next day.
I know of no prior trouble with Fritz. [*The further re-direct
and re-cross examination of this witness developed nothing
of consequence*].

MAJ. RENO HERE RECALLED

LT. EDGERLY
for further

CROSS EXAMINATION

I saw Maj. Reno the night of the 25th about 9 o'clock.
He came along toward where I was from the direction of
Capt. Benteen's line, and was perfectly sober. There was no
evidence that he had been drinking at all. It was at that time

that I reported the gaps in the line and he told me to have them filled up.

I saw him again at two o'clock, and he was perfectly sober then. I never heard the faintest suspicion of intoxication until I came here to Chicago this time. If he had been stammering and staggering and acting like a drunken man the officers would not have permitted him to exercise command.

RE-DIRECT EXAMINATION

I saw him for about a half minute at 9 o'clock, and again 5 hours later. I also saw him a few minutes before dark, when we first came back from downstream. *[The further re-direct and re-cross examination of the witness developed nothing more]*.

MAJ. RENO THEN RECALLED

CAPT. BENTEEN
for further

CROSS EXAMINATION

I may say I was with Maj. Reno all the time the night of the 25th. I saw him every fifteen or twenty minutes till 3 A.M.; I laid down in his bed. He was sober as he is now. He is entirely sober now and he was then. There was no time during the 25th or 26th when there was any indication of drunkenness on the part of Maj. Reno. He could not have been staggering and stammering without my knowing it.

RE-DIRECT EXAMINATION

I know nothing about any altercation with a packer except by hearsay. I know they robbed the packs and robbed me, and I also know there was not whiskey enough in the whole command to make Reno drunk. I saw him every 15 or 20 minutes throughout the night, except after the last time I left him, about 2:30. The Indians opened up about 3, and there may have been a half to three quarters of an hour that I did not see him.

RE-CROSS EXAMINATION

If he had been drunk between 9 and 10 o'clock I would have known about it; and had I known he had any whiskey I would have been after some myself.

THE RECORDER THEN CALLED

CAPT. E. S. GODFREY,
7th Cavalry

AS HIS SEVENTEENTH WITNESS.

DIRECT EXAMINATION

I commanded "K" Company during the 25th and 26th of June 1876; after about 12 that day I was under Capt. Benteen and in the afternoon we joined Maj. Reno and served under him thereafter. Capt. Benteen's command separated from Gen. Custer directly after crossing the divide between the Rosebud and the Little Big Horn. I was directed by Lt. Cook, the Adjutant, to report to Capt. Benteen for duty with his battalion. I was not present when either Benteen or Reno received their orders.

[BENTEEN'S MARCH]

We moved out to the left at an angle of about forty-five degrees to the direction of the trail. We marched generally about that way till we came to where the bluffs were so abrupt that we could not go over them without fatiguing the horses more than by going round the foot of the hills; and that took us more in toward the trail. I presume our distance from the trail when we began our return march was about 5 miles. Our gait was pretty rapid. My company was in the rear, and I often had to command a trot to keep up. I should say it was three or four miles to the bluffs. I think we had travelled 12 or 15 miles before we again struck the trail. The gait was so irregular it was impossible to gauge it. We halted about two o'clock to water at a little morass that crossed the trail. We halted there twenty minutes to half an hour. The head of the packtrain came up to the watering place just as we pulled out. Some of the mules plunged in and we had difficulty in getting many of them out.

From the water hole, Capt. Weir, who had been second, led the column and just after we passed the tepee with the dead Indian in it we met a sergeant who came back going toward the pack train; and he called out to some of the men

[CUSTER'S MESSENGERS]

in the company "We've got em," leaving the inference that they had captured the village. I did not understand anything more he said to the men; he passed on to the rear. I afterwards saw Trumpeter Martin of "H" Company coming toward the column. I don't know what he reported. My recollection is that the tepee is four or five miles from the river. We came to within a mile of the bottom when we met some Crow Indians and they signalled us to go to the right and we followed their direction. I don't know whose trail we were then on. At the place Martin came up, the packtrain was three or four miles back.

["I HEARD HEAVY FIRING"]

I heard firing. It was in the direction generally towards our front as we were marching: at first I only heard a few shots—then I heard quite heavy firing. Our gait was then increased to a trot and we kept to that till just before we met the Crow Indians. We were close to the Little Big Horn when I heard the firing.

I saw a good many horsemen in the bottom and saw smoke from the burning prairie—we did not stop long enough to take a good view; but I had thought from what I saw and what the sergeant said that they were burning the village and did not look particularly to see.

Soon after bearing to the right and passing out there I saw troops on the hill. I supposed they were troops put out for a picket guard as a protection to working parties. I thought so from Gen. Custer's habit; he had done so at other times to protect the command.

["WE JOINED RENO ON THE HILL"]

I think it was three quarters of a mile from where we left the trail that we joined Reno on the hill. It was my understanding that we were following the direction of the firing rather than the trail. I cannot fix the time, but think it was between three and four o'clock. I was ordered by Capt. Benteen to dismount my company and put it in skirmish line on the bluff toward the river.

["GOT WHIPPED LIKE HELL!"]

Lt. Hare, my second lieutenant, who had been detached to serve with the scouts, came up and said he was "damned glad to see me"—that they had "had a big fight in the bottom and got whipped like hell."

I saw Maj. Reno about that time. He gave me no instructions. Capt. Benteen gave me all my orders at that time. He seemed to be giving the commands. Maj. Reno was making arrangements to go down after Lt. Hodgson's body or get his effects.

[700 WARRIORS IN THE BOTTOM]

There was some firing by Indians at that time. I could not see many—they were in the ravines. The most I saw were in the bottom. I judge there were not less than six or seven hundred Indians in that bottom that I saw there—a great many starting up on our left, that is, going up the Little Big Horn above us. They soon came back and went down the river until the bottom was nearly cleared and I saw none at all. They all seemed to go down the river, not more than 10 minutes after our arrival. When my company was first put out the firing was pretty heavy, but the Indians that could be seen were so far away that it seemed like a waste of ammunition and I ordered the troops to stop firing. The heavy firing was on the part of the command principally.

I looked back when we were going toward Reno's command for signs of the packtrain, but did not see any dust
from it. Soon after we joined, however, I saw the dust coming from the column, and I judge it was three or four miles
away in a straight line.

Some of the ammunition mules came up in a half or three
quarters of an hour after we joined Maj. Reno. Lt. Hare
borrowed my horse and went there by Maj. Reno's orders
and brought them up on a run.

I saw Maj. Reno soon after we got there, coming up to
Capt. Benteen; or perhaps they were talking together. He
had a handkerchief tied around his head and seemed somewhat excited. I think he was making arrangements to go
for Lt. Hodgson's body or effects. I did not notice him long;
my attention was on the skirmish line.

[TWO DISTINCT VOLLEYS]

After Lt. Hare had returned from going after the packs,
we heard firing from below. I heard two very distinct volleys;
still, they sounded a long distance off. Then we heard
scattering shots afterwards, not very heavy. Lt. Hare and
myself were together and I called his attention to it. I don't
remember any conversation between us. I asked him if he
heard that firing. The supposition was it was done by Gen.
Custer and his command. That volley firing was loud enough,·
I think, to be heard by the command generally. I was about
as far away from it as anybody in the command, and besides
I am a little deaf naturally and was, at that time.

[WEIR MOVED OUT]

Capt. Weir with his company moved down below to a
high point probably three quarters or a mile in advance of
the command. He reached it before any other part of the
command moved out. The balance were together on the hill.
It was some time before the rest of the command advanced.
I don't know by whose orders, but Capt. Weir moved down
below to a high point before the ammunition mules arrived;
the command moved soon after they arrived. My recollection

is that it was put in readiness to move soon after the ammunition came up; and it was then stopped to wait till the whole train came up so as to take everything along. I know my company was taken from its position on the skirmish line, and we were dismounted again to wait for the packs to come up. I do not remember by whose order the movement was made.

[THE COMMAND FOLLOWED]

After the packs came up the command mounted and moved down the stream, till the advance company came to that high point on the ridge indicated by the figure 9 on the map. Three companies were up to that point. My company was a little below on the hillside. I went to the top to see, and while there the Indians started toward us from some position three or four miles down. The companies were ordered to dismount. Mine was placed in skirmish line on the crest of the bluff next the river and above that high point connecting with "M" Company, which was on the high point. Soon after getting in position I saw the packs and part of the command moving to the rear. I remained in position—did not receive the order to retire. The general rule is that when part of a command moves the rest follow if they don't receive orders to the contrary. I waited there some time. The companies on the ridge and on the high point were firing. Lt. Hare then came to me and told me the command was ordered back, and to mount my company and follow. About the time we started down the river Maj. Reno had said to me "Excuse me, Capt. Godfrey, I am going to use Lt. Hare as my Adjutant; Lt. Hodgson, my Adjutant, has been killed."

[THE RETREAT]

I drew in the skirmish line, mounted my company and started back. I had gone but a short distance when Capt. French's company came down the hill, passing to the rear very rapidly; and soon after, Lt. Edgerly with "D" Company came down also quite rapidly. The Indians followed them to the crest and began a heavy fire on them. As soon as I saw the Indians I dismounted my company and threw it out as skirmishers and when "D" Company had passed, commenced firing on the Indians and drove them back behind the hill. I then received orders from Capt. Benteen through Lt. Varnum to send in my led horses and fall back. In executing that movement I had just ordered Lt. Hare to take 10 men and occupy a ridge facing the Indians. He was selecting the men when Trumpeter Pennell came to me with Maj. Reno's compliments, saying I should fall back as quickly as possible. I recalled Lt. Hare and fell back to the line where the command was. Some of the command advanced beyond where Capt. Weir went. They went below, down toward the ford "B".

At the time we got to the advanced point, no Indians confronted us. We could see lots of them down the river; they appeared to be watching something downstream: and as I heard only an occasional shot, I supposed that Gen. Custer had been repulsed and that they were watching his retreat. They were three or four miles away. There was no severe engagement at the point; no casualties till we started back, which was soon after the deployment. The Indians only fired occasional shots. On the retreat I was between them and Reno's command, with my company. They were not visible at the time I was holding the Indians back.

[At this point in the proceedings the witness Churchill requested that his testimony be corrected to read: "I heard the volley firing down the river soon after we arrived on the hill with the packs."

Captain Godfrey also requested that the record be amended to show that he wished to convey the impression that when Lt. Hare came back after going to the packs, he did not remain, but went on ahead, and the packs came up on a run by themselves."]

[THE FIGHT ON THE HILL]

Upon joining the command I was asked by Maj. Reno to get into line quick. I was not assigned a position; my men were mixed in with those of "B", "M", "G" and "D". The attack began immediately. In fact it began before I got there; it followed me right in. It was then after 6 P.M., and the engagement lasted until dusk.

I don't recall seeing Maj. Reno on the hill during the fight that afternoon. I had no orders from him. When the fire of the Indians ceased that night, we dug rifle pits and put the men in them, and the companies were changed around so as to have them in order, and each was assigned to a position.

There was a gap between the corral and the line; and Capt. Weir and I agreed that it ought to be filled. But he would not do it without orders. Lt. Edgerly came along then and I told him if he filled the gap nothing would be said, and he could see it ought to be done. He spoke to Maj. Reno about it and his company was moved.

[WEIR AND GODFREY CONFER ABOUT CUSTER]

Capt. Weir and I had a talk about Custer. We thought he had been repulsed and unable to join us, and that we ought to move that night and join him as we then had fewer casualties than we were likely to have later. I did not see Reno that night, or receive any orders from him that I remember.

[THE 26TH AT DAYBREAK]

The fight began again at daybreak, about three o'clock or earlier. We did not have the local time: our watches were not changed. During the morning Capt. Benteen came over to our line and said he was being hard pressed on his side, and it was necessary to have another company. Maj. Reno, who was in a pit with Capt. Weir, replied that the Indians were pressing us too, and he could not spare another company. Capt. Benteen insisted, as his company was getting very thin from casualties, and so Capt. French was directed to go and reinforce him. Reno remained where he was.

Capt. Benteen came over during the forenoon of the 26th and said we would have to drive the Indians from our front because they were firing over on the rear of his line. He had to repeat the request several times to Maj. Reno before the charge was ordered. But it was made, Capt. Benteen giving the order.

Some time afterwards he came to the rear of my position and said he was going over to look for a new position. We started across together. While going over the rise, the Indians set up a pretty heavy fire on us. Reno dodged and said in a laughing manner: "Damned if I want to be killed by an Indian. I've gone through too many fights for that." Then he went on over to Benteen's line.

I had no talk with him on either day as to what had become of Custer. I saw very little of him the first day or night. I was not particularly impressed by Reno's qualifications as to courage, coolness or efficiency. There was little to do the 26th except to lie and shoot—no supervision was required; but what was done outside the line was done by Benteen. I don't think Reno's conduct was such as tended to inspire the command with confidence in resisting the enemy. It was my opinion that Capt. Benteen was principally exercising the functions of commanding officer.

[THE VILLAGE MOVES AWAY]

I saw the hostile village move away. It was getting dusk and it seemed a very large mass. We thought it between two and three miles long. Its width we could not tell, but on the outside were a number of Indians riding and also in the advance and on all sides. It was very compact. We could only distinguish figures on the outside; the bulk appeared as a moving mass. I estimate the fighting force of the village

[AT LEAST 3000 WARRIORS]

to have been at least three thousand.

I made no examination of the Custer trail, but I helped bury the dead on the field. Where the bodies lay I found many .45 calibre cartridge shells but no cartridges. I went off from the command to see if there was evidence of any escapes, looking for tracks of shod horses.

I went to the middle ford "B", and thought I saw evidences of shod horses having crossed, and made up my mind at the time that Custer had tried to cross there: but I saw no evidences of fighting near there. The first body was a long distance off—a half or three quarters of a mile. The bodies where I found the shells, were some distance from Custer's body. I think they had attempted to make a stand; there were fifteen or twenty bodies buried in one place by my company. All the troops I found appeared to have made a stand, though they were scattered. I supposed they had been dismounted and fought there.

[CUSTER'S HORSES]

The horses of Gen. Custer's column were not in as good condition as those of the other companies. They had been on a scout some days before under Maj. Reno and were much ridden down as compared with the others. But the general condition of the horses was good.

CROSS EXAMINATION

I have been an officer since '67, and a Captain two years. Reno had 300 men and 5 captains on the hill, two of whom had been colonels in the volunteer service during the war. All were abundantly able to command companies and there was nothing in the character of the struggle to which they were unequal. The duties were elementary and the exigency of a simple nature, consisting mainly of defense.

I have described only such acts and doings of Maj. Reno

[OFFICERS' OPINIONS DIFFER]

as came under my personal observation, and necessarily, among a large number of officers there are differences of opinion as to how best to conduct an engagement. Any difference between the opinion of Capt. Weir and myself and that of the Commanding Officer as to moving out that night does not indicate anything wrong with the Commanding Officer.

As to the charge made by order of Capt. Benteen, he was in a position to see the Indians and Maj. Reno was not. The latter accompanied the charge as did also Lt. Edgerly.

["CUSTER'S DESTRUCTION DID NOT CROSS MY MIND"]

The firing I heard was not sufficiently severe or continued to make me believe that Gen. Custer and his command were destroyed. Such a thought did not cross my mind at all.

I do not know how many Indians were about Reno the 25th and during the night; but there were a great many during the day and a few throughout the night.

During the night of the 25th a few shots were fired outside our lines; but in the village there was a great deal of firing; they were having a war dance and had a big fire.

The shod horses, tracks at the middle ford "B" might, of course, have been made by cavalry horses captured by the Indians and driven into the village.

["NERVOUS TIMIDITY—NOT FEAR"]

Maj. Reno's hesitation in accepting Capt. Benteen's suggestion did not, in my opinion, indicate cowardice; nor did his dodging bullets when he said he didn't want to be killed by Indians indicate fear. I probably thought it was nervous timidity. When he crossed over to Benteen's position, he went to an exposed part of the line, but the Indian fire was then letting up.

RE-DIRECT EXAMINATION

When there are differences of opinion between officers in a place of danger it is the place of the Commanding Officer to decide what shall be done.

[BENTEEN EXPOSED HIMSELF]

When Benteen came over to ask that the Indians be driven out, he was in so exposed a position that I told him he'd better come away—he would get hit. He said that the bullet had not been moulded yet to shoot him; that he'd been through too many dangerous places to care anything about their shooting. Benteen was standing where he could see the Indians and in a rather exposed place. Reno was not, but he could have seen them had he gone where Benteen was.

He hesitated some time when Benteen told him the Indians must be driven out, and it was not until Benteen told him that unless they were, they would come in on us, that Reno told him "all right, to give the command." Benteen gave a couple of whoops and the command started out. So far as I know, no effort to contact Custer was made during the night of the 25th, though I heard by grapevine, that scouts had been sent out.

["THE MEN THOUGHT WE WERE ABANDONED"]

There was an impression among the men that Custer had been repulsed and had abandoned them. I don't think there was any impression that he would do so if it were possible for him to get to us.

CROSS EXAMINATION

Capt. Weir and I did not communicate our opinion about moving to Maj. Reno and he was exercising his own judgment in deciding that the command should remain where it was.

The tracks I saw at the middle ford might have been made by Benteen's party on the 27th. I went there on the 28th.

EXAMINATION BY THE COURT

When at Weir's point I could see the general lay of the ground at the place of massacre, but could see no bodies or persons except Indians. I saw no evidences of fighting at that time.

THE EIGHTEENTH WITNESS CALLED BY THE RECORDER WAS

JOHN FRETT,
Civilian Packer

DIRECT EXAMINATION

I was a citizen packer. The horses and mules of the command were in average condition. On the 25th we had several reports of fighting which proved untrue; the first one sometime between 11 and 1. When we were at the watering place, a sergeant came and said we should hurry up, that Gen. Custer was attacking the Indians. We moved about two and a half miles and halted and then were ordered forward again. The halt was to close up the train. Then we went on as fast as the mules could walk. We did not trot them any.

We went to the big hill where Reno and Benteen were; and then down the river, and came back again to the hill. The Indians came around us and corraled us there. We unpacked the mules and put the packs into breastworks.

Several officers came where we were unpacking and working—I mean I saw them on the line, fighting. Lts. Varnum, Mathey and Edgerly came down there. Lt. Edgerly encouraged us and told us it would come out all right.

["I SHOULD CALL HIM DRUNK"]

The first time I saw Maj. Reno was after the firing ceased. I went over where we put the packs into breastworks and passed an officer. When almost in front of him I saw it was Maj. Reno. I saluted and said "Good evening." The first he said was "Are the mules tight." I said "tight," what do you mean by "tight". He said "Tight, God damn you"; and with that slapped me in the face and leveled a carbine at me and said "I will shoot you." Then a friend of mine named Churchill pulled me back and that was the last I saw of him till the next day.

He had a bottle of whiskey in his hand and as he slapped me the whiskey flew over me and he staggered. If any other man was in the condition he was I should call him drunk.

We had gone over there to get blankets and something to eat; we had had nothing that day and had no blankets. I had lost my horse and everything I had was stolen.

I never had any previous trouble with Reno.

Cross Examination

Capt. Benteen at no time to my knowledge came to the packs to drive out skulkers. At least I did not see him.

I know of no complaints made about stealing in the pack train.

I have no bitter feeling against Reno because he slapped me in the face—not in a place like this.

I would say he was drunk—very drunk. He staggered and stammered; his language was not very plain and he braced himself against a pack.

I did not see him the next morning; not till the afternoon. That was the only time I saw him drunk there.

[*In further re-direct and re-cross examination this witness was heckled by both examiners, but nothing of consequence was developed.*]

HERE MAJ. RENO RECALLED

CAPT. BENTEEN
For further

Cross Examination

I had occasion to go to the pack train many times during the 25th and 26th to drive out skulking soldiers. I did not go there for that purpose the afternoon of the 25th: but I did many times on the evening of the 25th and during the day of the 26th.

There was much complaint about stealing in the pack train: they stole everything I had.

THE NINETEENTH WITNESS CALLED BY THE RECORDER WAS

CAPT. E. G. MATHEY,
7th Cavalry

DIRECT EXAMINATION

I was in charge of the pack train from June 22 to June 28, 1876.

Early in the morning of the 25th we were in some timber where we stopped before daylight. We marched about two hours and halted. During that long halt I slept. I was wakened for officers call and I went to see what the orders were. The officers were coming away. Gen. Custer had given his orders, and supposing there were no further orders for me I went back. I followed the command. After about two miles Capt. Benteen turned to the left with his column. That was near the divide.

That morning Lt. Cook sent back an order to keep the pack mules off the trail on account of dust. I sent a man to attend to it. While the order was being executed Lt. Cook came to see if I got the order. I said "Yes" and asked Lt. Cook "How's that?" He said that was better, that they were not kicking up so much dust. That was the last order I ever got from that source.

We had about 160 mules, and I had 5 men from each company. I had about 70 men and four or five citizen packers.

["WE HAD TO RE-PACK A GREAT DEAL"]

We followed the main trail. Capt. McDougall urged me to get the packs along as fast as possible. I did so, but had to repack a great deal. We pushed along with great trouble, as the command had not had much to do of that before. After I had gone an hour or so, I went to the head of the train to see how things were. In a short time I came to where a mule had been in a morass. The packs were very much scattered—2 or 3 miles from front to rear. Three or four mules got stuck in the mud, but the train was not much delayed at the morass. I did not see Benteen's column at all.

It was about twelve [noon] when Capt. Benteen diverged to the left; four or five miles from the morass. We [the pack train] followed the trail made by Gen. Custer and Maj. Reno together.

"[THEY WERE TOO MANY FOR CUSTER"]

After passing the morass about 3 miles, we came to a tepee with a dead Indian in it. After passing the tepee two or three miles I saw somebody coming; one I remember was a half-breed. I asked him if Gen. Custer was whipping them and he said they were too many for him. I saw a great deal of smoke. When I first knew they were fighting I stopped the head of the column and sent back word to Capt. McDougall that there had been fighting and I would wait for him to bring up the rear. When it came up we went ahead after a halt of about 15 minutes.

I received no orders from Custer, Reno or Benteen on that march; only from Capt. McDougall. No sergeant reported to me with orders.

[HARE WANTED AMMUNITION MULES]

Where I made the halt, it was two or three miles from Reno's position on the hill. I saw smoke and thought I saw men on the hill—it turned out to be Reno. After we started I met Lt. Hare who said he wanted the ammunition mules and I detached two and ordered them to go with him. They carried two boxes each with 1000 rounds to a box.

We then moved on at a fast walk till we got to Reno.

I think it was about 3 P.M.; I saw a few scattered Indians in the bottom—no great numbers at all. There was then no firing around Reno's position.

Somebody gave me a glass, and about 3 miles away I could see Indians circling around, but no soldiers. That was downstream where the village was; on the left bank.

I saw Maj. Reno soon after my arrival on the hill; he was giving some orders to Capt. French about burying Lt. Hodgson and some men at the foot of the hill. Capt. French wanted more men but Maj. Reno told him to go on. Shortly after, he gave an order to Capt. French to come back. I heard Maj. Reno say we must try to find Custer and something about going in the direction Gen. Custer had gone.

[THE COMMAND MOVED DOWNSTREAM AND BACK]

The packs got no orders till the command started; then we followed about half an hour after. I don't know why they waited. I heard Capt. Moylan say it would be difficult to move his wounded. We moved very slowly. I don't know who ordered the movement. I received no orders, just followed the command.

There was one company in front—Capt. Weir's. When we got near the top of the high hill there seemed to be some halt and then I saw the troops turning back and, of course, I turned back with the pack train. I judge we had gone about one mile.

When we got back to the hill it seemed a good position and they halted. I was about to corral the mules when I received orders from Capt. Benteen to put the men from the different companies on the line and I gave the order and let the mules go. The firing was very heavy, and kept up till dark. There was quite a depression and the firing from that direction heavy. Maj. Reno ordered me to put boxes out for protection and I did so. Capt. Moylan's company was in that direction. I had no trouble with the packers and there were no complaints made in the command that I remember. Dr. Porter and I selected the place to put the wounded.

[A PICKET LINE IMPROVISED]

The next morning I got all the lariats I could and made a picket line, tying it to dead mules and horses, and tied up the living animals. There was no room for all of them. The firing recommenced early, soon after daylight.

I saw Reno about 10 o'clock walking around the line. He was down by Capt. Moylan's company in front of the packs. The fire was pretty heavy then, but it slackened about three or four o'clock and ceased about 5 or 6.

We had no ration issue the night of the 25th: nobody ate much. The packs were all mixed up and it was not possible then to separate them. I heard some talk about stealing rations, but no more were taken by the packers than by the soldiers. If they were hungry they helped themselves: there was nobody to prevent them.

[RENO WAS EXCITED]

When Maj. Reno first came up, he was somewhat excited, as any man would be under such circumstances. It was not long since he came out of the fight and that would be the natural condition for a man to be in. I did not think to question his courage and saw no act to indicate lack of courage, or cowardice. I received orders from both Reno and Benteen. The latter was second in command and I obeyed his orders without question.

I don't know of any effort on the night of the 25th to communicate with Custer. I heard that Maj. Reno tried to get the scouts to go and that they refused. I don't recall any expressions of opinion as to what had become of Custer and his command. My own impression was that Gen. Custer was surrounded, and in the same fix we were and that he could not leave his wounded. I thought if he could get away with his wounded he would certainly break for his own command. I don't know what others thought.

On the 26th Maj. Reno had a bottle with a little whiskey in it. Some one spoke of being thirsty and he said he had some to wet his mouth with to keep from getting dry. I don't know whether it was a quart flask or a pint. There was very little in it the morning of the 26th.

CROSS EXAMINATION

I saw no indication of drunkenness on his part, and never heard any intimation of it till last spring. I do not think excitement means fear; a man can be excited and not afraid.

[CAPT. NOWLAN ASKS ABOUT RENO'S CONDUCT]

I don't know whether all the officers had confidence in Maj. Reno. Capt. Nolan (Nowlan), on the 27th asked me about his conduct; someone seemed to have said something about it. I declined saying anything, though he seemed to have information from some source. The most they seemed to question was his conduct during the charge, and I knew nothing about that. I don't know whether there was any belief in the command that Custer needed support more than we did. We had so many wounded that we could not have moved with safety. Nobody seemed to think Custer had been destroyed.

The night of the 25th we had all we could attend to. I was so exhausted that I went to sleep standing up. I heard no bugle calls the 25th.

RE-DIRECT EXAMINATION

On the morning of the 26th, a call was sounded, but I forget the time.

RE-CROSS EXAMINATION

The first intimation I heard as to Reno's using liquor on the hill was in the spring of '78. Girard, the interpreter, made it at Ft. Lincoln.

CAPT. THOS. M. McDOUGALL,
7th Cavalry

DIRECT EXAMINATION

On June 25th, about 11 A.M., I reported to Gen. Custer for orders. He told me to take charge of the packs and to act as rear guard. That was on the divide between the Rosebud and the Little Big Horn. My company was composed of about forty-five men, and there were about 80 men with the train and 5 or 6 citizen packers.

I did not see Benteen diverge until he was eight hundred yards away. The regiment was divided into 3 columns, and I kept as near the center as possible. After they got seven or eight hundred yards ahead, I saw no more of any of them until I got on the hill.

[THE MARCH OF THE PACK TRAIN]

We started about 20 minutes after the command left. Lt. Mathey in advance with the mules made the trail, and we followed in the rear. We proceeded along till we came to a kind of marshy watering place where I found 5 or 6 mules mired. I dismounted my company to assist the packers and got them out in about 20 minutes. We adjusted the packs and proceeded. About 4 miles from there we came to a tepee. I dismounted and looked inside and found 3 dead Indians and a fire built around. From that point I saw in the distance a large smoke and told Lt. Mathey to halt for a few minutes till we could close up and prepare for action.

About a mile from there Lt. Mathey sent word that the fight was on. I told him to hurry with the mules as fast as possible. I went on about 2 miles and saw black objects on the hill in a mass and thought they were Indians.

I told my company we would have to charge them and get to the command. We drew pistols. I put one platoon in front and one in rear of the train and charged to where those persons were. I found then that it was Maj. Reno and his command. I should state that about quarter of an hour before reaching there I heard firing to my right, and as soon as I arrived I reported this to Maj. Reno.

[FIRING TO THE NORTH]

The firing I heard was to the north, on my right as I went toward the Little Big Horn, downstream. It was just two volleys. I told Maj. Reno about it and he said: "Captain, I lost your Lieutenant and he is lying down there." Then I left Maj. Reno and threw out a skirmish line. I waited about half an hour when I heard the bugle call "Mount". I mounted up and followed the command in single file toward a high mountain downstream. After going about a quarter of a mile Capt. Moylan met me and said he could not keep up on account of the wounded. I told him if he would take the responsibility, I would let him have one of my platoons. He said "all right" and I took the second platoon in person down to where he was. Upon returning I saw the men "left about" to go back to our original position.

["HOLD THAT POINT AT ALL HAZARDS"]

Capt. Benteen then put me in position on a kind of ridge facing this hill, or down the river facing the Indian village. Then Maj. Reno came by and said "Captain, be sure to hold that point at all hazards." The troops were then being assigned to their different places and the general engagement ensued. Very heavy fighting commenced and we fought till about 9 o'clock: the heaviest kind of fighting, and officers and men displayed great courage. Then I went at nightfall to get some hardtack for my men and a box of ammunition. The engagement began about 2:30 the next morning, being very heavy until about 1 o'clock when they made a general sally on us, but we stood them off and drove them back.

["YOU WILL HAVE TO CHARGE THE INDIANS"]

About 2 o'clock Capt. Benteen came down bareheaded

and said "Captain, you will have to charge the Indians with your company, as they are firing into me pretty heavily with arrows and bullets; so get your men ready and start out"; which I did, going about 60 yards when the firing was so heavy on our right and rear that I had to retire to our original position. Maj. Reno then came up and said "Captain, how are you getting along?" I told him "Very well." He asked me which way I thought the Indians were going and I said "Downstream." He then invited me to walk around with him which I did. He informed me that he wanted to change the position that night as the stench, the flies and the filth were so great that the men would probably get sick.

[INDIANS WITHDRAW: TERRY ARRIVES]

The Indians withdrew about 5 o'clock, when Maj. Reno put us in a new position. The next morning, the 27th, Gen. Terry arrived and we were informed of the annihilation of the other part of the regiment.

I cannot form any idea of the times or distances. I was too busy looking after animals and resisting attack.

I received no orders on the march and no word except when Lt. Mathey sent me word that the fight was on. I received no notification to hurry up the packs. I think Lt. Mathey got that order: he told me about it and I told him to hurry up. I was very anxious about it. I judge I was about two miles away when I saw the objects on the hill that I took to be Indians. The front mules were going about a dog trot and the rear ones were being pulled with lariats and whipped with blacksnakes to get them along. I think it was about 4 o'clock when we reached Reno.

["I REPORTED THE FIRING TO RENO"]

The firing I heard was about 4 to 4½ miles away. We were about the same distance from it as was Reno. It was not loud—a dull sound that resounded through the hills, just 2 volleys. I thought it was some of the command; that it must be Gen. Custer and the Indians. I reported it only once to Maj. Reno, as soon as I arrived with the train. All was quiet then, and I did not know anything was going on at all with the command until I had thrown out the skirmish line and went back and heard the officers talking about it.

I saw a very large herd of ponies and tepees downstream to the left in the bottom—a regular city of them. To the left where Maj. Reno had been engaged in the timber I saw only a few men, whether Indians or not I do not know. There was a large force in the village; but we did not see any large number till we took position on the hill finally.

I do not know by whose order the return movement from downstream was made. I was returning from Capt. Moylan's command and saw the left about, and I continued until Capt. Benteen put me in position. At the time Maj. Reno asked me to walk around with him the next day, the fire was not ceasing—the bullets were flying fast. It decreased about 4 o'clock.

[SHELTER FOR OUR HEADS]

During the night of the 25th I told the men to take their butcher knives and tin cups—we had no axes—and throw up some dirt and make some kind of barricade for their heads, so the Indians could not see our heads. We had no breastworks; merely shelter for our heads. This was done by my order. I received no orders that night from Maj. Reno or his Adjutant. In the charge on the Indians that I spoke of, Capt. Weir, Lt. Varnum and Lt. Hare also took part.

[RENO'S CONDUCT]

As to Maj. Reno's conduct, when I found him he seemed perfectly cool; had nothing to say; and during the day I did not see him till he asked me to go round with him. He was perfectly cool then. He had no enthusiasm as far as I could observe, but was as brave as any man there; they were all brave; I saw no officer or man show the white feather.

I think Maj. Reno would make as stubborn a fight as any man, but don't think he could encourage men like others.

Men are different; some are dashing and others have a quiet way of going through. I think he did as well as anyone could do. I thought when he asked me to walk around with him that he had plenty of nerve. The balls were flying around and the men in the intrenchments firing. We took it easily and slowly.

[3000 TO 4000 WARRIORS]

I saw the village move away. It seemed to be a mile and a half away, an immense village, as large as a division or two of mounted men—5000, at least, including men and women. I don't think there were many children. The mass was two or three miles long and very broad. Three or four thousand ponies were mounted. We gave them 3 cheers as they moved away. I think the fighting strength was in excess of three thousand, probably three or four thousand warriors and about a thousand women.

On Custer's field I only went to where I presume the skirmish line was killed. Maj. Reno then ordered me to go to the village and get implements to bury the dead. On returning he ordered me to bury Company "E" which I had formerly commanded for five years and to identify the men as far as possible. I found most of them in a ravine; about half were in the ravine and half on a line outside. All the men were lying on their faces and appeared to have been shot in the side. I thought they had fought as best they could and were attacked from both sides.

[CONFERENCE WITH GODFREY]

I did not converse much during the 25th-26th, except with Capt. Godfrey. During the night of the 25th the conclusion was that Custer had met the same crowd and they were either following him or else he had gone to join Gen. Terry. That was only my opinion, based on the fact that we had heard firing down there, and all the Indians had come back after us, and I thought perhaps he had retreated to Gen. Terry and they had come back to finish us.

I understood during the night of the 25th Maj. Reno tried to send a scout through to Custer—just hearsay. Reno had about 280 men, I think after the forces joined.

CROSS EXAMINATION

We had no idea that Custer's command was destroyed. It was no more reasonable to think they were than ourselves —we supposed our positions were about similar. We did not know what had become of him until Terry arrived. At the time we reached Reno no firing was going on and I saw no skirmish line, though I did not visit the entire command. I threw out my own merely as a precaution against possible attack by Indians.

["NO COMMAND EVER FOUGHT HARDER"]

No command ever fought harder; there was no cowardice, and no need of inspiriting the men. Some commanders go around to see their troops and others don't: that is a matter of temperament and disposition.

On the advance downstream I was in the rear. We would all have been killed if we had gone as far as the hill where Capt. Weir went. The position we took was the best position we could get in that country. We retired because we could go no farther and were attacked within 5 minutes by an immense number of Indians. I saw no evidence of drunkenness on Reno's part and never heard any intimation of it.

[The further re-direct and re-cross examination of this witness developed nothing of consequence.]

THE RECORDER AT THIS POINT OFFERED AND READ IN EVIDENCE THE FOLLOWING DOCUMENTS:

(a) An official copy of Maj. Reno's report dated 5 July 1876, which was received and marked "Exhibit No. 4."

(b) An official copy of a letter from Maj. Reno to Gen. Terry, dated 27 June 1876, which was received and marked "Exhibit No. 5," as follows:

EXHIBIT NO. 5

Camp on Little Big Horn,
20 miles from its mouth.
June 27".

General Terry:

I have had a most terrific engagement with the hostile Indians. They left their camp last evening at sundown moving due south in the direction of Big Horn Mountains. I am very much crippled and cannot possibly pursue. Lieutenants McIntosh and Hodgson and Dr. DeWolf are among the killed. I have many wounded and many horses and mules shot. I have lost both my own horses. I have not seen or heard from Custer since he ordered me to charge with my battalion (3 companies) promising to support me.

I charged about 2 p.m., but meeting no support was forced back to the hills. At this point I was joined by Benteen with 3 companies and the pack train rear guard (one Co.). I have fought thousands and can still hold my own, but cannot leave here on account of the wounded. Send me medical aid at once and rations.

(signed) M. A. RENO,
Maj. 7th Cavalry.

As near as I can say now I have over 100 men killed and wounded.

———

Headquarters Dept. of Dakota.
Saint Paul, Minn., January 9", 1879.

A true copy:

GEO. D. RUGGLES,
Assistant Adjutant General.

————————

(c) An official copy of the list of casualties in the 7th Cavalry at the battle of the Little Big Horn, which was received and marked "Exhibit No. 6."

The Recorder thereupon announced to the Court that he had no further testimony to bring before the Court in his capacity as Recorder.

THE PROSECUTION RESTED

MAJ. RENO THEN CALLED TO THE STAND, AS A WITNESS FOR THE DEFENSE

LT. GEORGE D. WALLACE,
7th Cavalry

DIRECT EXAMINATION

I kept the itinerary. The march commenced at 8:45 A.M.; first halt 10:07 A.M., marched 11:45 A.M. Second halt 12:05 P.M., when division into battalions was made. Marched 12:12 P.M. No further record. No more halts were made until we went into the fight. I estimate the commencement of Reno's fight in the timber at about 2:30. The division into battalions was made at 12:05, after we had passed the divide about a quarter of a mile, and when we were 12 to 15 miles from the crossing "A".

[THE ATTACK ORDER AFTER 2:00 P.M.]

Adjutant Cook's attack order to Reno was given after 2 o'clock, nine or ten miles from the place of division into battalions. I neither saw nor heard Gen. Custer give any order in person to Reno. I was riding to the left of Lt. Hodgson who rode at Reno's left: and was within a few yards of Maj. Reno all the time.

Benteen got his orders and moved to the left almost immediately after the division—about two hours before the attack order to Reno.

I heard no order to Maj. Reno to unite with Benteen, or any statement to him that Benteen would support him: and had there been any communication between Gen. Custer and Maj. Reno, or any meeting between them, I would have known it.

["I SAW THE AMMUNITION REPLENISHED"]

As to the replenishment of Reno's ammunition, I saw one box split open with an axe, and the men came up and helped themselves until it was all gone; this was before the command moved downstream in the direction of the Custer battlefield.

I saw no evidence of inebriety on Reno's part at any time during the 25th and 26th of June, and the first mention of it I ever heard was during this inquiry here in Chicago.

[The witness at this point, in an attempt to describe the terrain of Reno's final stand on the hill, made a pencil sketch of the ground and the position of the troops, which was exhibited to the Court, but was not introduced in evidence.]

The ground was an elevation with a little rise in the center, and the men grouped around that. An officer stationed at any point in the line could only see a portion of the command.

[RENO DID HIS DUTY]

At no time did I observe any failure upon Maj. Reno's part to do the duty expected and required of a commanding officer.

CROSS EXAMINATION

I heard the order of Lt. Cook to Maj. Reno, and I am positive Gen. Custer gave him no order in person; I saw no one but Lt. Cook approach him and I saw and heard no other order given.

["I SAW CUSTER BECKON RENO"]

I saw Gen. Custer beckon Maj. Reno to come to the opposite side of the tributary. That was when I pulled out my watch and looked at it, and it is my impression that an orderly came about the same time with Gen. Custer's compliments and asked him to go over to the other bank.

He moved over with his battalion and the two moved along from 10 to 15 yards apart, the heads of the columns about opposite each other. There was some mingling together

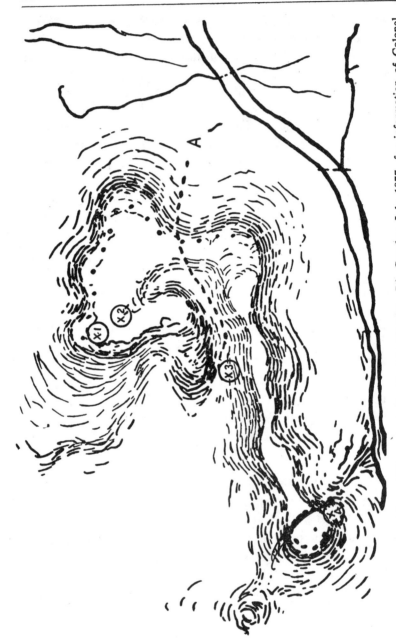

Map of Custer and Calhoun Ridges drawn by Captain Nowlan, 7th Cavalry, July 1877, for information of Colonel Sheridan. It shows the location of the following graves: 1—Calhoun; 2—Crittenden; 3—Keogh; 4—Custer.

of the men, and some of Gen. Custer's officers started [toward the river] with us.

["THE INDIANS FIRED ON HIM HEAVILY"]

During the hill engagement, the only time I saw Maj. Reno that impressed itself upon my memory was on the 26th when he said he was going over the ridge, and that when the Indians opened fire on him, to return it and keep them down as much as possible; and I remember they did fire on him heavily.

In that position, if the Commanding Officer wished to see his command frequently, he could do so only by crossing the ridge frequently.

[Nothing of consequence was developed by re-direct and re-cross examination.]

THE NEXT WITNESS CALLED BY THE DEFENSE WAS

LT. COL. M. V. SHERIDAN
Military Secretary to the Lieut. General

I visited the Custer field in July 1877 to bring away the bodies of officers killed there. I crossed at the middle ford "B" several times—it was a good ford. Right at that point there was a dry ravine and a gradual slope and there would be no difficulty to horsemen in crossing. The nature of the country near it was such that twenty to twenty-five men could protect the ford against a large number of Indians. The map [Exhibit 2] represents very much more timber than there was on the left side of the stream.

The sketch, 4 x 7, made by Capt. Nolan (Nowlan) shows where the named bodies were found. It is not made with reference to any scale. *[At this point Maj. Reno offered in evidence the sketch referred to, which was received and marked Exhibit 7.]* The first point in the dotted line shows where the first body was found back from the middle ford; it is nearly a half mile back. I did not notice any more, except one or two till we came to the ridge and there we found Lt. Calhoun's company in skirmish line. There was no other place where there was evidence of resistance. There were other men killed in various positions and in every direction. Behind the position in which I found Calhoun's body, was that of Lt. Crittenden. From a quarter to half a mile in rear of that I found Capt. Keogh's body—then they continued in a scattered condition to the point of the ridge where we found the remains of forty or fifty officers and men, including Gen. Custer, Col. Custer, Capt. Yates, Lt. Smith and others.

The place where Custer and the others were found is a ·rough point or narrow ridge not wide enough on top to drive a wagon—not a position where successful resistance could be made. Across that ridge were five or six horses apparently in line; looked as if they had been killed for purposes of resistance, but the remains were in a confused mass.

From the position of the bodies of Capt. Calhoun's company it looked to me as though that was the only point where resistance was made at all. I don't think the struggle could have lasted over an hour.

Cross Examination

The positions of the bodies were where I found them buried. I do not know that this was where they fell.

Three quarters of a mile below the middle ford "B" is another good crossing. It had evidently been used by Indians or buffalo.

Examination by the Court

I approached the field from the north, up the valley. I went up to the point known as Reno's crossing (Point A) and rode over it and then went over what is called Reno's position, but not back beyond the crossing "A."

For several hundreds of yards above the middle ford "B"

it would not be possible for a command to cross against resistance. It would be difficult on account of bluffs, to get down there even without resistance.

Re-direct Examination

It would not be practicable to cross against resistance anywhere between Reno's crossing "A" and the middle ford "B."

Re-cross Examination

I went down the ravine from Point "B" about two miles, and crossed it. It has steep cut banks for two miles, after you get 30 or 40 yards from the mouth, and it would be difficult to cross them.

[The Court now retired to consider and decide a request by Maj. Reno that certain witnesses who had appeared and had departed for their stations, be required to answer certain questions to be propounded by telegraph. The Court denied the request.]

THE RECORDER AT THIS POINT RECALLED

CAPT. MATHEY
for the Prosecution

Direct Examination

I have heard officers discuss the fight a great many times and express varied opinions. Some think it would have been better to have remained down below; others have expressed themselves in different ways. One expression particularly impressed itself on me; it was—"If we had not been commanded by a coward we would all have been killed."

I have heard officers say that they thought Maj. Reno lost his head, or words to that effect. Lt. DeRudio was the one who used the expression I remembered, and that impressed me so.

CROSS EXAMINATION

Lt. DeRudio has always told the same story to me. I know that there has been some question as to the reason he stayed in the timber: some doubted his story. I don't know whether he brought out the guidon or not.

THE RECORDER THEN RECALLED

CAPT. McDOUGALL
for the Prosecution

DIRECT EXAMINATION

On the night of the 26th I took Pvts. Ryan and Moon and got Lt. Hodgson's body and carried it to my breast-works, and on the 27th buried it, after sewing it up in blankets and a poncho.

CROSS EXAMINATION

The body was lying near where Maj. Reno crossed the river.

THE RECORDER THEN CALLED AS HIS TWENTY-FIRST WITNESS

GEN. JOHN GIBBON
(Col., 7th Infantry)

DIRECT EXAMINATION

I reached the battlefield the morning of the 27th, in command of the column under the direction of the Department Commander, Gen. Terry.

[RENO'S VALLEY POSITION]

I made very little examination of Maj. Reno's valley position, though I was there an hour or two. My camp was in a bend of the river, below where he crossed the river going back. I examined the banks from there down to the point of woods, where it was said he had his forces dismount. Just below where he crossed, there commences a series of crescent shaped curves on the left bank of the river; and beyond these curves is what is called the second bench of the valley; the main open valley extending off to the bluffs. These curves are irregular in shape, formed by the water when much greater than at present, and these curves continued in crescent shape, generally connecting with each other. This point of timber had enclosed in it, a considerable open space. The connecting slope between the second bench and the first, was covered by timber and thick brush. Some of the timber was of considerable size. The lower end of this crescent shaped slope nearly reaches the stream, to what is called a cut bank, where the stream has worked in to the second bench, and there the stream is 10 to 12 feet lower than the level of the country. Just behind this position the water is deep; and a short distance above is a ford that I crossed in coming back from down river. The bend in the river opposite this is filled with tangled brush and fallen timber, and directly behind that, and close to the bank of the river, there was more timber, in which we found a number of dead horses. The upper curve just below the ford where Reno crossed, was occupied by my troops when we first arrived. The next curve below was occupied by the 7th Cavalry the morning of 28 June. I think the third one was the point of timber I speak of. It was the third or fourth of the crescent shaped curves below the ford.

[THE BLUFFS TOO FAR AWAY]

With regard to the low place opposite where Reno had his command, there was a wide flat there through which the stream passes in a very crooked way, and the bluffs directly opposite were considerably back from the river. Gen. Terry and I started from my camp to go to the scene of the Custer fight, and we crossed opposite the camp and made our way to the foot of the bluffs; and in coming back we got involved in brushwood and were obliged to come back and cross above that point of timber. I don't think this map pretends to be correct in the curves of the river, and does not represent the position of those places.

The bluffs did not command the position in the timber; they were probably within long rifle range, but too far for any practical purpose.

[MAGUIRE'S MAP INCORRECT]

The map does not correctly represent the village. Most of the tepees were down near the stream or a short distance from it. There were no signs of tepees to the left, except two about the middle of the plain which I understand were filled with dead Indians. I cannot tell how near the village was to Reno's position. There may have been scattered tepees, but judging from appearances, the main camp was below the deep gulch.

[RENO'S HILL POSITION WEAK]

Reno's position on the hill was an exceedingly weak one for defense naturally. It was commanded at tolerable long range by bordering hills on the downstream side. The country was broken by a succession of little rolling hills and valleys behind which attacking parties could conceal themselves. The manner in which the animals were exposed was very bad. I counted 48 dead horses in one little valley; and the place was practically cut off from water which made it weak for any prolonged defense. This is a general opinion only. I did not go over the whole line, but had a view of it from the top of the hill.

[THE TIMBER NOT CORRECTLY SHOWN]

The map is not correct at all as to the timber. My decided recollection of that point of timber is that it was just above where the stream cuts into the second bench a considerable way so as to leave the bank almost as high as the ceiling of this room—above the water; around this bend there is no timber at all. The extent of this piece of timber I don't know. Inside the timber was a clearing about 50 yards wide; I don't know how long. It appeared to have been an Indian camp.

The distance from the front of the bend, that is, the point farthest to the south from the stream, varied very much. From the point where we crossed the river, to the ford, must have been two or three hundred yards. Then there was another open glade looking toward the prairie to the left and rear of the position. I cannot estimate the size of the enclosed space on the lower side, but don't think there was any connection with the timber on the upper side. There was some scattered timber up the river. On the opposite side of the river there was very little timber; there was brushwood and small trees, thick and tangled in places, with much fallen and dead timber amongst it.

Cross Examination

We arrived on the 27th, coming up the valley on the left hand side of the river on the left bank. The examination I made of the terrain was leisurely and deliberate. I cannot describe the right bank between Reno's position and Point "B" except where I crossed from my main camp. There I found a good ford, easily passed over. The bluffs from just below Reno's position for some distance downstream, were high. I suppose they extended almost to Point "B."

Examination by the Court

I cannot state the length of the bend I have described. It was a place where you could not see any great distance while in the timber. I rode down through a mere path and had to stoop on my horse to get through. I did not go to the lower end, and only know there were cut banks by approaching it from the other side of the river, where the bank is considerably lower. Right in the bend of the river opposite the position it was flat from there to the stream: it swept around and the bank was not more than two feet above the water. If an enemy got possession before that point was occupied, they would have to be driven out, because the brush was thick and tangled, and they would be almost perfectly concealed.

_____

At this point Maj. Reno asked the advice and decision of the Court as to whether he should himself take the witness stand. The Court held that he could not so appear except at his own formal request as provided by law; and expressed opinion that his position as an officer would not be prejudiced by failure to make such request, nor would it in any sense be indelicate for him to make it.

Counsel for Maj. Reno now asked that the record show that Maj. Reno by direction of his counsel was called to testify. The Court held that this would not be a compliance with the law.

Counsel for Maj. Reno then asked that the record entry be as follows: "Counsel for Major Reno in open court directs him to make request to appear before the Court as a witness," and asks decision of the Court upon this request. The Court thereupon again held that Major Reno could not testify except at his own formal request.

MAJOR RENO THEN PRESENTED TO THE COURT HIS FORMAL REQUEST TO BE ALLOWED TO TESTIFY, WHICH WAS RECEIVED AND MARKED "EXHIBIT NO. 8," AS FOLLOWS:

EXHIBIT NO. 8

To the Honorable,
    the Court of Inquiry.

In accordance with the Act of Congress approved 16 March 1878 I have the honor to request that I be allowed to testify before your honorable Court of Inquiry which has been convened upon my application.

                                M. A. RENO,
                                Maj. 7th Cav.

*   *   *

MAJOR RENO
Thereupon took the stand in his own behalf

DIRECT EXAMINATION

On the morning of the 25th, Col. Benteen came over to where I was, and while he was there, I discovered that the column was moving. I was not consulted about anything. I never received any direct orders, and exercised the functions of what I imagined were those of a lieutenant colonel. The division into battalions and wings had been annulled before we left the Yellowstone, and when the command moved out I followed it. At daylight, after we had marched some distance, the command halted, and I was informed only that the Commanding Officer had gone to the top of the mountain to make observation with regard to the Indians which the

[CUSTER DISCREDITS HIS SCOUTS]

scouts had reported to be in sight. He called the officers together and I attended, of course. He said the Indian scouts reported a large village in view from the mountain; that he did not believe it himself, as he had looked with his glass. He then announced that the column would be formed by companies in the order in which they reported ready, and this was done. I continued as before for two or three hours.

[THE BATTALION ASSIGNMENT]

About 10 o'clock Lt. Cook came to me and said, "The General directs that you take specific command of Companies "M," "A" and "G." I turned and said "Is that all?" He replied "Yes." I made no further inquiry but moved with my column to the second ridge; and between myself and Custer's column was a small ravine which developed into a tributary of the Little Big Horn. I moved parallel to Gen.

[BENTEEN DEPARTS]

Custer for some time. Previous to that Capt. Benteen had started to the left up the hill. I had no instruction as to him and asked him where he was going and what he was going to do. His reply was to the effect that he was to drive everything before him on the hill. That was all that passed between us. He had Companies 'H," "D" and "K." He went over to the hills and was soon out of sight. The other two columns continued moving on opposite banks of the stream until we came in sight of the tepee that has been referred to, when the

[CUSTER BECKONED WITH HIS HAT]

Commanding Officer beckoned to me with his hat to cross to the bank where he was. When I got there the battalion was somewhat scattered and I was about opposite the rear of his column. I there received an order from Lt. Cook to move my command to the front. When I got up there, there was a tumult going on among the Indian Scouts. They were stripping themselves and preparing to fight. I understood that they had refused to go forward and Gen. Custer had ordered them to give up their guns and horses. I moved forward to the head of the column and shortly after Lt. Cook

[THE ATTACK ORDER RECEIVED]

came to me and said "Gen. Custer directs you to take as rapid a gait as you think prudent and charge the village afterward and you will be supported by the whole outfit."

My Adjutant, Lt. Hodgson, was on my left and Lt. Wallace on his left. He came up and said, laughing, that he was going as volunteer aide. He was not at the time on company duty.

["INDIANS IN FRONT IN STRONG FORCE"]

I took a trot and proceeded to carry out my orders. I crossed the creek and formed my battalion with two companies in line and one in reserve. I had been a good deal in Indian country and was convinced that they were there in overwhelming numbers. I sent back word twice; first, by a man named McIlargy, my striker, to say that the Indians were in front of me in strong force. Receiving no instructions, I sent a second man, Mitchell, a cook. They were the nearest men I could get hold of quick. That was some minutes after and I was convinced that my opinion was correct. I still heard nothing to guide my movement and so proceeded down the valley to carry out my orders.

My first thought was to make my charge with two companies and hold the third as a rallying point, but when I saw the number of Indians I sent my Adjutant to bring the third company on the line. I was in front near the centre and to the right. The Indian scouts had run away, except three or four, and we did not see them again until we got to Powder River, 90 miles away.

[INDIANS DEBOUCH FROM RAVINE]

We were then at a gallop and I was about 40 paces in advance. I could see a disposition on the part of the Indians to lead us on, and that idea was confirmed when upon advancing a little further I could see them coming out of a ravine in which they had hidden. The ravine was eight or nine hundred yards ahead on what are called the foothills on the left bank. There were also straggling parties of Indians making around to my rear. I saw I could not successfully make an offensive charge; their numbers had thrown me on the defensive. The village was stretched along the bank to the front and right. There were times going down when I could not see it at all.

["DISMOUNT TO FIGHT ON FOOT"]

I dismounted by giving the order to the company officers. Lt. Hodgson gave it to Company "G" and myself to "M" and "A." I gave the order to dismount and prepare to fight on foot and shelter the horses in the point of timber.

I had an idea of the number of Indians from the trails, and I saw five or six hundred with my own eyes; all the evidences through the bottoms and over the trails showed Indians there. The dust on the trail I followed was four to six inches deep and there were several other trails showing that numbers of animals had gone there.

We were in skirmish line under hot fire for fifteen or

["I COULD NOT STAY UNLESS FOREVER"]

twenty minutes. I was on the line near Capt. Moylan when word came to me that the Indians were turning my right. I left Lt. Hodgson to bring me word of what went on there and went with Company "G" to the banks of the river. I suppose there were 40 men in the Company. When I got there I had a good view of the tepees and could see many scattering ones. It was plain to me that the Indians were using the woods as much as I was, sheltering themselves and creeping up on me. I then rode out on the plain. Lt. Hodgson came to me and told me they were passing to the left and rear and I told him to bring the line in, round the horses. After going down to the river and seeing the situation, I knew I could not stay there unless I stayed forever. The regiment evidently was scattered, or someone would have brought me an order or aid; and in order to effect a union of the regiment, which I thought absolutely necessary, I moved to the hill where I could be seen, and where I thought I could dispose the men so they could hold out till assistance came. The men had 100 rounds each, 50 in their belts and 50 in the saddle bags; their firing for 20 minutes was what I call quick fire.

["THERE WAS NO PLAN"]

At the time I was in the timber I had not the remotest idea where either the packtrain or Benteen's column were. There was no plan communicated to us; if one existed the subordinate commanders did not know of it.

I left the timber, sending Lt. Hodgson to give the order to Capt. French and giving it in person to Capt. Moylan and Lt. McIntosh, to mount their men and bring them to the edge of the timber and form in column of fours. I had no other means of accomplishing the formation.

["I MADE UP MY MIND TO GO THROUGH THEM"]

Where Bloody Knife was shot I stood about ten minutes

while the formation was going on. I had nothing to do with it. They had their orders to form the men in column of fours out of the timber. I had made up my mind to go through those people and get to the hill for the purpose of getting the regiment together, so as to have a chance to save those who got through. There was no use of staying in the timber when I could assist no one, and create no diversion. I acted on my best judgment and I think events proved me right.

The Indians were increasing, particularly on the right bank, skipping from tree to tree, keeping themselves as much under shelter as possible. They were much more cunning in woodcraft than the soldiers.

[700 WARRIORS: 112 SOLDIERS]

The Indians are peculiar in their manner of fighting; they don't go in line or bodies, but in parties of 5 to 40. You see them scattering in all directions. My opinion is that six or seven hundred Indians were there; and I had but 112 men. I thought it my duty to give those men the best chance I could to save themselves; and it was impossible to have a victory over the Indians. I thought it my duty as a military movement, and I took the responsibility.

The column was formed to go through the Indians on that side. I felt sure that some of us would go up; we were bound to; some would get hit and I would lose part of my command. I was willing to risk that in order to save the lives of the others from the desperate position we were in.

[COLUMN FORMED TO LEAVE TIMBER]

I saw Bloody Knife shot, and also a man of "M" Company to whom the attention of the Doctor was at once directed. Bloody Knife was within a few feet of me; I was trying to get from him by signs where the Indians were going. I did not immediately leave the glade and the timber and go on a gallop to the river. I had given orders for the formation and I went through the timber and up on the plain to satisfy myself about the Indians there. Capt. Moylan was at my

side. Before Bloody Knife was killed the formation was
being made to leave the timber. The column was formed,
"A" in front, "M" in rear, and "G" in center. I was at the
head of the column and the gait was a rapid one. I thought
it my duty to be there, to see about the direction of the
column and for observing the ford and the hill on the other
side; I would be on the hill to rally and reform the men. I
stopped at the river a moment. The men crossed hurriedly
and it threw the rear into confusion. They were exposed to

["THE INDIANS HAD WINCHESTERS"]

heavy fire and I lost many there. The Indians had Winchester
rifles and the column made a big target and they were
pumping their bullets into it. I did not regard the movement
as a triumphant march, nor did I regard it as a retreat. When
I reached the hill, after a glance about, I thought it as good
a position as I could get in the time I had; and I immediately put in the command in skirmish line, through the company commanders.

At the time I left the timber I did not see Benteen's column,
nor had I the remotest reason to expect him to unite with
me. But in a short time after reaching the hill I saw him
not far off and rode out to meet him. I told him what I
had done. He moved his battalion to where mine was.

In crossing, Lt. Hodgson, my Adjutant, and a great favorite and friend, had been shot. In the hope that it might be
only a wound, and that I might do something for him, I
went to the river after Benteen's arrival with some men I
called together. Sergeant Culbertson was one of them. I was
gone about a half hour. Capt. Benteen was in command while
I was gone, and I had complete confidence in him.

["BENTEEN: COME ON"]

He showed me the order from Lt. Cook about bringing
up the packs. It was about this effect "Benteen—come on—
big village—bring packs" and then a postscript "bring packs,"
and signed "W. W. Cook." He had not had time to add his

official designation as Adjutant. I took a ring and some keys from Lt. Hodgson's body and went back on the hill. The Indians had withdrawn from my front and around me, except for a scattering fire.

Ten wounded had been able to get on the hill with their horses. Most of them men of "A" Company, which led the column. I told Capt. Moylan to make them comfortable and do all that could be done.

[AMMUNITION SENT FOR]

The packs were not yet in sight; one of the men was sent after them to get the ammunition mules up as soon as possible. When I had time to look around I told Lt. Hare to act as my Adjutant and I sent him to the pack train to hurry it all he could. He went and returned and reported what he had done. In about an hour the packs arrived. I am not positive about the time; I had other things to do than looking at my watch. Before they came up the command was put in position: it was on this hill which I thought would enable everybody to see it, and I kept it there as a nucleus about which the scattered parties could gather, till all came together. That was the purpose for which I went there.

["TELL WEIR TO COMMUNICATE WITH CUSTER"]

When Lt. Hare returned I told him to go to Capt. Weir, who on his own hook had moved out his company, and to tell him to communicate with Gen. Custer if he could, and tell him where we were. I knew in which direction to send him, as Gen. Custer's trail had been found back of the position on the hill.

The main body was kept in hand and after the packtrain came up I formed the column with three companies on the left, the packs in the middle and two companies on the right, and started down the river.

["WE ADVANCED A MILE AND A HALF"]

We went perhaps a mile or a mile and a half. I was at the head of the column, and skirmishers were thrown out on the flanks and some on the river bank. I regarded Weir as an advance guard and if anything came there he could check it and give us time to take position.

["HARE USED MY NAME"]

Lt. Hare came back and said he had taken the responsibility of using my name and ordered the return of the command on account of the number of Indians he saw. The orders were then communicated to the other officers. Capt. Weir, I was afterwards told, left one of his men down there.

I had been impressed with the position I first reached on the hill; it was nearer water and if the companies in the rear could hold the Indians in check we could get there. The column moved both down and back by my orders.

["I SELECTED THE POSITION"]

I remained at the rear as the column was put about by fours. I thought, as the Indians were coming, I would be where I could get first information. I remained there a few minutes and then galloped to the head of the column to make disposition of the troops. Capts. French and Godfrey were sent to Capt. Benteen who gave them directions while I was gone to the head. I selected the position; it appeared to me the best I could get in the time I had. I knew I would have to fight dismounted, and that I would have all I could do to take care of myself. I said to Benteen "You look out for that side and I will of the other." I took "D" Company with me; I spoke to the men and told them to come with me. It was the strongest company we had and I put them in position where I thought the main attack would be made. I remained there most of the time as I knew the other flank was in good hands.

[THE INDIANS ATTACKED IMMEDIATELY]

We hardly had time to dispose of the horses and get the men on the line before we were attacked in large numbers. The men threw themselves on the ground, having no protection except the "grease weed" which was no protection whatever. I cannot fix the time, except that the sun was high enough to see it over the hills below us.

The fire commenced immediately. It was very heavy and lasted till about nine o'clock P.M. Between 6 and 9 I went over the line and felt satisfied we could hold it, and then I went to the left of "D" Company. About 9:00 the fire ceased and the Indians went down and made a huge bonfire in the village, where we could see them dancing and scampering about. After 9 I went around and made further dispositions; moved some of the companies and told the company commanders to protect themselves all they could and get all the shelter possible as they had to stay there; I remember saying many times that we could not leave the wounded, and we had got to stay there until relief came, that I knew could not be long as I knew Gen. Terry was in the country and

["I KNEW OF TERRY'S PLAN"]

I was sure to get information soon. I had been informed by one of Terry's staff that there had been a plan agreed upon between himself and Gen. Custer to meet in the vicinity of the Little Big Horn. He was to come up the Little Big Horn; so I expected to be relieved either by Terry or Custer.

The men and officers were very tired: they had been hard marched. It had been harder on the men than on the horses. The men were badly in need of sleep because they had been up in the saddle.

[CUSTER'S WHEREABOUTS DISCUSSED]

That evening the whereabouts of the Commanding Officer of the regiment was discussed by Capt. Benteen and myself, while he was lying on my blankets.

There was not the slightest belief or suspicion that Custer had been destroyed. It was supposed that he could take care of himself as well as we could. He had nearly as many men as I had; more than when I opened the fight.

[DAYBREAK ON THE 26TH]

On the morning of the 26th I went around the line and

could see the Indians moving up the valley, about daybreak; the attack commenced about 2:30, after they had formed a circle around me. The first thing I heard was two rifle shots, which attracted attention as everything was quiet. These were immediately succeeded by firing from all round the position. It was only when they fired that their position was indicated; by puffs of smoke and by the sound. There was one point behind which there were about 25 who fired together. They were the nearest Indians to us, and the ones who hit most of the horses. The fire was as severe as I ever experienced.

[2500 WARRIORS ATTACKED]

The time periods I stated in my official report were fixed by gathering information from various persons in the command. I got the best approximations available. But the 9 and 2:30 times I fixed myself and think they are about right. I stated in my official report that from the best information I had, I estimated the number of attacking Indians about 2500. I think now I was below the mark. I think they were all there on the hill. The firing continued intense till about 10:30, and then slackened; they were removing to the bottom in the direction of the village. I thought they were gone for ammunition or reliefs. They were raising a big dust, and had set the prairie afire, so it was difficult to see what they were doing, because we could not see behind the dust and smoke. I now think they left me to meet Gen. Terry, who encamped that night 8 or 9 miles from where I was. In fact I know they did.

[SHARPSHOOTERS REMAINED ALL DAY]

There were some high points which perfectly sheltered some of their sharpshooters who remained all day; and a few were left to annoy the command who stayed all day, annoying us particularly in the matter of getting water.

The weather was very warm. I and some other officers had gotten broad-brimmed straw hats from a trader at the mouth of the Rosebud and I wore one of these on the march. I lost it in the bottom, in the timber.

I brought my carbine with me to the hilltop. I never told anyone I had lost it. I did not fire my pistol on the hill, though I did several times while coming across the bottom; I don't think it had a charge in it when I got on the hill.

["WHY I LEFT THE TIMBER"]

My motive in leaving the timber was, that we had an immense force against us, and nobody came to our assistance. I was not certain that anybody knew where I was, unless directed by the firing. The position, in my judgment, was not tenable, and I thought by placing my command on the hill, the scattered portions of the regiment could get together. It was my opinion that was the only means of getting anybody away alive. The guidon planted by Capt. Benteen on Weir's hill was put there with the thought that it might be discovered by scattered men and detachments.

["I HEARD NO FIRING FROM DOWN RIVER"]

I heard no firing from down river till after we moved out in that direction and then only a few scattering shots. I thought they were from the village. It did not impress me as coming from a general engagement. Nothing that came to my attention on the 25th or 26th led me to suspect that Custer was destroyed.

My official report was made up in the manner such reports are generally made—from the best information I could obtain. There must have been matters of which I had no personal knowledge as to which I considered my information reliable; especially in regard to time.

["I WAS NOT DRUNK"]

I had some whiskey in a flask that I carried in the inside pocket of my uniform sacque; it held about a pint. I did not touch it until about midnight of the 25th. I was not drunk at any time; and the flask was not emptied till the 28th when on the Custer field; it was a most disagreeable sight and officers and men alike were much affected. The stench was sickening. I took one drink on the night of the 25th, but it did not affect me at all. I think it was the only whiskey in the command, except what the Doctor had.

On the 25th I went around the line and came to the packs, and found there a great many skulkers, and drove them out. I did this several times. The horses and mules were safe and I thought these men had no business there. The last time was after the packs had been taken off and I asked one of the men what he was doing there. I was annoyed. I cannot recall his reply, but I know it angered me and I hit him; and I may have told him if I found him there again I would shoot him. This was about 10 P.M., or between 9 and 10.

["I DID NOT KNOW WHERE BENTEEN WAS"]

I never had any intimation that Benteen was to support me in my attack on the bottom. I did not even know where he was.

During the night of the 25th I completed the line by moving some of the companies, and I told all the company commanders to shelter themselves as well as they could, as it would be impossible to leave. I went round the line several times. The Indians that were firing into the herd were able to reach the animals best through the depression, and I tried to fill that up with everything belonging to the packs. I had boxes of ammunition placed along the lines of the different companies, so the men could have all they wanted. Those were about all the orders I gave, and I went around afterward to see that they had been complied with.

On the 26th I moved about, but stayed most of the time with "D" Company near Lt. Wallace. I crossed the ridge several times, and recall being out in front of Benteen's line, and in Moylan's line; in fact, I was around all. After the heaviest firing was over, I was outside Benteen's position with Sgt. DeLacy, to shoot at some Indians we could see galloping around.

[FREQUENT ORDERS NOT NEEDED]

I took every means to inform myself that the officers and troops were behaving as well as possible in the circumstances. Frequent orders were not needed; and after the morning of the 26th I did not think any were necessary. I saw no occasion for encouraging either officers or men.

I remained in command after Gen. Terry's arrival, and he sent me to bury the dead, which I thought a proper duty for the 7th—to care for the wounded and bury our comrades, whom we were best able to recognize.

I received no communication from Girard at the ford "A"; he had no right to speak to me officially. I had had trouble with Girard, and discharged him because I thought he was stealing from the Government.

My effort to communicate with Custer the night of the 25th was as much for my benefit as for his. I had no more concern, nor as much, about his position as for my own.

There were two Indians, Half Yellow Face and a Crow, who I thought would be able to go through. I would not order a soldier to go to certain death. These Indians talked about it but would not go.

I made an effort on the 26th to communicate with Gen. Terry by a Crow scout. He took the note and left the lines but came back shortly. I do not know what became of the note. I finally got one to Gen. Terry on the 27th.

["I DO NOT FEEL THAT I FAILED"]

The only expectation of support I had from the order I received, was from the rear. I do not feel that I failed in my duty and think the results of those two days justify me.

CROSS EXAMINATION

The heavy dust I spoke of was on the trails we followed from the Rosebud, and which enlarged for miles before we reached the Little Big Horn. Lt. Cook put a portion of the command off the trail because we were making so much dust.

When troops are on an expedition of this kind, it is a general order always to carry 100 rounds of ammunition if they expect to meet anything, and I suppose all companies had that amount, as that was Gen. Custer's order.

["I DO NOT THINK THAT THERE WAS ANY PLAN"]

When I say that no plan was communicated to us I mean to the regiment. I do not think there was any plan. The trail I spoke of as Custer's was one of shod horses, and could not have been made by Capt. Benteen's command.

I do not remember the exact phraseology of the message to Benteen: as near as I can recall it was "Benteen; Come on; big village; big thing; bring packs. P. S. Bring packs," and now that you call it to my attention, I remember that it also contained the words "Be quick." It did not make any great impression on me at the time, because I was absorbed in getting those packs together, and did not intend to move until I had done so. It did not occur to me that Custer with 225 men needed anyone quickly; his force could hold off quite a number of Indians if properly disposed. I mean the number I saw.

[HARE ORDERED THE RETURN]

Weir moved out on his own hook; and when I sent orders to him to communicate with Custer, which I did immediately after I got hold of the pack train and the wounded were cared for, Lt. Hare told me that Weir took him out and showed him the impracticability of going any further; and it was then Lt. Hare used my name and ordered the return. I had thought he could cut through; I regarded him as the advance guard, as the whole column started toward him when the order was sent.

[FROM 1800 TO 2500 WARRIORS AT A TIME]

I do not mean to be understood that all the Indians engaged me on the hill at one time; there was not room enough; but I think there were from 1800 to 2500 engaging at a time. But I think they all came there. I imagine the circumference of the circle they formed around us was about 4000 yards, and they were all the way from 10 yards to 1200 yards from us.

I had no reason to believe that Gen. Custer would support me in any other manner than from the rear; in my opinion there was no other way. An attack on the flank would not have been a support under the circumstances, though I may have stated in my report that he intended to do so. I did not know where Benteen was; he might have gone to the mouth of the Rosebud for all I knew.

[RELATIONS WITH CUSTER FRIENDLY]

My relations with Gen. Custer were friendly enough; and if my own brothers had been in that column I could not have done any more than I did.

[*At this point the following colloquy occurred, and as it is difficult to abstract without losing its significance, it is reproduced verbatim*].

"Q. The question is, did you go into that fight with feelings of confidence or distrust."

"A. My feelings toward Gen. Custer were friendly.

"Q I insist that the question shall be answered.

"A. Well, sir, I had known Gen. Custer a long time; and I had no confidence in his ability as a soldier. I had known him all through the war."

The Indians I alluded to in my report as having been driven were the 40 or 50 decoys sent out there. I saw no ponies being driven about. Every pony I saw had an Indian on him.

[600 TO 900 INDIANS TO LEFT AND REAR]

I suppose there were from six to nine hundred Indians on my left and rear when I left the timber, and there were plenty in front, between me and the village. And they were in force on the other side of the river, in sheltered places, within close range, less than 100 yards away.

My casualties, before I decided to get out of there were, one scout killed, Sgt. Hynes [Sic. correctly spelled Heyn] of "A" Company hit, and two or three of "M" Company; that was before I mounted. The scout's name was Isaiah, a negro who had lived among the Sioux and had a Sioux wife.

The least number of men who could have held that timber was six or seven hundred; they would have to hold the outer edge all around, otherwise the Indians could creep up and get at us. I think the regiment could have done it, but not 120 men—and I did not have 120. To cover the necessary space, that number of men would be beyond speaking distance apart and their fire would be no support at all.

[THE INDIANS KILLED THE WOUNDED]

I suppose the Indians killed the wounded left in the timber. I could make no effort to take them out; and none was made. I do not know what became of the wounded left on the plain; the Indians would not permit me to take care of them.

I received no communication from Girard at the crossing: I would not have believed it if I had. I should have listened to him, but I repeat, I should not have believed him.

I tried to communicate with Custer the night of the 25th. I was quite as anxious to get him to aid me as I was to aid him. I did not call for volunteers; and I would not order a soldier on a mission of that kind, for I believed that would be sending a man to his death. I would have sent an Indian out, because of his peculiar ability to skulk along and get through a country without being seen when a white man would be seen.

["THE RESULTS JUSTIFIED MY ACTS"]

I consider that the results of the battle justified my every act, and with the same knowledge I then had, I would again do the same thing under the same circumstances. I believe that when I came out of the timber Custer's command was all dead. This belief is based on after information: I did not think so then.

I do not remember anybody reporting to me that he heard firing on the right. If I had heard this firing as they represent it, I should have known he was engaged while I was on the hill; but I heard no such firing. Perhaps I was not in a position to hear the firing when I was down the hill by Lt. Hodgson's body, though I was nearer the battlefield then than the command was.

["I WAS RESPONSIBLE"]

I consider that I obeyed orders. I did not charge into the village, but I went far enough to discover that it was impossible. Of course, ten men could be ordered to charge a million; a brilliant illustration is the battle of Balaklava. I then knew nothing of the topography, but it afterwards developed that had I gone 300 yards further the command would have been thrown into a ditch 10 yards wide and 3 or 4 feet deep. The Indians were in it; and the command would never have gotten that far; but by the time they had got within a few yards most of the saddles would have been emptied and the horses killed.

I was responsible for the union of my battalion with the rest of the regiment, and I believed I would find them on the other side of the river. I knew they were not on my side, as "M," "A" and "G" were the only companies that got on the left side of the river.

RE-DIRECT EXAMINATION

I had 112 soldiers and officers when I crossed the river going to the attack, and about 27 Indian scouts who didn't remain with me long.

["I DID EVERYTHING I COULD"]

I did everything I could to assist and cooperate with Gen. Custer as much as if he were my own brother. Never in my life did I feel more interest in the success of an engagement, because the Seventh was essentially my own regiment. I feel that I did everything possible short of sacrificing my command.

The principle that actuated me in returning to the hill was that of reuniting with Custer, not leaving him unsupported. I went out of there as much to aid him as to secure aid.

[A CONVICTION FORMED AFTER THE FIGHT]

When I said in my report that Gen. Custer meant to support me by a flank attack, it was a conviction formed after the fight. I expected my support to come from the direction I had crossed. I did not see how it was possible, on account of the high banks on the other side, for support to come from the flanks. I didn't think it was practicable to get down below me.

The number of wounded had nothing to do with my action in the timber. I should have done the same thing if no man had been hit. There was no communication to me that Custer's command had been sighted from the timber.

EXAMINATION BY THE COURT

When I retreated from the bottom I had no idea where Custer was. I knew he was not on the side where the village was, and if there was any chance for him to see me it was on this hill. I had no doubt that I could explain the retreat from my position; but I did not give it a thought. I never thought it would be questioned.

———————

Major Reno then offered and read in evidence a portion of Gen. Sherman's report, as follows:

"In this engagement the five companies of the 7th Cavalry led by Lieut. Col. Custer in person, viz: "C," "E," "F," "I," and "L," were literally obliterated, and the remaining seven companies were saved by the brave and prudent conduct of Major Reno, and the timely arrival of General Terry."

Maj. Reno then offered and read in evidence Exhibits 9, 10 and 11, being (9) an official letter of the Adjutant General transmitting a copy of (10) a petition signed by 235 of the enlisted survivors of the battle, addressed to the President and the Congress, and asking the promotion of Maj. Reno to the rank of Lieut. Col. to fill the vacancy caused by the death of Gen. Custer; and the promotion of Capt. Benteen to the rank of Major to fill the vacancy caused by the promotion of Maj. Reno, and (11) General Sherman's endorsement upon said petition.

THE DEFENSE RESTED

DID OFFICERS CHANGE THEIR STORIES?
[W.A.G.]

The Court of Inquiry had not yet completed its session when Frederick Whittaker, who styled himself "the accuser of Major Reno," saw the handwriting on the wall, and began to inveigh against the vindication he sensed was on the way.

His plan of attack was by innuendo to foster in the public mind, a suspicion that the members of the Court itself, and Colonel Wesley Merritt in particular, were more interested in suppressing facts than they were in exposing them. And he did not hesitate to charge, after the Court had finished its labors and dissolved, that Merritt was the real author of the Court's findings ("The Custer Myth," p. 328-9), which in his opinion, failed to clear the name and fame of Custer as he had planned, and had resulted in a whitewash instead of the purge he had schemed to bring about.

Nor did Mr. Whittaker hesitate to excoriate the witnesses who, he said, were allowed to slander Custer, while nothing against Reno was permitted. He was especially critical of Benteen, whose testimony he described as a series of malignant sneers against the dead hero.

This attempt by Mr. Whittaker to discredit the conduct and findings of the Court even before the latter were promulgated, resulted in reviving once again all the old animosities and disputes that the Army, doubtless, had hoped would soon be buried and forgotten. But it was not to be.

To let sleeping dogs lie has ever been the Army policy, especially when to waken them would inevitably result in a public clamor critical of the Service. And here there were no sleeping dogs. Whittaker and his following had seen to that; and that they did the job thoroughly is proven by the fact that not since 1879 have any of the dogs enjoyed one fleeting wink of sleep: on the contrary, each year has seen more and more of the public engaged in an effort to keep them stirred up and in a fighting mood.

In later years, though Whittaker has been forgotten, his work lives on. Its influence is apparent in the charges one hears and reads from day to day that the officers of the Seventh changed their stories; that they talked one way and swore another when put under oath to tell the truth. These charges are not new; they have been going the rounds for years; the one thing new about them is to be found in the variations that from time to time are added to the theme.

Few battles have been fought that have not produced their critics, and it has been the habit of soldiers from time immemorial to differ in opinion as to the efficiency with which military commanders have conducted them. The battle of the Little Big Horn was no exception—on the contrary it was one that produced, and still produces, more differences of opinion than have followed most of the combats in which our Army has engaged.

The fact is that there were bound to be many differences. Some thought Custer was to blame: some thought Reno lost his head, and Custer with it: some thought he should have marched at once to the sound of the guns, without waiting for the ammunition or the packs. But those most critical of his conduct in the valley were not with him in the valley; and those who held that he should have marched at once ignored his lack of ammunition.

But when these same men took the witness stand and swore to tell the truth, all, as good soldiers, even the more experienced Benteen, to whom Reno himself looked for advice and counsel, recognized and acknowledged that it was Reno and not one of them who was Commanding Officer; that it was he, not they, upon whom rested the duty and responsibility of decision. They might, as some did, sharply disagree with his decisions, but they could not question his authority to make them, an authority which carried with it the obligation to use his best judgment and to accept the consequences if that judgment proved unsound. And not one of them, not even the unfriendly Godfrey, was able to put his finger on any act that he was willing to stigmatize upon his oath, as cowardice.

During my debate with Capt. R. G. Carter ("The Custer Myth," p. 316), in answer to my challenge to name the "equally credible witnesses" whose statements he claimed would offset the testimony at the Inquiry, he named one man—John Merrill— son of Major Lewis Merrill of the Old Seventh.

It so happened that I knew Merrill well. He was a temporary or "emergency" officer of the Ordnance Corps during World War I, who had been a practising lawyer in Philadelphia, and was then about 60 years of age. Pending discharge, he was detailed to the Judge Advocate General's Office, and was assigned to the Contracts Section, of which I was Assistant Chief. I was then engaged in copying, in longhand, the record of the Inquiry proceedings, and he saw the record as it lay upon my desk. He talked to me many times about the Inquiry, and the burden of his remarks was always the same; the officers of the Seventh didn't testify the way they talked at Ft. Lincoln when as a teen-aged youth, he had heard them discuss the battle on numerous occasions at the Post Trader's store.

Which officers, I asked. O—all of them, said he. And what did they say? O—that Reno should have charged the village; he should have stayed in the timber; he ought to have marched at once to Custer's aid. He could have saved Custer and he didn't try. And which officers said that? O—all of them. Did Benteen say it? He didn't remember about Benteen. Did Moylan, or French, or Wallace, or Varnum or Hare say it? He didn't know about them either. Did he know what any particular officer had testified? No, he didn't. Could he name any officer who had changed his story? No, he couldn't, but he was sure they all did.

This shotgun method of impeachment was not too convincing. Indeed, it was not at all convincing to me; yet here was Carter's star witness; the only one he was willing to name. I did not tell him that I knew Merrill and had learned all he knew about the matter, which was nothing.

With the exception of the none-too-reliable DeRudio, quoted by Mathey as having said, "If we had not been commanded by a coward we would all have been killed," I found no evidence that any officer of the Seventh materially changed his story when called to the witness stand. Some of them were evasive—Benteen, for example; some generalized more than an expert examiner would have permitted them to do; and I think all were more or less reluctant, for understandably enough, they were not proud of the Little Big Horn. They answered what they were asked; but no more. They did not volunteer testimony, and only an expert examiner could have done better with them than did Recorder Lee.

But when their testimony is taken by the four corners and analyzed, in my opinion it stands up. That they were not in perfect agreement always is nothing strange. Honest men invariably differ on details, and one of the surest badges of perjury displays itself when witnesses tell precisely similar stories. Recorder Lee believed they told the truth: so also do I.

The testimony concluded, the Court was now addressed on behalf of the defense by Major Reno's counsel, Mr. Gilbert, excerpts from whose remarks follow. Mr. Gilbert's eloquent address was filed in written form for the record.

The case * * * commenced as an examination of the courage shown by Major Reno, during a time when General Custer and his column could be affected by his conduct.

It extended itself until it included his behavior long after General Custer and those under him had ended with honor their lives as soldiers, and it ended with a question into the sobriety of Major Reno, at a time when the Indians were with savage joy holding their scalp dance over their defeat of Custer and his command.

These charges so varied and unlike, so distant and remote

from the real charge which provoked this Court of Inquiry, have been the subject of testimony from many witnesses. These represent different degrees of character, and will I am sure be properly discriminated between by the Court. It is not so much of them as of the principle which underlies testimony applicable to all cases of a military character that I wish to speak. A military court is always, so far as I am informed, composed of officers higher, or at least equal in grade, to the one who is interested in its proceedings. The reason for the rule is, I think, plain. It is found not merely in the greater impartiality which higher rank confers, not merely in the greater knowledge and ampler experience which attends it, but also in the fact that the independence of every officer requires that those who live in the suburbs of the Army, to whom he must give peremptory orders to which the only answer is unquestioning obedience, shall not be his judge in matters which concern his life, or his honor.

Apply the reason which governs the selection of military courts to the kind of testimony by which you, as members of this court, would be governed, and you will see that some of the testimony requires a rule of rigid construction.

Let it once be understood that an orderly—a private soldier of limited intelligence, who follows at the heels of his commanding officer, is evidence to establish an important order, as much as the officer who rides by his side; that an Indian interpreter on his first expedition can give reliable testimony upon military matters, or after being dismissed for stealing can sit in judgment on the courage of his superior; or that a mule-packer struck in the face by an officer for being where it was thought he had no duty to be, can originate a charge of drunkenness against that officer, and unsupported by any other witness save that of another mule-packer, can insist on this story in a Court of Inquiry—let it once be understood that name and character and fame lie in the keeping of these followers of any army, and the sense of subordination is gone—and the desire to conciliate becomes stronger than the desire to command. The character of an officer will then depend on the favor of the camp followers and they will profit by that knowledge.

The charges against Major Reno rest largely on the testimony of two mule-packers, a doctor, an Indian scout, a sergeant, and an Indian interpreter. When we remember that about three hundred men saw his behavior at the times when these witnesses have objected to it, we are appalled by this number.

*   *   *

Dr. Porter, within the limits of his duty, I greatly respect. But if he has the gift of courage, he did not have it with him at all times on the 25th day of June. * * * The men whom Falstaff saw in Kentish Green never multiplied themselves so rapidly to his vision as did the Indian lodges to the Doctor's eyes, when he saw 1000 lodges from the timber.

His judgment of the military movement differs from that of many of the officers, and perhaps its value would have been understood by John Randolph who, when Chairman of the Military Committee in Congress said, in answer to a member, formerly a watch-maker, who criticised the bill, that the gentleman might understand tic-tacs, but certainly did not understand tac-tics.

Of the two mule-packers who try to establish the drunkenness of Reno on the night of the 25th of June, 1876, but little shall be said. * * *

Mark their story—Reno is drunk, is staggering, is stammering; and yet beside Girard—the non-combatant—no one of all that command on the hilltop even imagines him to be in that condition until they reach Chicago, more than two years and a half after the time they fix. They made a mistake in making him too drunk. Drunkenness has a beginning, an existence, and an end, and with the frequent contact Reno had with officers and men, he must, if in any of the stages of it, have been detected and exposed. * * *

It was hardly necessary to summon Edgerly, and Benteen, and Wallace, and Mathey and McDougall to contradict them and to propose to have Hare and Varnum and Moylan telegraph their knowledge upon this subject. It was only dignifying falsehood and putting honesty to unnecessary labor.

The question of time and distance about which such differing evidence has been given is not to my mind of great importance except as it determines the relation of one command to another. And this relation and position can, as the court has no doubt already observed, be fixed independently of watches. Where Custer's column was with reference to that of Reno can be definitely placed without regard to the time of day. There will be I think but little difficulty upon that point.

The Court will also, I am sure, remember that Reno's duty was made difficult by the fact that surrender was impossible, and therefore the whole course of his conduct was different from what it would have been against a civilized foe.

The history of this case presents some difficulty with regard to distance and to time, but none so serious but that a very little consideration will remove them all. As far as the testimony exhibits, the Seventh regiment of Cavalry was on the 25th day of June 1876 moved from the divide between the Rosebud and the Little Big Horn rivers in the direction of the latter stream. With several halts it reached a point at about 12 o'clock upon that day where a division of the command was made into battalions. * * * If we rely, as I think we can with the greatest safety, upon the testimony of Lieut. Wallace who kept the itinerary, this point of division was about fifteen miles distant from the Little Big Horn river, and the point where Maj. Reno afterward crossed it. Immediately after the division was made, Col. Benteen diverged to the left, and after going a distance which no one states to be greater than two miles, was lost to the view of the rest of the column. The command thus diminished in number by the separation of Col. Benteen, continued in the direction in which it had been marching until it reached a point about ten or twelve miles lower down, where there was a burning tepee containing the body of a dead Indian. At this point Reno received an order from Gen. Custer as commanding officer, which governed his future action. It has been stated in several ways, but all of them unite in declaring that he was to charge the Indians, who had already been discovered in the bottom on the left side of the Little Big Horn, under a promise of support from Gen. Custer's command. * * *

After the command was received, Reno gave the order to trot and his battalion moved down to the crossing of the river. The Indians had already been seen on the river bottom. * * * When the crossing was reached * * * the battalion went to the other side of the river, and passing through a fringe of timber such as follows the water courses on the western prairies, halted to reform. * * * Before advancing from this point, Maj. Reno saw enough of the Indians who were approaching him, to judge of their numbers and their disposition. He knew as Benteen knew, as Girard says he knew, that Gen. Custer believed that the Indians were retreating, and he could fairly presume that the order he had received from Gen. Custer had predicated on wrong information. He sent back word by a private soldier who served him in the capacity of a body-servant, * * * that the Indians were all before him and that they were very strong. Not receiving an answer * * * he again sent back word by a man named Mitchell, and as neither of them ever returned or were ever again seen alive, it is fair to infer that they succeeded in reaching the main column. Girard himself testified that he saw Indians advancing up the valley in such large numbers that he called Maj. Reno's attention to the fact; * * * that he turned back from the river's edge and met Adjutant Cook and told him of that fact, and that the Adjutant promised to inform Gen. Custer of it. Adjutant

Cook died on the lower hills with Gen. Custer and it is safe to say that he performed his promise.

* * * Without any further delay, Maj. Reno formed two companies into line, and throwing the third company in their rear in line, moved down the valley. On his right was the river with its growth of trees, on his left was a line of foothills that stretched and lost itself far to the southwest. There was a large column of dust before him, and there were Indians coming out of the dust to meet him. He skirted the timber and went a distance that, according to the statements of witnesses, varies from a mile and a quarter to about two miles. He was then satisfied that the Indians were not only not fleeing, but that they were preparing an ambush to receive him, and therefore he ceased his charge, and ordered the men to dismount and deploy as skirmishers.

Was he justified in doing so? He was already at a considerable distance from the point from which he expected to receive his support. The Indians, instead of continuing on his front, had commenced to separate and were already circling along the hills on his left in order to cut him off from the crossing. This circumstance in itself, I submit to the Court, justified an officer who was responsible for the lives of his command in believing that the enemy * * * were in such force that they invited an attack, for Reno was then between the village and the river, and the love of the hearthstone, though different in degree, is the same in principle in civilized and uncivilized men; and the Indians, if they had felt distrustful of their strength, would undoubtedly have presented a united resistance to any approach toward the village; but when they gave way, and invited an attack that if successful would have destroyed their homes, they declared to the commanding officer that they were not only able to protect themselves, but were able to destroy his command. In this act of judgment Maj. Reno is confirmed by the opinions of the officers who accompanied him. * * *

The wisdom of Reno's action is still further seen in the fact that as soon as he did dismount, Indians to the number of four or five hundred, * * * appeared in his front from out a ravine into which his command must certainly have plunged if he had continued charging. Not only does the result which we now see would have followed, prove that he acted rightly in dismounting where he did, but it was his duty as an officer who expected not merely to be supported by another portion of the command, but to support it by making a diversion, not to throw away the lives of his battalion until the supporting column was near enough to him to receive the benefit of the attack that he would make. If he had continued on at this point, his entire command would have been destroyed without any benefit being received by any supporting command. He deployed the men on skirmish line, and if we can believe the officers whose duty called them to that part of the field, the command continued to advance on foot and fired as they advanced.

What now was Reno's position? The Indians were close to him and increasing in number. They were on his front and were circling to his rear between him and that point from which the expected support must come. The river was close to the edge of the timber. On its other side rose high bluffs which stretched a number of miles to such a height that from them no assistance could come. Between the hills on the opposite side and the river, there was some low land covered with timber and brush, into which the Indians had already commenced to come, and from which they were sending a fire into the timber. He had one hundred and twelve men under his control, not counting the Indian scouts and the noncombatants. The force was too small to occupy the timber with any hope of resisting the number of Indians that he saw attacking and preparing to attack him. At this point his attention was called to a fire that was being received on the side of the timber next to the river, and with part of his force he enters the timber with a view to dislodging the Indians. While there word is brought to him that the Indians have turned his flank, and he goes out with Capt. Moylan to see the situation for himself. He becomes convinced that it is his duty to retire the men from the skirmish line and bring them into the timber, and in that act he is abundantly confirmed by the judgment of those who were with him. * * * Reno, unsupported as he was, was then forced to decide what duty he owed his command and his commanding officer, and he decided to leave the timber.

* * *

A number of questions were asked the witnesses with regard to Maj. Reno's ability to continue in the timber if he had been joined by Col. Benteen. A sufficient answer to this is that Maj. Reno knew that Benteen had been ordered away from the column before he (Reno) had been directed to make his charge—that he was in entire ignorance of the orders given to Benteen and therefore had no reason to expect him to support him; and Benteen further says, that Reno was not justified at all in expecting that he (Benteen), under orders given him by Gen. Custer, could render him any support whatever.

In addition to the increasing number of Indians and the threatening positions that they occupied on his rear and flank, Maj. Reno found another difficulty. And that was the want of ammunition. It is in evidence * * * that some of the men had already expended half the number of cartridges that they had brought across the river, and therefore if there was to be a prolonged resistance, that long before it could be successful, the troops would be left with empty carbines.

Up to this point let us inquire what had been Maj. Reno's conduct. He had certainly led the charge up to the point where the men were dismounted. * * * The mere act of leaving the timber was itself an evidence of courage. A timid man would have remained there. Even Girard testified that with the number of Indians in the bottom he thought it was an excess of bravery to leave the timber, and he stayed behind because he expected the command would return.

Now if there was nothing more in this case than this, we would claim that Maj. Reno was certainly open in no way to censure as an officer and a soldier. But it is claimed that he showed cowardice in the way in which his command started from the timber to go to the hilltop. It is said that no bugle calls were given and that was an evidence of fear. * * * Unless Capt. Moylan is virtually incorrect, Maj. Reno came to the edge of the timber and there consulted with him before any movement of the troops was made, and that it was their joint judgment that a higher point should be sought on the other side of the river, at which the force under Maj. Reno could contend on more nearly equal terms with the force that was brought against him. It is in evidence * * * that the command was passed down along the line for the men to mount and to make a charge. It is in evidence * * that the column was undoubtedly formed before the men left the timber, and that if they all had been in their places, as it was the expectation of the commander that they should be, they all would have returned in as good order as did Moylan's company.

Maj. Reno led the charge to the river. He was justified in thinking that after the company officers had received the word to mount and charge, the men in their companies would be properly informed and fully obey him. He was seeking to cross an unknown river, and over country to which he was a stranger, to find a place where he might ascend the high land on the other side of the river. * * * To me it seems plain that where a ford is to be selected and a crossing is unknown, it is the duty of the commander to be there to use his discretion and his judgment with regard to the manner in which the troops shall pass from one side of the river to the other, and rise to the new place that they shall occupy for defense. It is a strange thing in this case that those eyes which saw the most demoralization in the column as it moved to the river, were not those of military men, and it is undoubtedly true that the column may not have been in perfect order, but the circumstances forbade it being so. It was not a triumphant march. It was the departure of a command from a place in which destruction was believed to be sure, to a spot in which it was hoped the danger would be less great. If Reno was doing his duty at the head of the column, I submit that he should not be charged with want of duty at its rear.

At this point it may perhaps be well to pause and to meet another charge that Reno in some way failed of his duty because of the untimely fate which befell Gen. Custer and his command, and which it is claimed would have been averted if Reno had continued in the timber. I think there is no truth in this belief. The Indians were certainly there in number that in the minds of military men justified the belief that they were able to overcome at one and the same time each portion of the command that then engaged them. * * * The fact that Reno's withdrawal from the timber had no influence whatever upon the fate of Gen. Custer is seen by two considerations. It is plain from the testimony that Reno was at least forty five minutes in the timber. During that time Gen. Custer with his command was thrice seen. Lt. Varnum saw the Gray Horse Company on the bluffs above the right bank of the river about thirty minutes before Reno left the timber. He believed that Custer had certainly time to reach the point on the map known as ford "B" before Reno reached the top of the hill. DeRudio, who saw with straining eyes, Custer with Cook standing on the high land overlooking Reno in the timber, states that the firing he heard down the river was almost simultaneous with Reno's reaching the top of the hill. If that proves anything, it proves that the diversion that Reno made, lasted until Custer had reached within striking distance. Martin, the trumpeter, testified that he left Custer at a considerable distance lower down the river than the point where Reno made his stand. * * * Custer having promised to support Reno and having had a view of him attacking the Indians under his order, would undoubtedly in turn have charged the Indians at the first point where he could have reached them. That point was the ford "B."

It cannot be doubted by this court that the testimony that they have heard, not merely from officers of Reno's command, but also from the evidence given by Lt. Col. Sheridan, who made a careful examination of that point and found a gravel bottom at the river there, over which he several times sent a wagon, that there was a proper point for Gen. Custer to give his promised support to Reno, if it was in the power of his command to support him at all. If the mind can believe testimony and draw any inferences from it, it is overwhelmingly clear that Custer had reached the ford "B," where he could have crossed to the Indian village, before the Indians whom Reno was diverting by his attack in the timber could have reached that point; and from the known character of Custer for valor and for bravery, it was equally plain that notwithstanding the thousand Indians whom Reno detained at the upper end of the village, there were Indians at the ford "B" in such overwhelming number as to make it a matter of madness for Custer and his command to engage them there. That explains the fact of the sleeping village which Martin says that Custer saw.

So far then as Reno's retreat from the timber was concerned, it had no effect whatever on the fate of Gen. Custer, for not a man nor a horse were found dead at the ford "B," and the first indication that Custer had found his enemy was at least eight hundred yards below the ford on the right bank of the river.

Another consideration proves this. Custer and his men were found in such position, with such separation and with such disorder, that it proves that whatever resistance they made, brave and heroic as it was, was in the nature of a defense and not of an attack. Competent judges have shown, not merely that the struggle could not have lasted more than an hour, but that from its very beginning it was hopeless. So far, then, as Reno is concerned, we hold that he was justified by the appearances as they presented themselves to him at the time he halted, in doing what he did; that he was further justified in this conduct by the result as it afterward declared itself; that he showed no cowardice whatever in the timber, that his retirement from it was not only within his discretion as a commanding officer, but was the result of consultation with one of his tried and approved officers and endorsed by many of the officers of his command; but that both on account of the number of the Indians and the manner in which Custer and his command were destroyed, it had no effect whatever upon any other command than his own.

It has not escaped the attention of the Court that when Benteen came up to the point where he afterwards joined Reno, he saw the Indians still in the bottom and that he thought that they were at least eight hundred or nine hundred in number. Sgt. Culbertson, a most careful witness, fixed their number at about a thousand; Lt. Varnum said that a great many Indians remained in the bottom, when he came up with Benteen; and it is the statement of Lt. DeRudio, who watched them from the timber in which he had remained, that they did not retire because Reno left the timber, but because Benteen was seen to approach on the other side of the river. * * *

When Reno reached the river, he decided * * * that this was no place to halt and reform the men. It was his duty as a commanding officer to select the new position from which the new struggle should be made, and he accordingly went to the top of the hill.

Much has been said of the manner in which the men

followed him. It is needless for me to say to this court that in no other way than a straggled way, even under circumstances of perfect peace, can a battalion of cavalry climb a steep bank. And yet, it was not demoralized. * * *

* * *

What now was the duty of Reno? He had had three companies engaged in the timber whose ammunition had been largely expended and needed to be replaced. He had wounded men whom he could not leave to the mercy of the Indians. He certainly ordered Hare back to the pack train to hurry the ammunition, and after receiving his report and making direction with regard to the care of the wounded, he sent an order to Weir, who had already moved out with his company, that he should endeavor to communicate with Custer. If, as we believe, Custer and his men had by this time been destroyed, anything else that was done thereafter could have no possible effect upon that command.

But it is urged that the message carried to Benteen by Martin exacted of him a duty. If it did, it was the duty of assistance, and that, he (Reno) prepared to render in the most effective way. He did this by replenishing his ammunition and by bringing up the pack train which the order to Benteen twice commanded him to do. The fire that had been heard in the direction of Custer's battlefield was not such, as was proven by every witness who gave testimony upon the subject, as to excite any grave distrust of Custer's condition. * * *

* * *

After the pack train came up, after the wasted ammunition was replaced, and the wounded—seven or eight in number—were properly cared for each with six attendants, the main column, by Reno's order and with him at the head, moved down the right bank of the stream to follow the advance guard of Capt. Weir. It reached a point where it was met by Lt. Hare, Reno's acting Adjutant, who returned from giving the order to Weir, to say that the Indians were so many in Weir's front that he had used Reno's name to order a return.

Of the ability of this command to force its way further down the river, there is but one opinion, all unite in saying that a forward movement would have been its destruction.

There was no firing to indicate an engagement below. That which had already been heard had ceased, and it had not awakened any belief whatever that Custer's command was any less able to take care of itself or had met with any greater opposition than the command under Reno. And yet, at the last moment, at the furtherest point in the advance, Benteen placed the guidon of the 7th Cavalry. It was at a place where * * * if visible, it would have carried no message to those who had fought on the hills and valleys below, because they had passed away from the region of human sense.

Slowly, and compelled by overwhelming numbers, the command moved back to a point which Reno selected and made its final stand. The disposition of the troops was made under the Indian fire and by Reno and Benteen, and then commenced a struggle which for tenacity and bitterness has never I believe been surpassed in the history of Indian warfare. * * * All save Gen. Gibbon unite in declaring that it was the best position that could have been selected; * * * and to his objection there is the overwhelming answer that a resistance was made from the afternoon of the 25th day of June until the evening of the 26th, and that when Gen. Terry came up with Gen. Gibbon * * * they found that portion of the 7th * * * on the unsurrendered heights.

I shall not linger to describe that height. The character of the place, the arrangement of the troops, were such that no man could have a full view of the acts and conduct of the Commanding Officer. His duty was of a simple kind. The commands that he gave were abiding ones, and after their places had been taken, the duties of the soldiers and of their officers were of a simple and an elementary kind. They were those of self-defense. * * *

And on the score of courage there is but one voice. * * * Testimony like that no award can obtain. It is a record of duty done with quietness, but with effect, without display, but with success. His command needed no inspiriting. The promptings of their own high natures sufficiently told them their duty. Think who gathered around him on the hilltop. Men who had the endorsement which our great Military University gives only to soldiers. Others were there, graduates of that trying school, the Civil War, to whom death was a familiar thing and bravery an instinct. * * * And with these, I gather up and bring to remembrance those who, lowlier in place, fought with such prodigious constancy; men like Culbertson, whose type is found in the two sergeants who gathered about the wounded Keogh and died with him. And with them all and over them all was Reno; not surpassing them in bravery, but in that not unequal to them; and better record than that need no man make.

Many times I have wondered as I sat before you whether if Custer could come back, he would own those, who standing in his shadow, claim to represent him; whether to the survivors of the 7th Cavalry he would not say, as they would say to him, "Our efforts failed to be mutual supports because of the overwhelming force that confronted each of us, and your honor takes no stain." Of the report made a few days after the battle and now submitted in evidence I need say nothing to a court familiar from long personal experience, with the manner in which such reports are written. They give a general statement of many matters of which the Commanding Officer cannot have a personal knowledge, and which may prove, under the minute examination of a Court of Inquiry, to rest on the recollection of others than himself, and for which he is not entirely responsible.

The statement of Gen. Custer made to his officers before Benteen diverged from the column, showed that after fullest care he disbelieved in the presence of the Indians. The announcement made by Girard just before Reno left the tepee, a short distance from the river, disclosed the belief that the Indians were running away. The sleeping Indian village seen by Martin, and, as he testifies, also by Gen. Custer, when the command of the latter was so close to the place of its heroic but final struggle, further attests the ignorance of the number and plans of the Indians, and of the preparations they were making for resistance.

The large number of Indians, about 1500, seen by Girard to be advancing up the valley to meet Reno while at the ford; their sudden disappearance; the small number that appeared then in his front; the dust behind them indicating a still larger number in their rear; the circling of the Indians away from the village, which they would not have left if in feeble strength, and their effort to reach Reno's rear, and to intercept his crossing and the support he expected to reach him, told to the practised eye of an Indian fighter, the story of an Indian ambush. The halt before the ravine, which was then seen four hundred yards away in the front; the skirmish line deployed after the firing began, were overwhelmingly justified even before the Indians, in number about three to five hundred, commenced to emerge from the ravine into which they had hoped the command would plunge in its continued charge.

The withdrawal of the skirmish line, when its continuing on the plain would have been its quick destruction, the charge through the timber by Reno himself to see the position of the Indians on his flank, attest the excellence of his wisdom and judgment. The retreat from the bottom, not made because of loss of life, but to save life, when its destruction was without value to any command, * * * is unmarked * * * by any act of cowardice. The support expected * * * from the rear had not come, and could not come from the other side of the river except after a delay * * * which would have rendered it worthless.

The diversion made by Reno lasted until the brief battle which Custer and his men heroically fought against such prodigious odds had begun, and the Indians he had detained so much longer than if in one brief mad rush he had sacrificed his command, were unneeded to complete it, and too far away to effectively take part in it. The well chosen place on the hilltop; the attempted march to Custer; * * * the sustained valor with which the position was defended, until it was delivered unsurrendered to Gen. Terry, * * * are part of Reno's history. And through it all, differing as were the demands made upon his character and capacity as a soldier, no man entitled to credit in any human court seeks to say aught against his courage. Aye, even the privates and non-commissioned officers, on what was almost the field of battle, with one voice commend him and his brother officers for promotion for soldierly bearing—and the General of the Army receives with approbation their high praise of his conduct.

* * *

Upon the conclusion of Mr. Gilbert's address, the Recorder, Lt. Lee, addressed the Court on behalf of the prosecution. Excerpts from his argument follow. The Recorder's address was also filed in writing for the record.

It would be useless for one unaccustomed as I am to that which pertains to the legal profession, to attempt to rival the eloquence and learning displayed so brilliantly by the gifted counsel of Maj. Reno. I make no pretensions in that direction, and it were useless for me to have any ambition of that character; but I shall be content to present my views to the court in as clear and plain a manner as possible.

First; permit me to say that in any comments I may make in regard to any persons who have been connected with this case either as witnesses or otherwise, I trust that nothing may be misconstrued, for most certainly I have no personal interest in this case, and whatever I may say will be from a sense of duty; and if I err, I hope it will not be attributed to any bias or prejudice. As far as I am able to discover, this investigation has brought out all the material facts—if any remain undeveloped it is certainly no fault of mine, for I have endeavored to elicit everything that might have a bearing on this matter. * * *

The order convening this Court issued from the War Department at the request of Maj. M. A. Reno to investigate his conduct at the battle of the Little Big Horn River on the 25th and 26th of June, 1876, and the Court is ordered to "Report the facts and its opinion as to whether from all the circumstances in the case, any further proceedings are necessary." Maj. Reno's request is accompanied by a copy of a letter emanating from Mr. Frederick Whittaker of Mount Vernon, N. Y., and addressed to the Hon. Mr. Corlett, of Wyoming Territory, urging a similar request to the House of Representatives. Maj. Reno in his application refers to that letter, and asks an investigation thereon; thus making it the very basis of his application. That letter charges Maj. Reno with various military offences, all of which are within the scope of this inquiry as ordered by the War Department, and that letter has been taken as the basis in part, of this investigation, which however, under the order constituting the Court, extends to the whole of Maj. Reno's conduct as an officer on the days mentioned.

* * *

I have no attacks to make on any witness before this court, and my honest conviction is, that every witness examined has told the truth as to the facts within his knowledge as he saw them, and his opinions are more or less correct in proportion to his means of information, and perhaps his prejudices too. * * *

I believe it to be my duty, however, to represent to the Court, and to counsel for Maj. Reno as well, that prejudice either for or against a witness on account of his relations to the Army, whether officer, enlisted man or citizen, cannot for an instant be allowed to influence this inquiry in any manner whatever. To believe or disbelieve a man on account of his position solely, would pervert the ends of justice and render a trial or an inquiry a farce. I imagine that this Court will divest its mind of all such distinction and will decide this case on its merits as disclosed by the testimony.

The bias, interest, or prejudice of witnesses as far as they appear in the testimony are proper subjects of consideration in weighing the evidence, but I believe that no extraneous matters can sway this Court in giving its opinion as to Maj. Reno's conduct. The evidence of even mule-packers as to matters of fact, such as words, blows, threats to kill, and the presence of whiskey, is as good as that of anyone, however exalted, until it is contradicted. There is no material contradition in this case, even by the testimony of Maj. Reno who gives evidence in his own behalf.

The question before the Court reduced to the simplest form is as follows:

> *Was the conduct of Major Reno at the battle of the Little Big Horn, that of a brave, efficient, prudent, and obedient officer?*

This question involves:

First—The orders under which he was acting, and his obedience to those orders.

Second—His responsibility in any manner for the defeat of the 7th Cavalry in that battle and the massacre of Gen. Custer and his troops.

Third—Whether he manifested cowardice, timidity, or misbehavior in the face of the enemy in that battle, or any portion of it.

Fourth—Whether he knowingly or through negligence, abandoned Gen. Custer to his fate?

Fifth—Had he any means of informing himself as to the danger in which Gen. Custer's command was placed, and did he take all measures and make proper efforts to obtain information and act upon it?

Sixth—Were his relations or feelings toward Gen. Custer, his commanding officer, such as would lead him to obey the orders he received from that officer in a hearty spirit of vigorous and unhesitating support, or—were they those of distrust and suspicion, leading him to criticise and evade those orders, or neglect his duty; and

Lastly—Was Major Reno's conduct during those two days in any other respect unofficer-like and contrary to what should be expected or required of an officer occupying such a responsible position and at such a time?

* * *

* * * *First.* The question as to the orders under which Maj. Reno was acting is settled by the concurrent testimony of a number of witnesses all of whom swear to having heard the words. These witnesses mainly agree as to the terms of the order, though there is some variance as to the exact phraseology.

* * *

When we take into consideration the lapse of time—over two years—since these events occurred, it is reasonable to believe that the witnesses who heard this order, have stated its purport as correctly as it is possible to state it in the nature of human recollection; and it is undisputed that the tenor of the order was a clear and explicit direction to Maj. Reno to attack the Indians, with no provision expressed in words for a retreat at the discretion of that officer. The only allowance for discretion as stated by Maj. Reno himself, was with reference to the rapidity of the advance—*"at as*

fast a gait as you think prudent." In all other respects the
order was positive and peremptory.

*   *   *

We need go back no further than our late war to illustrate
the vital necessity of full and complete obedience to orders.
The failure of one subordinate commander has not infre-
quently brought disaster and defeat to an army. Boldness,
vigor and confidence have, times without number, won victory over an overwhelming foe, and seldom can it be shown
that these essential qualities of a soldier have brought defeat.

But it is urged that there was no plan; that Maj. Reno
was not consulted; that he did not know the ground. Now
a plan to attack an Indian village must of necessity be quick
of conception and rapid in execution. Gen. Custer's plan
seems to have been to strike his enemy wherever he found
him. The plan of attack was communicated to Maj. Reno
as soon as matured by his Commanding Officer and the part
assigned him was definitely stated in the order to *"move
forward as fast as you can and charge them as soon as you
find them, and we will support."* Did Maj. Reno obey that
order as fully as he could, taking into consideration the
means at his disposal and the resistance opposing him? * * *

* * * All agree that the advance to the ford was made
rapidly, that a short halt was made at the river, some of the
horses were watered there. After crossing, the companies
were soon formed in line, and ultimately galloped toward
the village in line of battle, three companies abreast. * * *

* * * After advancing down the valley Maj. Reno halted
near a point of timber and deployed a dismounted skirmish
line in the open, within long range of part of the Indian
village. This line had a support for its right flank in the
timber which bordered the stream, but its left was in air
and liable to be turned. Meantime the enemy seems, from
all the testimony, to have been hovering on his front, and

the only positive testimony given, * * * fixes it at the time the line of skirmishers was deployed and halted.

There is some conflict in testimony as to whether the skirmish line advanced after it deployed, but as there are positive statements that a part of it did advance, it seems that at least the right company moved forward for a short distance, but very soon after this the left of the line swung back, and the weight of the testimony seems to show that this was done without orders, though I believe it is not claimed by any witness that the enemy actually drove it back. The concurrent testimony of several witnesses shows that straggling parties or squads of Indians were passing to the left through the bluffs.

During the swinging back of the line Maj. Reno seems to have been on the right in the timber with a carbine, and among the men on foot. It further appears that after the withdrawal of the line from the open or the plain, the Indians who had been circling at long range became emboldened and closed in nearer the timber, passing the command and crossing its line of retreat. A party of Indians seems to have circled entirely around the command, concealing themselves in some timber very near the bank of the river in rear of this second position of the command. A very short contest then ensued at the edge of the timber after the left of the line fell back, and then Maj. Reno ordered the company commanders to withdraw their men to their horses in a small opening in the midst of the timber and to mount in column of fours. The column headed up stream and away from the Indian village. During the execution of this movement the fire of the command seems to have entirely ceased; and no definite means appear, by the testimony of any witnesses, to have been taken to cover the movement or keep back the Indians. No examination of the timber, by any person, appears to have been made by Maj. Reno's order; and he himself by his own testimony visited only that portion facing the Indian village. He states that he had made up his mind to leave the timber and get back to the right bank of the river to a high position from whence he might see the rest of the regiment or be seen by them. This he says was his determination before the men mounted. * * *

At or about the moment of starting, the party of Indians who had concealed themselves in the timber near the river, fired into the column, killing Bloody Knife and wounding a soldier. The uncontradicted testimony * * * is that Maj. Reno then shouted, "Dismount!" and immediately after "Mount!" when the whole command, or what was there, left the timber without further orders, Maj. Reno taking the lead. * * *

The manner of leaving the timber and reaching the hill is a matter of dispute among the witnesses. The companies of Capts. French and Moylan seem to have left in column of fours, headed by Maj. Reno; but "G" Company, which was originally on the right flank of the skirmish line appears to have received no definite orders to mount, beyond a rumor that the balance were leaving the timber. Maj. Reno states that he gave the order for "G" Company to Lt. McIntosh, but there is no evidence to show that it was properly communicated to the company except by rumor, the result being that many of the men of that company did not succeed in mounting and joining the column.

Lt. Varnum testifies that he heard some men say "They are going to charge! They are going to charge!" and that is the way he got the information the troops were going to leave the timber! The horses were reported to be in danger, but Lt. Varnum found them all right. It is an undisputed fact that one officer (Lt. DeRudio), at least fourteen soldiers and two citizens (Herendeen and Girard)—were left in the timber or ran back to it from the plain upon finding they had no chance of escape, and another officer—Lt. Hare— would have been left but for the merest chance or accident of having a faithful orderly. Some who attempted to escape and overtake the rapidly receding column were ridden down and butchered by a savage foe.

It is also a fact not controverted that no Indians barred or met the front of that column on its way to the river, but they harassed its right flank and rear—killing 27 men and wounding seven or eight more who succeeded in clinging to their horses until they reached the top of the hill. Maj. Reno in his official report says: "I succeeded in reaching the top of the bluff with a loss of three officers, 29 enlisted men killed and seven men wounded." Maj. Reno says nothing in his report of the wounded men left in the timber, nor of the 14 soldiers who also remained there for some time. It is quite clear that every wounded man who could not cling to his horse, and every man who was dismounted by having his horse killed under him, fell an easy prey to the Indians and are doubtless accounted for under the heading "killed." Upon reaching the river at an unknown ford, considerable confusion ensued—says Maj. Reno—Indians circled above stream within easy range and deliberately shot the men in the river and on the banks. No formation is made on the opposite bank to protect the men whose horses are plunging and rearing to get out. Even a sergeant asks why somebody don't form and keep those Indians back.

* * * All the witnesses agree that there was confusion at some part of the column, that it suffered heavily in the rear, that all the killed and wounded on the left bank of the river were abandoned to the enemy; that nothing was done to cover the crossing, and that the movement ceased on the hill when the Indians no longer pursued. It is also not disputed that Maj. Reno headed the movement as far as the river and that he was among the first to reach the top of the hill.

Was this movement a charge, a retreat, or a stampede? Maj. Reno ordered it and it was executed under his direction. He alone is responsible for that movement and no officer nor man under his command can be held accountable in the slightest degree for any result of that move from the timber. There is no stigma or discredit that can be placed upon any officer or man—the officer who ordered the move is alone responsible. The plan was Maj. Reno's, and he should have all the credit or discredit which attaches to it. It is but natural however, that almost every officer and soldier who survived that disastrous move from the timber to the hill would in his own mind, by imperceptible degrees, ultimately arrive at a conclusion that after all it was the best thing to do—and results which could not be foreseen at the time may have been taken into consideration to excuse or palliate. *Esprit de corps* is a strong inducement to participants to do this, notwithstanding they may have no responsibility in the matter. There is necessarily in the minds of the participants a sort of community of interest and most certainly their judgment and opinions cannot remain absolutely impartial. Especially is this liable to be the case after a long lapse of time when many things are forgotten—and opinions become insensibly modified or changed.

* * * Maj. Reno took the responsibility of disobeying Gen. Custer's order. He left the timber not on account of the losses that had occurred, but of what might occur. The ammunition was not half gone, though there had been a free use of it at long range. * * * Maj. Reno * * * knew that Gen. Custer said he would be supported—but Maj. Reno could look to the rear and seeing no support, he made up his mind "to get out of that." He did not wait—he stood not upon his order of going, but went at once. His casualties did not occur in charging toward the village but in going away from it! His position in the timber threatened the village and held the bulk of the warriors, perhaps nearly all—in the vicinity of his command. He had but few casualties while there, and with a judicious use of ammunition might

have remained there for several hours.

Second, the question whether or not Maj. Reno is responsible for the defeat of the 7th Cavalry and the annihilation of Gen. Custer and his five companies can only be determined by such facts or indications as appear in the testimony, as to the plans and movements of Gen. Custer.

* * *

It is settled indisputably that Gen. Custer ordered the witness, Capt. Benteen, to scour the country to the left of the main trail and that he sent him three successive orders prescribing or limiting his movements in that direction. It is also undisputed that after Gen. Custer had given Maj. Reno his orders to attack the Indians he continued his course down the river on the right bank. The last words from Gen. Custer to Maj. Reno were, "we will support you." From the time Maj. Reno started to obey the order, Gen. Custer must have been possessed of that idea, that intention; not for one moment did he forget it. His route downstream lay behind the bluffs or ridge next the river, mainly unexposed to the view of the hostile Indians. He was hurrying on at a rapid gait to strike the foe. Maj. Reno's support might not come from the rear, but he would be supported still with the sound of Custer's guns and the cheers of Custer's men in front. Maj. Reno himself says that he had no reason to believe that Gen. Custer would remain out of the fight with his five companies. Had he reflected for a moment, he must have been satisfied that Gen. Custer was near the foe and had Maj. Reno waited twenty or thirty minutes before giving the fatal order to put the river between himself and the enemy, he would have seen Capt. Benteen with his column coming from the rear—and might have heard Custer's men in front. With Reno holding the Indians near him—Benteen coming up with 250 men and Custer striking in front, there was a glorious chance for a thrice glorious victory. Maj. Reno slipped his hold and *all was lost!*

But Maj. Reno says he had no confidence in Gen. Custer. With that feeling could he have gone into the battle strong-hearted? It scarcely seems possible that one could do so.

It is only occasionally that we see men under such circumstances rising high above all danger and by a heroic example infusing confidence and courage and thus grasping the laurel of victory from the very midst of defeat. When Gen. Custer waved his hat from the bluff, he had confidence that Maj. Reno would hold on, and down the bluffs rode Custer's column to support Maj. Reno by a strong attack in flank—or rear, of the village. Ancient proverbs tell us that "Obedience is not truly performed by the body of him whose heart is dissatisfied." True obedience neither procrastinates nor questions. * * *

*   *   *

The unimpeached testimony of all the witnesses who were left in the timber by Maj. Reno is in effect that Gen. Custer went into action near the place where his body was found, as indicated by the direction from whence the sound of firing came, and at a period of time distinctly after Maj. Reno had left the timber. The nature of the country as described by all the witnesses prevented Gen. Custer from seeing Maj. Reno's command after the time at which Lt. DeRudio saw the General and his Adjutant on the bluff.

The inference from the testimony is therefore perfect that the last view had by Gen. Custer of Maj. Reno's command was when the latter was engaged; that he waved his hat signalling to Maj. Reno's command, his own cheering words to his brave men; "Courage boys." He did this doubtless with the hope of being seen by someone, and then went back to his own column to make a flank attack in support of Maj. Reno. It is undisputed save by opinion that Gen. Custer's engagement did not commence till after Maj. Reno had left the timber to retreat to the hill.

It is an undisputed fact that Gen. Custer received no

support whatever from the seven companies of his regiment which remained on the hill under Maj. Reno's command. It seems that there was indecision and tardiness, and that the move that was made downstream was not begun by Maj. Reno's orders until after the pack train had arrived. Two pack mules were sent for, each carrying 2000 rounds of ammunition, * * * and none was issued. Lt. Wallace testifies that he saw *one box* opened and men helping themselves. So it appears that Maj. Reno's command was not so badly in need of ammunition after all. * * * Maj. Reno says he did not intend moving down towards where Gen. Custer was supposed to be until after the arrival of the pack train. It was then too late; the field was lost, and Gen. Custer and the last of his men were weltering in their gore.

The true character of the struggle on Gen. Custer's field can only be definitely ascertained from Indians, and their statements are generally unreliable in such matters. Leaving out mere matters of opinion it appears to me from all the testimony that Gen. Custer's column never attempted a crossing at the ford "B". He must have gone around the head of that ravine and evidently sought to cross and attack the village lower down. The route to ford "B" was inaccessible from the bluffs except for about fifty yards at the mouth of the ravine. It seems conclusive that his struggle began soon after Maj. Reno reached the hill.

The well-known capacity, tenacity and bravery of Gen. Custer and the officers and men who died with him forbid the supposition of a panic and a rout. There was a desperate and sanguinary struggle in which the Indians must have suffered heavily. From the evidence that has been spread before this Court it is manifest that Gen. Custer and his comrades died a death so heroic that it has but few parallels in history. Fighting to the last and against overwhelming odds, they fell on the field of glory. Let no stigma of rout and panic tarnish their blood-bought fame. Their deeds of heroism will ever live in the hearts of the American people, and the painter and the poet will vie with each other in commemorating the world-wide fame of Custer and his men.

*   *   *

Third—Whether or not Maj. Reno exhibited cowardice in the battle at any time is a matter which must be more in the nature of presumptive evidence than of direct or positive proof. Though the majority of witnesses have testified that they themselves saw no direct indication of cowardice yet it must be remembered that these statements are very much in the nature of opinions. * * *

*   *   *

In considering the opinions advanced by officers and men two things must necessarily be taken into consideration: *Esprit de corps,* and the personal interest which witnesses feel—these may unconsciously shape their opinions or bias their judgment, and the testimony of impartial witnesses unbiased by either must always weigh heavily against such opinions.

Fourth—Were Gen. Custer and his command through the cowardice or negligence of Maj. Reno abandoned to their fate? The uncontradicted evidence shows that Gen. Custer did in point of fact receive no assistance from Maj. Reno, who was in command of fresh troops on the hill. The question as to culpable negligence is a matter of opinion. * * *

Fifth—Could Maj. Reno have known Gen. Custer's danger? The means of information at command of Maj. Reno as to the danger of his commanding officer are settled by the testimony of every witness save himself and Capt. Benteen.

Maj. Reno stands alone in denying in 1879 that he was informed that there was fighting down the river after he arrived on the hill, June 25, 1876. He now states that he neither heard firing nor was it reported to him at that time. In his official report he states; "We had heard firing in that direction and knew it could only be Custer." Capt. Benteen heard disputes about firing, though he heard none himself from the Custer field. Even Capt. Godfrey, who admits to be somewhat deaf, swears that he heard more or less firing from that direction. The Indians had nearly all left Maj. Reno's front and great dust and smoke were seen by several witnesses in the direction of the hostile village.

It thus seems clear from the evidence and from the fact that Maj. Reno, by his own admission, already knew the presence of a heavy force of the enemy between himself and Gen. Custer, that he had every reasonable means of knowing that his Commanding Officer was in great danger.

Sixth—The question as to the spirit in which Maj. Reno entered the battle is settled by himself in his own testimony; he says: "I had known Gen. Custer as a soldier for a long time, and I had no confidence in his ability as a soldier; I had known him all through the war." It is for the Court to determine from his own open statement and from the facts developed from the evidence whether he heartily supported his commander. Obedience is born of confidence and respect, and for some reason Maj. Reno seems to have entertained toward Gen. Custer neither of these generous sentiments. When we remember the brilliant record of the gallant Custer; the continued confidence reposed in him during an eventful war; his rapid ascension in rank and esteem in the hearts of the American people we naturally pause with astonishment that any of his subordinate commanders should despise his ability as a soldier.

The final question, as to other matters affecting Maj. Reno's conduct during the battle of June 25 and 26, is plain and clear as to facts, while opinions are as various as it is possible for them to be. The bravery of the officers and men under Maj. Reno's command during the fighting on these

two days is without question. The gallant charges made by
Capts. Benteen, Weir, McDougall, and others, merit the
highest praise; but whether the conduct of Maj. Reno was
all that could be expected or required of a Commanding
Officer is for the Court to determine from the evidence
adduced.

I desire to especially invite the attention of the Court to
the great diversity of opinions as to the number of hostile
Indians—the estimates vary all the way from 1500 to 9000
warriors, one witness thinks there were from three to six
warriors to a lodge. The moving village is described as
2½ miles long and about ½ mile wide—a dense mass as
closely packed as could be to move along. Now allowing
54 square feet for each pony, that area would contain
1,134,220 ponies; but allowing 216 square feet for each
pony would give 283,555. If there were 28,000 ponies each
one would have a space of 2160 square feet which would
make them appear somewhat scattered. Maj. Reno in his
official report says: "I think we were fighting all the Sioux
Nation, and also all the desperadoes, renegades, half-breeds
and squaw men between the Missouri and the Arkansas and
east of the Rocky Mountains, and they must have numbered
at least 2500 warriors." It will thus be seen that there are
no means of arriving at anything like a reasonably correct
estimate of the number of warriors in that hostile village.
Judging from the variety of opinions that matter can never
be settled. I fear it will forever remain involved in doubt
and obscurity.

In conclusion I wish to invite the attention of the Court
to a few brief extracts from the official report of Maj. Reno.
* * * After describing the moving off of the Indian village
on the 26th, Maj. Reno says "We now thought of Custer,
of whom nothing had been heard and nothing seen since
the firing in his direction about 6 P.M. on the evening of
the 25th and we concluded that the Indians had gotten be-

tween him and us and driven him toward the boat at the mouth of the Little Big Horn River." Capt. Benteen, in reference to his move to the left, states in his report which accompanies that of Maj. Reno that "I had then gone about fully ten miles, the ground was terribly hard on horses so I determined to carry out the other instructions, which were that if, in my judgment, there was nothing to be seen of Indians, valleys, etc., in the direction I was going, to return with the battalion to the trail the command was following."

* * *

I believe that my duty is done and I wish to express to the Court my thanks for its patience and forbearance; and to the talented and accomplished counsel who has so ably represented Maj. Reno in this inquiry, I wish to say that his connection with this case has been to me most pleasant and instructive.

* * *

The addresses on behalf of both prosecution and defense having been heard and filed in writing, the Court then deliberated in closed session, and having arrived at the following findings, adjourned sine die.

THE COURT'S FINDINGS

The Court of Inquiry assembled by Special Orders No. 255, dated Headquarters of the Army, A.G.O. Washington, November 25th, 1878, reports in obedience to that order the following facts involving the conduct of Major Marcus A. Reno, 7th Cavalry, in regard to the Battle of the Little Big Horn fought June 25 and 26th, 1876:

1st. On the morning of the 25th of June 1876 the 7th Cavalry, Lieutenant Colonel G. A. Custer commanding, operating against the hostile Indians in Montana Territory, near the Little Big Horn River, was divided into four battalions, two of which were commanded by Colonel Custer in person, with the exception of one company in charge of the pack train,—one by Major Reno and one by Captain F. W. Benteen.

This division took place from about twelve (12) to fifteen (15) miles from the scene of the battle or battles afterwards fought.

The column under Captain Benteen received orders to move to the left for an indefinite distance (to the first and second valleys) hunting Indians with orders to charge any it might meet with.

The battalion under Major Reno received orders to draw out of the column, and doing so marched parallel and only a short distance from the column commanded by Colonel Custer.

2nd. About three or four miles from what afterwards was found to be the Little Big Horn River where the fighting took place, Major Reno received orders to move forward as rapidly as he thought prudent until coming up with the Indians who were reported fleeing, he would charge them and drive everything before him, and would receive the support of the column under Colonel Custer.

3rd. In obedience to the orders (given by Colonel Custer) Captain Benteen marched to the left (south) at an angle of about forty-five degrees, but meeting an impracticable country, was forced by it to march more to his right than the angle above indicated, and nearer approaching a parallel route to the trail followed by the rest of the command.

4th. Major Reno, in obedience to the orders given him moved on at a fast trot on the main Indian trail until reaching the Little Big Horn River, which he forded, and halted for a few moments to reform his battalion.

After reforming he marched the battalion forward towards the Indian village, downstream or in a northerly direction, two companies in line of battle and one in support, until about half way to the point where he finally halted, when he brought the company in reserve, forward to the line of battle, continuing the movement at a fast trot or gallop until after passing over a distance of about two miles, when he halted and dismounted to fight on foot, at a point of timber upon which the right flank of his battalion rested.

After fighting in this formation for less than half an hour, the Indians passing to his left rear, and appearing in his front, the skirmish line was withdrawn to the timber and the fight continued for a short time, half an hour or forty-five minutes in all, when the command, or nearly all of it, was mounted, formed and at a rapid gait was withdrawn to a hill on the opposite side of the river.

In this movement one officer and about sixteen soldiers and citizens were left in the woods besides one wounded man or more, two citizens and thirteen soldiers rejoining the command afterwards.

In this retreat Major Reno's battalion lost some twenty-nine men in killed and wounded, and three officers, including Doctor DeWolf, killed.

5th. In the meantime Captain Benteen having carried out as far as was practicable the spirit of his orders, turned in the direction of the route taken by the remainder of the regiment and reaching the trail, followed it to near the crossing of the Little Big Horn, reaching there about the same time Reno's command was crossing the river in retreat lower down, and finally joined his battalion with that of Reno on the hill.

Forty minutes or an hour later the pack train which had been left behind, on the trail, by the rapid movement of the command, and the delays incident to its march, joined the united command, which then consisted of seven companies, together with about thirty (30) or thirty-five (35) men belonging to the companies under Colonel Custer.

6th. After detaching Benteen's and Reno's columns,

Colonel Custer moved with his immediate command on the trail followed by Reno to a point within about one mile of the river, where he diverged to the right (or northward) following the general direction of the river to a point about four miles below that afterwards taken by Major Reno, where he and his command were destroyed by the hostiles. The last living witness of this march, Trumpeter Martin, left Colonel Custer's command when it was about two miles distant from the field where it afterwards met its fate. There is nothing more in evidence as to this command, save that firing was heard proceeding from its direction, from about the time Reno retreated from the bottom up to the time the pack train was approaching the position on the hill.

All firing which indicated fighting was concluded before the final preparations in Major Reno's command for the movement which was afterwards attempted.

7th. After the distribution of ammunition and a proper provision for the wounded men, Major Reno's entire command moved down the river in the direction it was thought Custer's column had taken, and in which it was known General Terry's command was to be found.

This movement was carried sufficiently far to discover that its continuance would imperil the entire command, upon which it returned to the position formerly occupied, and made a successful resistance, 'till succor reached it.

The defense of the position on the hill was a heroic one against fearful odds.

The conduct of the officers throughout was excellent and while subordinates in some instances did more for the safety of the command by brilliant displays of courage than did Major Reno, there was nothing in his conduct which requires animadversion from this Court.

OPINION

It is the conclusion of this Court in view of all the facts in evidence, that no further proceedings are necessary in this case, and it expresses this opinion in compliance with the concluding clause of the order convening the Court.

JNO. H. KING,
Colonel 9th Infantry
President

J. M. LEE
1st Lieutenant & Adjutant 9th Infantry
Recorder

*   *   *

The record of proceedings having been referred to the Judge Advocate General, the latter transmitted the same to the General of the Army, with his opinion and recommendation, as follows:

War Department,
Bureau of Military Justice,
February 21, 1879

HON. GEO. W. MCCRARY,
Secretary of War.

Sir:

I have the honor to submit the record of the proceedings of a Court of Inquiry convened by order of the General of the Army at the request of *Major Marcus A. Reno, 7th Cavalry,* "for the purpose of inquiring into that officer's conduct at the battle of Little Big Horn River on the 25th and 26th days of June, 1876."

After daily sessions with scarcely an omission for twenty-six days, and the taking of much testimony, the Court arrived at conclusions which are set forth at length in the second volume of the record. The testimony taken by the Court has been examined with sufficient minuteness to justify, it is believed, an entire concurrence in the results so reached.

The statement of facts with which the Court introduces its opinion of the inexpediency of further proceedings in the case, is regarded as a very accurate summary of the testimony which describes the movements of Major Reno's command from the time it was detached from the main column by Gen. Custer's orders, until its relief by the arrival of Gen. Terry in person, after the two days engagement with the Indians under Sitting Bull. I concur with the Court in its exoneration of Major Reno from the charges of cowardice which have been brought against him, and in its conclusion that no further action is required.

The object of Gen. Custer in detaching Major Reno is shown to have been to attack the Indians simultaneously on opposite sides of their encampment or village. Their number appears to have been far greater than Gen. Custer imagined, and very far in excess of the force under his command. On Major Reno arriving within striking distance, he appears to have attacked at once, but being met by overwhelming numbers, was compelled to fall rapidly back and intrench himself on the summit of a hill a short distance from the battle field. This hill was four and a half miles by measurement from the point at which Gen. Custer lost his life. Faint firing from the direction of Custer's command was heard by some, but not by all, of Major Reno's detachment. But the testimony makes it quite clear that no one belonging to that detachment imagined the possibility of the destruction of Gen. Custer's troops; nor, had this idea suggested itself, does it seem to have been at any time within their power, fighting as they were for life under the attack of a body of Indians vastly outnumbering them, to go to his assistance. The common feeling was at the time one of anger with Gen. Custer for sending them into so dangerous a position and apparently abandoning them to their fate. The suspicion or accusation that Gen. Custer owed his death and the destruction of his command to the failure of

Major Reno, through incompetency or cowardice, to go to his relief, is considered as set at rest by the testimony taken before the present Court.

It is respectfully recommended that the conclusions of the Court be approved.

(Signed) W. M. Dunn
Judge Advocate General

The record, together with the opinion and recommendation of the Judge Advocate General was then forwarded to the General of the Army, who transmitted the same to the Secretary of War, with the following action:

Headquarters of the Army, Washington, D. C., March 5th, 1879. The findings of the Court of Inquiry in the case of Major Reno are approved and the proceedings are respectfully forwarded to the Hon. Secretary of War.

W. T. Sherman,
General.

The Secretary of War thereupon spread upon the record, the following:

FINAL APPROVAL

The proceedings and findings are approved by order of the President.

Geo. W. McCrary,
Secy. of War.

March 5, 1879.

THE UNANSWERED RIDDLE
[W.A.G.]

When and where Custer's fight began and when and where it ended; whether he was among the first or among the last to fall, are interesting subjects for discussion; and when Little Big Horn fans foregather for an evening's chat, these questions almost invariably come before the house. They have never been answered with authority, because they cannot be, though conditions on the field of battle did afford some hints that might, if properly appraised, lead to an answer of sorts. My own views as to what occurred are well known, and are as stated fully in "The Story of the Little Big Horn." But I do not wish to labor them: rather do I prefer to present the views of others whom I know to be competent and unbiased, and who do not wholly accept my premises and incline to balk at some of my conclusions. I have the honor to be associated informally, with a small group of men who have made of the Little Big Horn a life-long hobby. All experts in their chosen fields, they have transformed it from a study into what amounts almost to an avocation. They know the terrain thoroughly, and visit it time after time in search of something they think is there, but which they cannot define. Here, as succintly as I can state it, is a composite of their ideas.

Custer had with him five companies of his regiment, whose average strength, exclusive of officers, ranged close to 55 men. The number he took into action, however, is not known, for due to last minute changes and details, the strength of each company had been whittled down, until altogether there remained in his ranks approximately but 225. That figure is as near the fact as anyone can get, for whatever memoranda were carried into action were destroyed by the Indians.

The officers, including General Custer himself, counted thirteen —surely an unlucky number that day; and as is well known, all in his column were killed, officers and men alike. The bodies of three subalterns, however, were never found, and this was true also as to the bodies of several enlisted men. Because of the uncertainty that exists (and always will), as to the exact number of enlisted personnel who went in to the action, the number of the missing can never certainly be known.

Custer led the column, as was his custom, his Adjutant by his side, while immediately behind him came his color bearer with his headquarters flag, a red and blue forked pennant embellished with naked crossed sabers in white. Beside the color bearer rode his orderly trumpeter, John Martin of "H" Company, and after these the non-commissioned staff. It is doubtful that any orderlies were detailed, for the first messenger sent back after Custer and Reno separated, was Sgt. Kanipe of "C" Company, and it was unusual to detail non-coms for orderly duty. His second, and so far as is known, his last messenger, was Trumpeter Martin.

The command when last seen, was in column of twos, the "Gray Horse Troop" in the center; and the fact that a "C" Company sergeant was Custer's first messenger, leads to the belief that this Company, under the General's brother Tom, was first in the column, followed by "F", under Yates, while Smith with "E's" grays was third. Following "E" came Keogh with "I", Calhoun bringing up the rear with "L".

Whether the doomed battalion came upon the battle ridge in that order, Custer leading, no one knows. It probably was so. The bodies of his men were found in an area that covered more than a mile square, with little semblance of organization or order. The companies of Smith, Yates and Custer appear to have been thrown out toward the river, to fend against attack upon the right flank. They formed an irregular line, if it could be called a line, extending south from the battle ridge, the end deflected to the left. At the extreme left flank Calhoun occupied a smaller ridge that ran almost at right angles to the main battle ridge, and here he and all his men were butchered. On Calhoun's right, extending up toward Custer's command post at the peak of the battle ridge, died Keogh and all his company, while between him and Custer, appears to have been slain a platoon of Yates' company.

Custer's own position was on the slope of a hill that marked the termination of the battle ridge proper, and here were found, with him, nearly half the officers of the battalion; Yates and Reily of "F", Smith of "E", Tom Custer of "C" and Cooke, the Regimental Adjutant. Except for the last, their presence here is hard to understand, for in a desperate action such as was the Little Big Horn, the duty of officers is with their commands. No explanation was ever made except that by Benteen, who thought that this abnormal situation, together with the general confusion, the lack of lines—the evidences of flight, indicated panic rout. Dr. Kuhlman, it is true, in his "Legend into History," advances a theory that the three company commanders were with Custer awaiting final orders when they were killed. No military man is known who endorses this idea as tenable. The indications are that the lines were broken, the men dispersed or killed, and that the officers rallied around their commanding officer as did many enlisted men, in a desperate effort to stave off the Indians' assault, killing their mounts, behind whose carcasses they might resist to the last man and the last cartridge.

If Trumpeter Martin may be credited, Custer met opposition before he was fairly on his way to Benteen with the message to "Come on and be quick." In 1921-2 he said that after Custer returned from the edge of the bluffs "we rode on, pretty fast, until we came to a big ravine that led in the direction of the river * * * about a mile down the river from where we went on the hill," and "about three miles from where we left Reno's trail. * * * The last I saw of the command *they were going down into the ravine.* The gray horse troop was in the center * * * in a few minutes I was back on the hill where the General and I had looked at the village; *but before I got there* I heard firing back of me, and I looked around and saw Indians, some waving buffalo robes and some shooting. They had been in ambush." ("The Custer Myth," p. 290).

The "big ravine" thus described can only have been the one known as Medicine Tail Coulee which ends at ford "B." Martin's statement, however, does not make clear whether the command was *crossing* the ravine, or was heading down it toward the ford: but he is the one eye witness who definitely places Custer *in* the ravine.

As no evidences of fighting were discernible at or near the ford, the safe conclusion is that if he did ride down the ravine, he did not follow it far, but left it lower down to gain the higher ground beyond. Doubtless, Martin heard some firing and saw some Indians, but that he saw any robe waving at this stage of the fight is incredible though undoubtedly he believed he did. His testimony at the Inquiry was of less value than it should have been, for his ideas of time and distance were very vague.

Custer had another ravine to traverse before he came to the battle ridge—North Medicine Tail. It also runs down to the ford "B," and there is some evidence that when at its head, he detached one platoon of the "Gray Horse Troop" to explore its lower reaches. As he rode out upon the battle ridge, warriors of the Cheyenne, the Ogalalla, the Sans Arc and the Minneconjou, concealed among the clumps of sage that everywhere abounded, crouching in the coulees that hid them from the ridge, their ponies concealed in the many draws and small ravines nearby—opened up against him a long range fire, and things now began to happen quickly.

How long this type of fighting lasted no one knows. Dr. Kuhlman thinks it was at least an hour and a half, but if its purpose was to cause dispersal of the troops, as we believe, it is unlikely that it continued after its purpose was achieved. The time element becomes now of first importance.

Custer and Reno separated at the lone tepee about 2:15. Custer followed two-thirds of the way to the river, then turned sharply to the right: Cooke had returned from Reno's column with the news that the Indians were not running. This information Custer had not later than 2:40. Almost immediately he left off following Reno and began his fatal ride downstream "trotting or galloping all the way." Once he stopped at a water hole, long enough to water his jaded horses, then rode on.

Reno, in the meantime, had crossed the river, halted and prepared for action. He started down the valley about the same time that Custer turned to the north. At about 3 P.M. he was dismounting to fight on foot, having advanced some two miles toward the village. At this moment Lt. Varnum glanced up at the bluffs across the river and saw the Gray Horse Troop. It was, he said, not quite so far down as Point 2 on the Maguire map.

Martin turned back from Point 8 perhaps 15 minutes later— or at 3:15. His horse was jaded; the best it could do was a jog trot, and Martin, following instructions, in another 15 minutes was back on the hill from which the General had scanned the village. Reno's line, not visible before, was now in the act of changing front.

We know that Benteen joined Reno on the hill about 4:20, and that Reno had been there about 20 minutes. Working backwards, this fixes the time of Martin's return to the observation hill at approximately 3:30. Then he rode on, delivered Custer's message to Benteen and returned to Reno Hill with him.

The testimony establishes that the heavy firing heard by many of the combined command, commenced very soon after the Benteen-Reno junction. It establishes further that Weir, perturbed by the sounds of battle, mounted and rode to the north, alone but for an orderly. Edgerly, seeing him go, and believing he had secured permission to advance, mounted "D" Company, and followed. This happened not more than a half hour after their arrival on the hill. They got about one-third of the way to where Custer was found two days later, and were stopped by an Indian horde. No battle was in progress. Custer and his men were dead.

Weir started about 4:45, Edgerly following at once. They advanced at most a mile and a half. It was a little after 5 o'clock when they reached the peak known ever since as Weir's Point. It follows that Custer was destroyed some time during the half hour between 4:30 and 5 o'clock.

Where did his fight begin? Nobody knows: but under such leaders as Crazy Horse and Gall, either right flank or left may have been the point of first attack—or, again, both may have been assailed simultaneously. Where did it end? Probably on the slopes of the hill where, barricaded with the carcasses of horses, his faithful few gathered for a last desperate stand, for here was the only place on the battlefield that evidenced sustained resistance.

When did his fight begin? Again, nobody knows: but some time between 3:30 and 4:00 P.M. He probably reached the battle ridge about 4 o'clock and was immediately attacked. How long did it last? Possibly an hour altogether. Certainly no longer; probably not so long.

To attempt a reconstruction of Custer's fight is but an idle task. It must depend too heavily upon conflicting stories told at various times by various Indians. We doubt that any individual Indian could tell a comprehensive story of the battle, conceding his desire to tell the truth. We think the best, and indeed the only way, to discover authentic Indian accounts, is to look for them in various volumes that throughout the years have been published over the names of responsible authors, who have sought for truth rather than for dramatic effect, to read them, compare them and appraise them. We recommend especially "My friend the Indian" by Major James McLaughlin, for many years Indian Agent at Standing Rock; "A warrior who fought Custer" by Dr. Thomas B. Marquis, the tale of a young Cheyenne who was in the fight; "Custer's Last Battle," by General E. S. Godfrey; "The North American Indian" by Curtis, "The Arikara Narrative," an official publication of the Historical Society of North Dakota. The collection of Sioux accounts in Colonel Graham's "The Custer Myth," is likewise a treasure trove. In all these one finds some portions of the truth, but not the whole truth in any.

EXHIBIT NO. 4

HEADQUARTERS 7TH U. S. CAVALRY,

CAMP ON YELLOWSTONE RIVER,

JULY 5, 1876.

Captain E. W. Smith,
A. D.C. and A. A. A. G.

The command of the regiment having devolved upon me as the senior surviving officer from the battle of the 25th and 26th of June between the 7th Cavalry and Sitting Bull's band of hostile Sioux on the Little Big Horn River, I have the honor to submit the following report of its operations from the time of leaving the main column until the command was united in the vicinity of the Indian village.

The regiment left the camp at the mouth of the Rosebud river after passing in review before the Department Commander under command of Brevet Major General G. A. Custer, Lieutenant Colonel, on the afternoon of the 22nd of June and marched up the Rosebud twelve miles and encamped:—23d marched up the Rosebud passing many old Indian camps and following a very large lodge-pole trail, but not fresh, making thirty-three (33) miles: 24th the march was continued up the Rosebud, the trail and signs freshening with every mile until we had made twenty-eight (28) miles, and we then encamped and waited for information from the scouts: at 9-25 p.m. Custer called the officers together and informed us that beyond a doubt the village was in the valley of the Little Big Horn, and in order to reach it, it was necessary to cross the divide between the Rosebud and the Little Big Horn, and it would be impossible to do so in the day time without discovering our march to the Indians; that we would prepare to march at 11 p.m.; this was done, the line of march turning from the Rosebud to the right up one of its branches which headed near the summit of the divide. About 2 a.m. of the 25th the scouts told him that he could not cross the divide before daylight. We then made coffee and rested for three hours, at the expiration of which time the march was resumed, the divide crossed and about 8 a.m. the command was in the valley of one of the branches of the Little Big Horn; by this time Indians had been seen and it was certain that we could not surprise them and it was determined to move at once to the attack. Previous to this no division of the regiment had been made since the order had been issued on the Yellowstone annulling wing and battalion organizations, but Custer informed me that he would assign commands on the march.

I was ordered by Lieutenant W. W. Cook, Adjutant, to assume command of companies M. A. and G.; Captain Benteen of companies H. D. and K., Custer retained C. E. F. I. and L. under his immediate command and company B, Captain McDougall, in rear of the pack train.

I assumed command of the companies assigned to me and without any definite orders moved forward with the rest of the column and well to its left. I saw Benteen moving farther to the left and as they passed he told me he had orders to move well to the left and sweep everything before him. I did not see him again until about 2-30 p.m. The command moved down the creek towards the Little Big Horn valley, Custer with five companies on the right bank, myself and three companies on the left bank and Benteen farther to the left and out of sight. As we approached a deserted village, and in which was standing one tepee, about 11 a.m. Custer motioned me to cross to him, which I did, and moved nearer to his column until about 12-30 a.m. [p.m.] when Lieutenant Cook, Adjutant, came to me and said the village was only two miles ahead and running away; to move forward at as rapid a gait as prudent and to charge afterwards, and that the whole outfit would support me. I think those were his exact words. I at once took a fast trot and moved down about two miles where I came to a ford of the river. I crossed immediately and halted about ten minutes or less to gather the battalion, sending word to Custer that I had everything in front of me and that they were strong. I deployed and with the Ree scouts on my left charged down the valley driving the Indians with great ease for about 2½ miles. I however soon saw that I was being drawn into some trap as they would certainly fight harder and especially as we were nearing their village, which was still standing, besides I could not see Custer or any other support and at the same time the very earth seemed to grow Indians and they were running towards me in swarms and from all directions. I saw I must defend myself and give up the attack mounted. This I did, taking possession of a point of woods, and which furnished (near its edge) a shelter for the horses, dismounted and fought them on foot. Making headway through the woods I soon found myself in the near vicinity of the village, saw that I was fighting odds of at least five to one and that my only hope was to get out of the woods where I would soon have been surrounded, and gain some high ground. I accomplished this by mounting and charging the Indians between me and the bluffs on the opposite side of the river. In this charge 1st Lieutenant Donald McIntosh, 2nd Lieutenant Benj. H. Hodgson, 7th Cavalry and A. A. Surgeon J. M. DeWolf were killed. I succeeded in reaching the top of the bluff with a loss of three officers and twenty-nine enlisted men killed, and seven men wounded. Almost at the same time I reached the top, mounted men were seen to be coming towards us and it proved to be Colonel Benteen's battalion, companies H. D. and K. We joined forces and in a short time the pack train came up. As senior my command was then A. B. D. G. H. K. M., about 380 men and the following officers, Captains Benteen, Weir, French and McDougall, 1st Lieutenants Godfrey, Mathey and Gibson, and 2d Lieutenants Edgerly, Wallace, Varnum and Hare and A. A. Surgeon Porter. 1st Lieutenant DeRudio was in the dismounted fight in the woods but having some trouble with his horse, did not join the command in the charge out, and hiding himself in the woods joined the command after night-fall of the 26th. Still hearing nothing of Custer and with this reinforcement, I moved down the river in the direction of the village, keeping on the bluffs. We had heard firing in that direction and knew it could only be Custer. I moved to the summit of the highest bluff but seeing and hearing nothing, sent Capt. Weir with his company to open communication with him. He soon sent back word by Lieut. Hare that he could go no further and that the Indians

were getting around him. At this time he was keeping up a heavy
fire from his skirmish line. I at once turned everything back to
the first position I had taken on the bluff and which seemed to
be the best. I dismounted the men and had the horses and mules
of the pack train driven together in a depression, put the men
on the crests of the hills making the depression and had hardly
done so when I was furiously attacked,—this was about six p.m.
We held our ground with a loss of eighteen enlisted men killed
and forty-six wounded until the attack ceased about 9 p.m. As
I knew by this time their overwhelming numbers and had given
up any hope of support from that portion of the regiment with
Custer, I had the men dig rifle pits; barricaded with dead horses
and mules and boxes of hard bread the opening of the depression towards the Indians in which the animals were herded, and
made every exertion to be ready for what I saw would be a
terrific assault the next day. All this night the men were busy,
and the Indians holding a scalp dance underneath us in the
bottom and in our hearing. On the morning of the 26th I felt
confident that I could hold my own and was ready as far as I
could be when at daylight about 2-30 a.m. I heard the crack of
two rifles. This was the signal for the beginning of a fire that
I have never seen equalled. Every rifle was handled by an expert
and skilled marksman and with a range that exceeded our carbine, and it was simply impossible to show any part of the body
before it was struck. We could see as the day brightened, count-
less hordes of them pouring up the valley from out the village,
and scampering over the high points towards the places designated for them by their chiefs and which entirely surrounded
our position. They had sufficient numbers to completely encircle
us, and men were struck from opposite sides of the lines and
where the shots were fired. I think we were fighting all the Sioux
nation, and also all the desperadoes, renegades, half-breeds and
squawmen between the Missouri and the Arkansas and east of
the Rocky mountains, and they must have numbered at least
twenty-five hundred warriors. The fire did not slacken until about
9-30 a.m. and then we found they were making a last desperate
effort and which was directed against the lines held by companies H. and M. In this charge they came close enough to use

their bows and arrows, and one man lying dead within our lines was touched with the coup stick of one of the foremost Indians. When I say the stick was only ten or twelve feet long, some idea of the desperate and reckless fighting of these people may be understood. This charge of theirs was gallantly repulsed by the men on that line led by Colonel Benteen. They also came close enough to send their arrows into the line held by Co's. D. and K., but were driven away by a like charge of the line which I accompanied. We now had many wounded and the question of water was vital, as from 6 p.m. of the previous evening until near 10 a.m., about 16 hours, we had been without.

A skirmish line was formed under Colonel Benteen to protect the descent of volunteers down the hill in front of his position to reach the water. We succeeded in getting some canteens although many of the men were hit in doing so. The fury of the attack was now over, and to our astonishment the Indians were seen going in parties toward the village. But two solutions occurred to us for this movement, that they were going for something to eat, more ammunition (as they had been throwing arrows) or that Custer was coming. We took advantage of this lull to fill all vessels with water, and soon had it by camp kettles full. But they continued to withdraw and all firing ceased soon; [except] occasional shots from sharp-shooters sent to annoy us about the water. About 2 p.m. the grass in the bottom was set on fire and followed up by Indians who encouraged its burning, and it was evident to me it was done for a purpose, and which purpose I discovered later on, to be the creation of a dense cloud of smoke behind which they were packing and preparing to move their village. It was between six and seven p.m. that the village came out from behind the dense clouds of smoke and dust. We had a close and good view of them as they filed away in the direction of Big Horn Mountains, moving in almost perfect military order. The length of the column was fully equal to that of a large division of the Cavalry Corps of the Army of the Potomac as I have seen it in its march.

We now thought of Custer, of whom nothing had been seen and nothing heard since the firing in his direction about six p.m. on the eve of the 25th, and we concluded that the Indians had gotten between him and us, and driven him towards the boat at the mouth of the Little Big Horn River. The awful fate that did befall him never occurred to any of us as within the limits of possibility.

During the night I changed my position in order to secure an unlimited supply of water and was prepared for their return, feeling sure they would do so, as they were in such numbers; but early in the morning of the 27th and while we were on the *qui vive* for Indians, I saw with my glass a dust some distance down the valley. There was no certainty for some time what they were, but finally I satisfied myself they were cavalry, and if so could only be Custer, as it was ahead of the time that I understood that General Terry could be expected. Before this time however, I had written a communication to General Terry and three volunteers were to try and reach him. I had no confidence in the Indians with me and could not get them to do anything. If this dust were Indians, it was possible they would not expect anyone to leave. The men started and were told to go as near as it was safe to determine whether the approaching column was white men, and to return at once in case they found it so; but if they were Indians to push on to General Terry. In a short time we saw them returning over the high bluffs already alluded to. They were accompanied by a scout who had a note from Terry to Custer, saying Crow scouts had come to camp saying he had been whipped but that it was not believed. I think it was about 10-30 a.m. that General Terry rode into my lines; and the fate of Custer and his brave men was soon determined by Captain Benteen proceeding with his company to his battle ground, and where was recognized the following officers who were surrounded by the dead bodies of many of their men: General G. A. Custer; Col. W. W. Cook, Adjutant; Captains M. W. Keogh, G. W. Yates, and T. W. Custer; 1st Lieuts. A. E. Smith, James Calhoun; 2nd Lieutenants W. V. Reily of the 7th Cavalry, and J. J. Crittenden of the 20th Infantry, temporarily attached to this regiment. The bodies of Lieutenant J. E. Porter and 2nd Lieutenants H. M. Harrington and J. G. Sturgis, 7th Cavalry and Assistant Surgeon G. W. Lord, U.S.A., were not recognized, but there is every reasonable probability they were killed. It was now certain that the column of five companies with Custer had been killed.

The wounded in my lines were during the afternoon and eve of the 27th, moved to the camp of Gen'l Terry, and at 5 a.m. of the 28th I proceeded with the regiment to the battle ground of Custer and buried 204 bodies, including the following named citizens: Mr. Boston Custer, Mr. Reed (a young nephew of General Custer) and Mr. Kellogg, a correspondent for the New York Herald. The following named citizens and Indians who were with my command were also killed: Charles Reynolds (guide and hunter); Isaiah Dorman (colored) interpreter; Bloody Knife who fell from immediately by my side; Bobtail Bull and Stab of the Indian scouts.

After traveling over his trail, it is evident to me that Custer intended to support me by moving further down the stream and attacking the village in flank, that he found the distance greater to the ford than he anticipated; that he did charge, but his march had taken so long, although his trail shows he had moved rapidly, that they were ready for him. That Co's. C. and I. and perhaps part of E. crossed to the village or attempted it, at the charge; were met by a staggering fire, and that they fell back to find a position from which to defend themselves, but they were followed too closely by the Indians to permit time to form any kind of line. I think had the regiment gone in as a body, and from the woods from which I fought advanced upon the village, its destruction was certain. But he was fully confident they were running away or he would not have turned from me. I think (after the great number of Indians there were in the village) that the following reasons obtain for the misfortune. His rapid marching for two days and one night before the fight; attacking in the daytime at 12 M and when they were on the *qui vive* instead of early in the morning, and lastly his unfortunate division of the regiment into three commands.

During my fight with the Indians I had the heartiest support from officers and men, but the conspicuous service of Bvt. Col. F. W. Benteen, I desire to call attention to especially; for if ever a soldier deserved recognition by his government for distinguished service, he certainly does. I enclose herewith his report of the operations of his battalion from the time of leaving the regiment until we joined commands on the hill. I also enclose an accurate list of casualties as far as it can be made at the present time, separating them into two lists: "A", those killed in General Custer's command; "B", those killed and wounded in the command I had. The number of Indians killed can only be approximated until we hear through the Agencies. I saw the bodies of 18 and Captain Ball, 2d Cavalry, who made a scout of thirteen miles over their trail says that their graves were many along their line of march. It is simply impossible that numbers of them should not be hit in the several charges they made so close to my lines. They made their approaches through the deep gulches that led from the hill top to the river, and when the jealous care with which the Indian guards the bodies of killed and wounded is considered, it is not astonishing that their bodies were not found. It is probable that the stores left by them, and destroyed the next two days, was to make room for many of them on their travois. The harrowing sight of the dead bodies crowning the height on which Custer fell, and which will remain vividly in my memory until death, is too recent for me not to ask the good people of this country whether a policy that sets opposing parties in the field armed, clothed and equipped by one and the same government should not be abolished.

All of which is respectfully submitted.

(Signed) M. A. RENO,
Major 7th Cavalry,
Com'd'g Regiment.

Official
(S'G'D) R. P. HUGHES,
Captain 3d Inf't'y. A.D.C.

A true copy:

Headquarters Department of Dakota,
Saint Paul, Minn., January 9", 1879

GEO. D. RUGGLES,
Assistant Adjutant General.

EXHIBIT NO. 6

LIST OF CASUALTIES IN 7TH REGIMENT OF U. S. CAVALRY
DURING THE BATTLES ON LITTLE BIG HORN RIVER WITH
SITTING BULL'S BAND OF HOSTILE SIOUX ON THE 25TH AND
26TH OF JUNE, 1876

KILLED

Company	Name	Rank
Field & Staff	George A. Custer	Bvt. Maj. Genl. U.S.A.
Field & Staff	W. W. Cook	Bvt. Lt. Col. U.S.A.
Field & Staff	Lord	Asst. Surg. U.S.A.
Field & Staff	J. M. DeWolf	Act'g Asst. Surg. U.S.A.
N. C. Staff	W. W. Sharrow	Sergt. Maj.
N. C. Staff	Henry Voss	Chief Trptr.
A	Henry Dalious	Corpl.
A	George H. King	Corpl.
A	John E. Armstrong	Pvt.
A	James Drinan	Pvt.
A	William Moody	Pvt.
A	James McDonald	Pvt.
A	Richard Rawlins	Pvt.
A	John Sullivan	Pvt.
A	Thomas P. Switzer	Pvt.
B	Benj. Hodgson	2nd Lt.
B	Richard Doran	Pvt.
B	George Mack	Pvt.
C	Thos. W. Custer	Bvt. Lt. Col. U.S.A.
C	H. M. Harrington*	2nd Lt.
C	Edwin Bobo	1st Sergt.
C	Finley	Sergt.
C	Finkle	
C	French	Corpl.
C	Foley	Corpl.
C	Ryan	Corpl.
C	Allen	Pvt.
C	Criddle	Pvt.
C	King	Pvt.

Company	Name	Rank
C	Bucknell	Pvt.
C	Eisman	Pvt.
C	Engle	Pvt.
C	Brightfield	Pvt.
C	Farrand	Pvt.
C	Griffin	Pvt.
C	Hawel	Pvt.
C	Hattisoll	Pvt.
C	Kingsoutz	Pvt.
C	Lewis	Pvt.
C	Mayer	Pvt.
C	Mayer	Pvt.
C	Phillips	Pvt.
C	Russell	Pvt.
C	Rix	Pvt.
C	Reuter	Pvt.
C	Short	Pvt.
C	Shea	Pvt.
C	Shade	Pvt.
C	Stuart	
C	St. John	Pvt.
C	Thadius	Pvt.
C	Van Allen	Pvt.
C	Warren	Pvt.
C	Wyndham	Pvt.
C	Wright	Pvt.
D	Vincent Charlie	Farrier
D	Patrick Golden	Pvt.
D	Edward Hansen	Pvt.
E	A. E. Smith	Bvt. Capt. U.S.A.
E	J. Sturgis*	2nd Lt.
E	Fred. Hohmeyer	1st Sergt.
E	Ogden	Sergt.
E	James	Sergt.
E	Hagan	Corpl.
E	Mason	Corpl.
E	Blorn (Brown?)	Corpl.
E	Meyer	Corpl.
E	McElroy	Trpt.
E	Mooney	Trpt.
E	Baker	Pvt.
E	Boyle	Pvt.
E	Bauth	Pvt.

Company	Name	Rank
E	Connor	Pvt.
E	Darring	Pvt.
E	Davis	Pvt.
E	Farrell	Pvt.
E	Hiley	Pvt.
E	Huber	Pvt.
E	Hime	Pvt.
E	Henderson	Pvt.
E	Henderson	Pvt.
E	Leddisson	Pvt.
E	O'Connor	Pvt.
E	Rood	Pvt.
E	Reese	Pvt.
E	Smith 1st	Pvt.
E	Smith 2nd	Pvt.
E	Smith 3rd	Pvt.
E	Stella	Pvt.
E	Stafford	Pvt.
E	Schoole	Pvt.
E	Smallwood	Pvt.
E	Tarr	Pvt.
E	VanSant	Pvt.
E	Walker	Pvt.
E	Brogen	Pvt.
E	Knicht	Pvt.
F	G. W. Yates	Captain
F	W. Van Reilly	2nd Lt.
F	Kenney	1st Sgt.
F	Nursey	Sgt.
F	Vickory	Sgt.
F	Wilkinson	Sgt.
F	Colman	Corpl.
F	Teeman	Corpl.
F	Briody	Corpl.
F	Brandon	Farrier
F	Manning	Blk. Smith
F	Atchison	Private
F	Brown 1st	Private
F	Brown 2nd	Private
F	Bruce	Private
F	Brady	Private
F	Burnham	Private
F	Cather	Private
F	Carney	Private

Company	Name	Rank
F	Dohman	Private
F	Donnelly	Private
F	Gardiner	Private
F	Hammon	Private
F	Kline	Private
F	Knauth	Private
F	Luman	Private
F	Losse	Private
F	Milton Jos	Private
F	Madson	Private
F	Monroe	Private
F	Audden	Private
F	Omeling	Private
F	Sicfous	Private
F	Sanders	Private
F	Warren	Private
F	Way	Private
F	Lerock	Private
F	Kelley	Private
G	Donald McIntosh	1st Lt.
G	Edward Botzer	Sgt.
G	M. Considine	Sgt.
G	Jas. Martin	Corpl.
G	Otto Hageman	Corpl.
G	Benj. Wells	Farrier
G	Henry Dose	Trptr.
G	Crawford Selby	Saddler
G	Benj. F. Rogers	Pvt.
G	Andred J. Moore	Pvt.
G	John J. McGinniss	Pvt.
G	Edward Stanley	Pvt.
G	Henry Seafferman	Pvt.
G	John Rapp	Pvt.
H	Geo. Lell	Corpl.
H	Julian D. Jones	Corpl.
H	Thos. E. Meador	Corpl.
I	M. W. Keogh	Bvt. Lt. Col.
I	J. E. Porter*	1st Lieut.
I	F. E. Varden	1st Sgt.
I	J. Bustard	Sergt.
I	John Wild	Corpl.
I	G. C. Morris	Corpl.
I	S. F. Staples	Corpl.

Company	Names	Rank
I	J. McGucker	Trptr.
I	J. Patton	Trptr.
I	H. A. Bailey	Blksmith
I	J. F. Broadhurst	Pvt.
I	J. Barry	Pvt.
I	J. Connors	Pvt.
I	T. P. Downing	Pvt.
I	E. C. Driscoll	Pvt.
I	D. C. Gillette	Pvt.
I	G. H. Gross	Pvt.
I	E. P. Holcomb	Pvt.
I	M. E. Horn	Pvt.
I	Adam Hetismer	Pvt.
I	P. Kelley	Pvt.
I	Fred. Lehman	Pvt.
I	Henry Lehman	Pvt.
I	E. P. Lloyd	Pvt.
I	A. McIhargey	Pvt.
I	J. Mitchell	Pvt.
I	J. Noshang	Pvt.
I	J. O'Bryan	Pvt.
I	J. Parker	Pvt.
I	F. J. Pitter	Pvt.
I	Geo. Post	Pvt.
I	Jas. Quinn	Pvt.
I	William Reed	Pvt.
I	J. W. Rossbury	Pvt.
I	D. L. Symms	Pvt.
I	J. E. Troy	Pvt.
I	Chas. VonBramer	Pvt.
I	W. B. Whaley	Pvt.
K	D. Winney	1st Sgt.
K	R. Hughes	Sgt.
K	J. J. Callahan	Corpl.
K	Julius Helmer	Trumpeter
K	Eli U. T. Clair	Pvt.
L	James Calhoun	1st Lt.
L	J. J. Crittenden	Lt. 20 **Inftry.**
L	Butler	1st Sgt.
L	Warren	Sgt.
L	Harrison	Corpl.
L	Gilbert	Corpl.
L	Seiller	Corpl.

Company	Names	Rank
L	Walsh	Trumpeter
L	Adams	Pvt.
L	Assdely	Pvt.
L	Burke	Pvt.
L	Cheever	Pvt.
L	McGill	Pvt.
L	McCarthy	Pvt.
L	Dugan	Pvt.
L	Maxwell	Pvt.
L	Scott	Pvt.
L	Babcock	Pvt.
L	Perkins	Pvt.
L	Tarbox	Pvt.
L	Dye	Pvt.
L	Tessier	Pvt.
L	Galvin	Pvt.
L	Graham	Pvt.
L	Hamilton	Pvt.
L	Rodgers	Pvt.
L	Snow	Pvt.
L	Hughes	Pvt.
L	Miller	Pvt.
L	Tweed	Pvt.
L	Vetter	Pvt.
L	Cashan	Pvt.
L	Keefe	Pvt.
L	Andrews	Pvt.
L	Crisfield	Pvt.
L	Harrington	Pvt.
L	Haugge	Pvt.
L	Kavanaugh	Pvt.
L	Lobering	Pvt.
L	Mahoney	Pvt.
L	Schmidt	Pvt.
L	Simon	Pvt.
L	Semenson	Pvt.
L	Riebold	Pvt.
L	O'Connell	Pvt.
M	Miles F. O'Hara	Sergt.
M	Henry M. Scollin	Corpl.
M	Fred. Stringer	Corpl.
M	Henry Gordon	Pvt.
M	H. Klotzbrusher	Pvt.
M	G. Lawrence	Pvt.

Company	Names	Rank
M	W. D. Meyer	Pvt.
M	G. E. Smith	Pvt.
M	D. Somers	Pvt.
M	J. Tanner	Pvt.
M	H. Turley	Pvt.
M	H. C. Vogt.	Pvt.
	Boston Custer	Civilian
	Arthur Reed	Civilian
	Mark Kellog	Civilian
	Chas. Reynolds	Civilian
	Frank C. Mann	Civilian

Indian Scouts

Bloody Knife
Bobtailed Bull
Stab

Total number of commissioned Officers killed 14

Act'g. Asst. Surg. 1

Enlisted men 247

Civilians 5

Indian Scouts 3

* The bodies of Lts. Harrington, Sturgis and Porter were not found, but it is reasonably certain that they were killed.

List of Wounded in 7th Regiment U. S. Cavalry during the Battle on Little Big Horn River with Sitting Bull's Band of Hostile Sioux on the 25th and 26th of June 1876

Company	Names	Rank
A	William Heyn	1st Sergt.
A	Jacob Deal	Pvt.
A	Samuel Foster	Pvt.
A	Frederick Homestead	Pvt.
A	Francis M. Reeves	Pvt.
A	Elijah T. Stroud	Pvt.
B	William M. Smith	Corpl.
B	Chas. Cunningham	Pvt.
C	Chas. Bennett	Pvt.
C	Maguire	Pvt.
C	Thompson	Pvt.
C	Whittaker	Pvt.
D	Patrick McDonald	Pvt.
E	Jas. T. Reilly	Sergt.
G	Jas. P. Boyle	Pvt.
G	Chas. Camell	Pvt.
G	John McVey	Pvt.
G	John Morrison	Pvt.
H	Joseph McCurry	1st Sergt.
H	Patrick Connelly	Sergt.
H	Thos. McLaughlin	Sergt.
H	John Pahl	
H	William Ramel	Trmptr.
H	Otto Voit	Saddler
H	Henry Bishley	Pvt.
H	Chas. H. Bishop	Pvt.
H	Alex B. Bishop	Pvt.
H	John Cooper	Pvt.
H	Henry Black	Pvt.
H	Wm. Farley	Pvt.
H	Wm. George	Pvt.
H	Thos. Hughes	Pvt.
H	John Muller	Pvt.

291

Company	Names	Rank
H	John Phillips	Pvt.
H	Samuel Severes	Pvt.
H	William C. Williams	Pvt.
H	Charles Windolph	Pvt.
I	David Cooney	Pvt.
K	Patrick Corcoran	Pvt.
K	Michael Madden	Pvt.
K	Max Milke	Pvt.
L	Thos Marshall	Pvt.
M	Patrick Carey	Pvt.
M	Charles White	Pvt.
M	Daniel Newall	Blksmith
M	Frank Braun	Pvt.
M	John H. Meyer	Pvt.
M	William E. Morris	Pvt.
M	Roman Rutten	Pvt.
M	Thos. P. Warner	Pvt.
M	Jas. Wilbur	Pvt.
M	Chas. Wiedman	Pvt.

The above is approximate. The absence of all company records and the loss of 7 1st Sergts. has rendered it almost impossible to account for all the men at the present time.

> M. A. RENO,
> *Major 7" Cavalry.*
> *Commanding Regiment.*

1ST ENDORSEMENT

Headquarters Department of Dakota—Saint Paul, Minn.

> July 10" 1876.

Respectfully forwarded to Headquarters Military Division of the Missouri—269 bodies have heretofore been reported buried. This report accounts for 260 only. I have understood unofficially that there are 23 men missing. Some of these 23 were undoubtedly buried but were not recognized.

> Signed GEO. D. RUGGLES,
> *Asst. Adjt. General.*

For and in the absence of the Brig. Genl. Commandg.

2ND ENDORSEMENT

Headquarters Mil. Div. Mo.
Chicago, July 13, 1876.
Respectfully forwarded to the Adjutant General of the Army.
(Signed) P. H. SHERIDAN
Lieutenant General.
Commanding.

Official copy
E. D. TOWNSEND.
Adjutant General.
A. G. Office,
Jan. 9, 1879

It is obvious that these lists were made up in the field, without records,
as some of the names listed do not appear at all in subsequent lists, and
many of the names correctly included are incorrectly spelled. Corrected
lists were made on muster rolls ante-dated to June 30, 1876.

EXHIBIT NO. 9

Headquarters of the Army,
Adjutant General's Office,
Washington, August 10, 1876.

Major M. A. Reno
7th Cavalry
(Through Headquarters Military Division of the Missouri)
Sir:

Referring to the petition of the enlisted men of the 7th Cavalry (forwarded by you the 15th ultimo) for the promotion of yourself and other officers of the regiment who participated in the engagement of June 25, 1876, I have the honor to enclose herewith, for the information of the officers and enlisted men concerned, a copy of the remarks of the General of the Army with reference to the request contained in the petition.

Very respectfully,
Your obedient Servant
(signed) E. D. TOWNSEND,
Adjutant General.

A true copy:

J. M. LEE
1st Lieut. and Adjt. 9th Infantry.
Recorder

EXHIBIT NO. 10

Camp near Big Horn on Yellowstone River,
July 4th, 1876.

To his Excellency the President and the Honorable Representatives of the United States.

Gentlemen:

We the enlisted men the survivors of the battle on the Heights of Little Horn River, on the 25th and 26th of June 1876, of the 7th Regiment of Cavalry who subscribe our names to this petition, most earnestly solicit the President and Representatives of our Country, that the vacancies among the Commissioned Officers of our Regiment, made by the slaughter of our brave, heroic, now lamented Lieutenant Colonel George A. Custer, and the other noble dead Commissioned Officers of our Regiment who fell close by him on the bloody field, daring the savage demons to the last, be filled by the Officers of the Regiment only. That Major M. A. Reno, be our Lieutenant Colonel vice Custer, killed; Captain F. W. Benteen our Major vice Reno, promoted. The other vacancies to be filled by officers of the Regiment by seniority. Your petitioners know this to be contrary to the established rule of promotion, but prayerfully solicit a deviation from the usual rule in this case, as it will be conferring a bravely fought for and a justly merited promotion on officers who by their bravery, coolness and decision on the 25th and 26th of June 1876, saved the lives of every man now living of the 7th Cavalry who participated in the battle, one of the most bloody on record and one that would have ended with the loss of life of every officer and enlisted man on the field only for the position taken by Major Reno, which we held with bitter tenacity against fearful odds to the last.

To support this assertion—had our position been taken 100 yards back from the brink of the heights overlooking the river we would have been entirely cut off from water; and from behind those heights the Indian demons would have swarmed in hundreds picking off our men by detail, and before midday June 26th not an officer or enlisted man of our Regiment would have been left to tell of our dreadful fate as we then would have been completely surrounded.

With prayerful hope that our petitions be granted, we have the honor to forward it through our Commanding Officer.

Very Respectfully,

The above petition was signed by 236 enlisted survivors. The original record does not indicate that the signatures were introduced in evidence. They are, therefore, not reproduced here. Photostatic copies of these signatures were made during 1922, but many were even then illegible, most of them having been signed with pencil. Neither the original petition nor any copy thereof was attached to the original record as an exhibit.

EXHIBIT NO. 11

Headquarters Army of the
United States, Washington,
D. C., August 5, 1876.

The judicious and skilful conduct of Major Reno and Captain Benteen is appreciated, but the promotions caused by General Custer's death have been made by the President and confirmed by the Senate; therefore this petition cannot be granted. When the Sioux campaign is over I shall be most happy to recognize the valuable services of both officers and men by granting favors or recommending actual promotion.

Promotion on the field of battle was Napoleon's favorite method of stimulating his officers and soldiers to deeds of heroism, but it is impossible in our service because commissions can only be granted by the President on the advice and consent of the Senate, and except in original vacancies, promotion in a regiment is generally if not always made on the rule of seniority.

(signed) W. T. SHERMAN,
General.

Official
(sgd.) E. D. TOWNSEND,
Adjutant General.
A true copy
J. M. LEE
1st Lieut. and Adjt. 9th Infantry.
Recorder

APPENDIX

MILITARY HISTORY OF MAJOR MARCUS A. RENO, SEVENTH CAVALRY
(Condensed from Cullom's Record of West Point Graduates)

Cadet Military Academy, Sept. 1, 1851 to July 1, 1857. Brevet Second Lieutenant of Dragoons, July 1, 1857. On frontier duty at Fort Walla Walla, Washington, 1858-59, scouting, 1859. (Second Lieut., 1st Dragoons, June 14, 1858). Fort Dalles, Oregon, 1859, and Fort Walla Walla, Washington, 1859-61.

First Lieutenant, 1st Dragoons, April 25, 1861; First Cavalry, August 3, 1861.

Service during the Rebellion of the Seceding States, 1861-1866. (Captain 1st Cavalry, November 12, 1861) in Defenses of Washington, January to March 1862; in Virginia Peninsular Campaign (Army of the Potomac) March to August, 1862; being engaged in Siege of Yorktown April 5 to May 4, 1862; Battle of Williamsburg, May 4-5, 1862; Battle of Mechanicsville, June 26, 1862; Battle of Gaines' Mill, June 27, 1862; Battle of Glendale, June 30, 1862, and Battle of Malvern Hill July 1, 1862. In command 1st Cavalry (Army of the Potomac), in the Maryland Campaign, September-October, 1862; being engaged in the Combat at Crampton's Gap, September 14, 1862; Battle of Antietam, September 17, 1862 and Skirmish at Sharpsburg, September 19, 1862. On Detached service October-November, 1862. In the Rappahannock Campaign (Army of the Potomac) December 1862 to March, 1863; being engaged in Action at Kelly's Ford, Virginia, March 17, 1863.

(Brevet Major March 17, 1863, *for gallant and meritorious services* in Action at Kelly's Ford, Virginia). On leave of absence, disabled by injuries received at Kelly's Ford, March 18, to May 1, 1863. On Recruiting service May 1 to June 20, 1863; as Chief of General W. F. Smith's Staff, with Pennsylvania Militia, June 20 to July 12, 1863; being engaged in a Skirmish at Hagerstown, Maryland, July 10, 1863; on Recruiting service July 12 to October 1, 1863. On the Rappahannock (Army of the Potomac) October 1863 to March 1864; as Assistant in the Cavalry Bureau at Washington, D. C., March-May 1864; as Acting Assistant Inspector-

General of 1st Division of Cavalry Corps (Army of the Potomac), in the Richmond Campaign, May to August 1864; being engaged in the Battle of Hawes' Shop, May 28, 1864; Battle of Cold Harbor, May 31 to June 1, 1864; Battle of Trevillian Station, June 11, 1864; Action at Darbytown, July 28, 1864, and various Skirmishes, June-July, 1864; as Chief of Staff of the Cavalry in the Shenandoah Campaign, August 9, 1864 to January 1, 1865, being engaged in the Skirmishes at Winchester, Aug. 16, Kearneysville, August 25 and Smithfield, August 29, 1864, and Battle of Cedar Creek, October 19, 1864.

(Brevet Lieutenant-Colonel October 19, 1864 *for gallant and meritorious services* at the Battle of Cedar Creek, Virginia); (Colonel, 12th Pennsylvania Cavalry Volunteers, January 1 to July 20, 1864); in command of Brigade January to July 1865; being engaged in a Skirmish at Harmony, Virginia, with Mosby's Guerillas, March, 1865.

(Brevet Colonel, March 13, 1865, *for gallant and meritorious services* during the Rebellion.)

(Brevet Brigadier-General, U. S. Volunteers, March 13, 1865, *for gallant and meritorious services* during the Rebellion.)

At the Military Academy, as Assistant Instructor of Infantry Tactics, August 31, to October 2, 1865; at New Orleans, Louisiana, in Freedmen's Bureau, December 4, 1865 to August 28, 1866; on leave of absence August 28, 1866 to February 8, 1867; in conducting Recruits to California, April, 1867; on frontier duty at Fort Vancouver, Washington, May 6 to June 22, 1867; as Acting Assistant Inspector-General, Department of the Columbia, June 22, 1867 to June 15, 1869.

(Major, 7th Cavalry, December 28, 1868); enroute to Headquarters of Department of the Missouri, and on leave of absence to August 1869; on Court Martial at Santa Fe, New Mexico, August 23 to November 1869; on frontier duty at Fort Hays, Kansas, December 19, 1869 to July, 1871, being engaged in Scouting in Colorado, May to August, 1870; as Member of Retiring Board at Fort Leavenworth, Kansas, August 1869 to February 1870; in garrison at Spartansburg, South Carolina, July 21, 1871 to August 2, 1872; as Member of Small-Arms Board, August 1872 to April 1873; in garrison at St. Paul, Minnesota,

April to June, 1873; in command of Escort to Northern Boundary Survey to October 22, 1873; on sick leave of absence, October 28, 1873 to May 1, 1874; in command of Fort Totten, Dakota, May 25 to June 1, 1874; and of Escort to Northern Boundary Survey, June 1 to September 1874; on leave of absence, September 22, 1874 to October 24, 1875; on frontier duty at Fort Lincoln, Dak., October 30, 1875 to December 15, 1876. (Commanding regiment, June 26 to October 18, 1876), except while engaged in the Sioux Expedition, May 11 to September 22, 1876; and Fort Ambercrombie, Dakota, December 17, 1876 to February 28, 1877; before Court Martial at St. Paul, Minnesota, to May 1, 1877, and undergoing sentence of two years' suspension, May 1, 1877 to May 1, 1879; in command of Fort Meade, Dakota, to July 17, 1879, and on duty thereat to October 28, 1879; and in arrest to April 1, 1880. Dismissed from the Army April 1, 1880, for "Conduct to the Prejudice of Good Order and Military Discipline."

Born, Illinois, 1832; died, March 30, 1889, at Providence Hospital, Washington, D. C., following operation for cancer of the tongue.

INDEX

The index of the original record is incomplete, and lists the witnesses in the order of their appearance. This index lists them alphabetically, and the exhibits, omitted from the original, are included.

Column 1 indicates order of appearance.

EXHIBITS

Column 1, page introduced; column 2, page reproduced

EDITORIAL COMMENTS

APPENDIX

ILLUSTRATIONS

BENTEEN'S BATTLE MAP

The following, in Benteen's inimitable handwriting, appears on the reverse side of the battle map drawn and annotated by him in the field shortly after the battle, and which appears on the back end paper:

"(If you see fit, Dr. Taylor can send this to N. Y. Heard [Herald?] in case nothing of kind has appeared.)"

"On the morning of the 25th of June, Custer, about 16 or 17 miles from the indian village, divided his regiment into 3 Battalions—Custer having Co's. "C.E.F.I.L.,," Reno getting Co's. "A.G.M."—Benteen, Co's. "D.H.K." Benteen, with his Battn. was started off at once to the left—to hunt for vallies, indians, etc. Custer with his own and Reno's Battn.—kept the main trail: on arrival near indian village—Reno with his Battn. was sent across Little Big Horn to charge down the valley—He got to the heavy grove of timber marked "★," There he dismounted, leaving horses in timber, throwing skirmish line across valley— He was driven back to horses, mounted and charged thro', getting to bluffs at the place marked "Ford" ====. It was at this place and time that I arrived on the field, and, seeing the cavalry retreating, reinforced them at once on bluffs. We awaited at this point until McDougal with Co "B," came up with the pack train— and at same point were corraled by the indians for two days. When Reno crossed river to charge indians, Custer promised to support him,—but instead, went to his own death by the line marked, as per margin. General Terry relieved us on the morning of the 27th June. It is my belief that no line was formed by Custer, but what was formed by each Co. commander on his own hook: and that the indians got him running and kept him at it until they all saw they were surrounded."

At the bottom of the map itself, also in Benteen's handwriting, occurs the following message:

"Kittie, I have hastily sketched for you the battle field of the 'Little Big Horn.' From it you can probably glean some idea of our situation."

Underneath the message, Benteen wrote (referring to the map):

"Scale; About one mile to one inch."

BENTEEN'S BATTLE MAP

The above battle map, drawn and annotated in the field by Benteen soon after "The Yellow Hair" and his men had passed into history, was discovered during May 1954. Never before published, it is especially valuable for its placement of Reno's positions. Benteen, whose part in the battle stands out more sharply than that of any other surviving

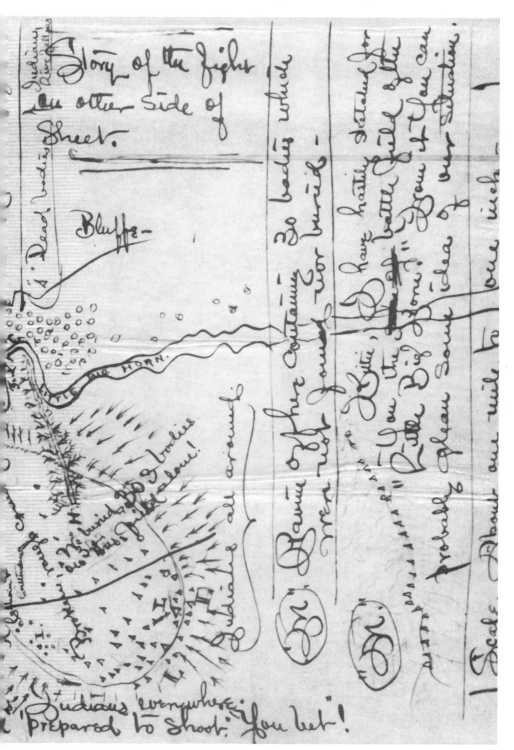

officer, had no need to speculate or guess. Crude and hastily drawn, the map contains errors, chiefly as to the number of bodies found. Reno's route down the valley, the position of his skirmish line, his line of retreat and the arrangement of his hill defense, are sketched with particularity and detail. As did Maguire, Benteen plots the route originally believed to have been taken by Custer, as to which his opinion later changed. (See pp. 143, 146 infra).

The Custer Myth
by W. A. Graham

✧

Legend into History **and**
Did Custer Disobey Orders
at the Battle of the Little Big Horn?
by Charles Kuhlman

✧

The Reno Court of Inquiry:
Abstract of the Official
Record of Proceedings
by W. A. Graham

✧

The Story of the Little Big Horn
by W. A. Graham

✧

Troopers with Custer
by E. A. Brininstool

✧

With Crook at the Rosebud
by J. W. Vaughn